Dave
Mize,

Thank you so much for all you do. for and did for the Shrine Bowl - thanks to your continued support of Coach Bowl

Best Chris Ridley

NEVER SEEN A FINER DAY

CHRIS RIDLEY

Never Seen A Finer Day

Softcover - 978-1-64318-094-6

Hardcover - 978-1-64318-095-3

703 Eighth St.

Baldwin City, KS, 66006

www.imperiumpublishing.com

NEVER SEEN A FINER DAY

IMPERIUM PUBLISHING
CREATE YOUR STORY

CHRIS RIDLEY

FOREWORD
by Mike Manns and Steve Rottinghaus

MIKE

First of all, let me say it's an honor for me to jot down some thoughts about Coach Ron Bowen. I have been broadcasting high school sports in the Topeka area for over 40 years and I consider Ron Bowen to be one of the best football coaches that I have had the privilege to know personally. I never met a coach who had the overwhelming will to win as well as genuine regard for his players. Ron Bowen's players would walk through fire for him. He told them that if they made a mistake in blocking or carrying out other assignments during practices to take it upon themselves to bear crawl back to the huddle. And they did just that. How many coaches today would ask and receive that from their players?

I always determine the success of a coach, not necessarily with their overall wins and losses, although Bowen was highly successful, but by what young men say about their coach after they leave the school. I have never met a player coached by Ron Bowen who had anything but praise for their former coach. How many boys did Ron Bowen help turn into young men?

I am proud to say that I not only admire Coach Bowen for his coaching abilities, but I most admire the "man" he is. I am one of the lucky guys to be able to call Ron Bowen a friend.

Mike Manns is a long-time radio broadcaster for Topeka-KMAJ radio who also coached football at a Topeka middle school. A good friend of mine and a friend of Topeka high school sports.

STEVE

When our family moved to the Auburn-Washburn school district the summer of 1976, we could see the Washburn Rural High School's McElroy Stadium light poles from our home a mile east on the corner of 61st street and Fairlawn Road. By the time I was a fifth grader at Pauline Central in 1978 and started paying attention to the sports section of the Topeka Capital-Journal, I became more aware of the WRHS brand of football, led by Ron Bowen, as the Junior Blues were emerging a perennial Centennial League power and eventual state champion contender. Starting in early September, when the stadium lights were brightly shining, I knew it was time for my parents to drop me off to watch must-see football at 61st and Wanamaker. As a manager of the ninth-grade Jay Shideler Junior High School football team, I recognized that squad had the potential for greatness by the time they reached their senior year. One of my managerial responsibilities was to be a part of the chain gang and flip the down marker. I seem to recall moving the chains a lot after repeated first downs. In their second year of playing tackle football, the ninth-grade squad finished 6-1 with four shutouts with it only loss to Lawrence South. Under the guidance of Ric Tubbs and Chris Ridley, the Class of 1986 was well positioned to continue to develop in Bowen's rising program.

The WRHS success in the early 1980s undoubtedly sparked my interest in sports journalism. As a sports editor of the Blue Streak (school newspaper), I fondly remember Coach Bowen being generous with his time, answering questions of aspiring reporters, verifying stats and spellings of player's names. After the 1985 Junior Blues claimed the city's first state championship, Blue Streak sports editor Tim Bisel and I thought we needed a special section to commemorate the victory and the season. We pitched the idea to our journalism teacher. It was an easy sale with Mary Lou Bowen, wife of the coach, as our newspaper adviser. In my 16 years in sports journalism, I always looked forward to contributing as a writer, editor and designer for football special sections, due in large part to my exposure to the winning football at Washburn Rural. Through the 1990s with Ron Bowen still manning the sidelines in his WR ballcap, I covered a handful of Washburn Rural games as a sportswriter and remained in awe of the consistency WRHS football had maintained since I first saw them play under the Friday night lights 20 years earlier. – Steve Rottinghaus

Steve Rottinghaus worked 20 years in the newspaper industry, including stints at the Topeka Capital-Journal, Dallas Times-Herald, Manhattan Mercury and Lawrence Journal-World, before serving 10 years as the public relations director at Baker University in Baldwin City, KS. He currently is the career and outreach coordinator at the William Allen White School of Journalism and Mass Communications at the University of Kansas, where he teaches a course in professional development to journalism students.

• *Rottinghaus was also a journalism student of mine and we continue to be friends*

Never Seen a Finer Day

I'VE NEVER
SEEN A FINER DAY

S o, folks asked, "when are you going to write another book? If you do, will it be another book about a football coach?" First, let me clarify something. I never thought I'd publish one book. When I started writing the last one, it was just a project, something to do. I like to write.

And let me tell you, it took me a long time to get used to someone calling me, an "author." I never pretended I was an author. But I enjoyed the process of writing and of self-publishing my first book– "Venable, Part Legend, All American." And, I must say, the response to that book was overwhelming. I can not thank folks enough. The first time I heard someone call me, "author", I looked over my shoulder and checked to see if someone else was in the room with us.

My process of writing is jotting down random thoughts and stories then do a little research. I tell stories. Lots of stories. I do my level best to add substance to my stories by researching. It's what I expected from my students when I taught journalism to high school freshmen. I learned a lot through my from writing my first book. I put my thoughts and research together in a manuscript and then I unscrambled it into some semblance of order. My dear friend and former Topeka Capita- Journal sportswriter, Rick Peterson, was the one who encouraged me to arrange my story into chapters. I owe him a debt of gratitude for that tip. The scattered and scrambled writing process seems to work for me- but eventually cutting and pasting into chapters helps put order to any story. It helps the reader make sense of what you share with them.

I suffer no pressure from thinking, "I have to write a book!" Then, at some juncture, if I get lucky, the piece may just become book worthy. I let good friends, who edit for me, be the litmus test. If a book is not the biproduct of this writing and a book does not come to fruition, at least the stories will be written down and recorded. Captured for others to share. A noble and worthwhile project indeed. I'll let those in my circle of trust read it. They'll determine if it's book worthy. If I get indications from them that it is, I will trust their judgement.

I did take the important first step in the fall of 2020 letting Coach Bowen and his wife, Mary Lou, know that I was starting my next writing project. I told them it was to be a story about Coach Bowen and his coaching career. After all, he was the most successful football coach EVER to lead the Washburn Rural Junior Blues. THE most successful football coach in Topeka's history as well. And he had some very good years at Valley Center before venturing to Topeka. I wanted the Bowen's collective blessing and their assistance of course. An anthology about Coach Ron Bowen's life and coaching career will be at least as popular as the one about Baldwin Coach Merle Venable. And the nature of this project was very similar to my first. It was a smooth transition with lots of parallels. This project contains a lot more facts because I lived it and, thanks to the Washburn Rural library/media center for collecting articles from the Topeka Capital-Journal. They had every year I needed and the scrapbooks date back as far in time as I needed to go. And the gifted reporters for the Capital-Journal wrote tremendous pieces.

I told Ron that, during this isolated, COVID time, it would be fun if he and I sat at his farm, reminisce a little and have some meaningful conversations. Like we always have. His long and storied career has lots of personal meaning and relevance to me. I intend to have my tape recorder on because those recordings may be fun to listen to some day as well. Conversations with Coach Bowen made the time spent more than worthwhile whether it becomes a book or not. And his wife, Mary Lou, her recollections were a real bonus.

Early in the writing process, I recognized that only writing about my years on his varsity staff (1985-1988) there were LOTS of MY football memories. Lots of great kids, great athletes to mention. I had the good fortune of being a small part of two state championships as an assistant coach. Just writing in depth about those two memorable years and talking about the outstanding players and the games they played will make this a pretty lengthy book, uh project. Then it donned on me it was not a book about me, it was about Coach Bowen's storied career. So, focusing on successes and good stories, determined the depth of the chapters. The three state championship years deserved the most ink. The championship runner-up year and the semi-final years deserved recognition. So, early on, I kind of prioritized chapter length based on either the successes of the teams or the interest level of the stories. Writer's privilege.

It was a process that, once I got into it, often required adjustments. I decided that the most detailed accounts of football seasons should be devoted to the state championship years. My years were 1985 and 1986. But then, if it is a book about WR football and the Bowen years, how could you leave off the undefeated 1989 state championship year. That year the players and coaches also deserve the same courtesy I extended to the '85 and '86 teams. Because I was no longer coaching, (I gave up the coaching to devote my time to being the athletic director) I missed the experience of coaching the '89 bunch.

Then, as I wrote extensively about the three state championship years, I thought, how could I say nothing about 1987, a tremendous bunch I coached who were 8-3 and reached the state semi-finals and lost in unusual fashion in what ended their hopes of defending their other two other championships. The class of 1988 contributed to three successive excellent seasons. So, I wrote a lot about the individual players, many of whom also deserve to have their story included.

And if I didn't write about my last year of coaching varsity, 1988, how would that be fair. Those players were up against a lot of expectations and they lived in the shadows of the three previous year's teams, faced a lot of adversity and misfortune, but finished their season so strong by making the playoffs again. And many of those juniors contributed to the '87 season and then went on to be seniors for the undefeated state championship year of 1989.

See how my thought process works? Anyway, I did my level best to give attention to ALL of the Bowen years. .

And to this day, I often reflect that the years I was on the coaching staff I had the good fortune of working directly with fantastic high school athletes and a coaching staff that was incomparable. When athletic director duties dictated that I quit coaching, I was still associated with the Washburn Rural football program. In addition to my own recollections, I wanted to share personal recollections from players and other coaches on the staffs. Sharing player and coach's perspectives and perspectives of folks from the school community was also important to me. They all have a story to tell. There were so many great players associated with the two back-to back championship seasons and on the 1989 team, I will do my best to mention many of them. I spent time as a school administrator and athletic director at Rural. I had the good fortune of being associated with nearly all of Coach Bowen's Washburn Rural years. In fact, I was only NOT there for the first three years (1975-1977). I will attempt to tell as much about those initial years of leading the Junior Blues and turning the program into one of the most respectable football programs in Kansas.

And Coach Bowen spent his early years at a couple of junior highs as well as three other high schools. So, we've established what I'll write. Why will I write it?

Well, if I've learned anything through publishing my first book, it's that the subject matter is likely the most important thing to ensure that your book will be popular and possess lots of readership potential. And dadgum, I'm awfully proud of my association and experiences at Washburn Rural High School in Topeka, Kansas. When you truly love something, it's not hard to write about it. At least not for me. I tell stories.

RONALD
STEPHEN BOWEN

Ron Bowen was born October 4, 1937 near Reserve, Kansas in Brown County. He was born in the log cabin portion of his family's homestead. There was no electricity or running water at the Bowen homestead. He was the third son of Philip and Edna Bowen. His oldest brother was Hillis and his next older brother Delayne.

According to Bowen, his childhood home was heated by a wood burning stove. His mother cooked on a wood burning kitchen stove. Coal oil lamps were used for lighting. Water was hand pumped from a well and brought inside the home with a bucket that held a dipper to dispense water. Bowen says, "There was a three-hole outhouse furnished with old catalogues." Humble beginnings indeed.

That house was Ron Bowen's home through fourth grade. Both he and his father suffered with asthma. His father had once traveled to California to visit relatives and the elder Bowen discovered he had no asthma when in the western state. Since the home and farm were rented by the Bowens, they had a sale, bought a very basic trailer home, and headed to California.

They used a 1936 one- ton truck to pull the trailer. While his father drove the truck, his mother followed in the family's 1937 Studebaker. Bowen's parents, his brother Delayne, Ron and a cousin all made the long journey to California. Ron's brother Hillis, who was nine years older than Ron, did not accompany the family.

The Bowen's took up residence in a Bellflower, California trailer park where they shared a community restroom facility and showers.

For Bowen to attend school he and his brother would climb over a corner of the fenced-in trailer park and walk to the elementary school. The California school was quite a bit different than the little one room schoolhouse he attended north of Hiawatha. According to Bowen, his former teacher in Hiawatha had discipline. At the California school the teacher had no discipline. Bowen remembers the things he learned the quickest were "ducking" and "dodging." He said the kids who attended the California school frequently threw things, jumped over their desks and chairs and it was utter chaos for a youngster with mid-western manners.

A family illness brought the Bowens back to Kansas. An aunt, his mother's sister, had become deathly ill.

So, Bowen finished his fifth-grade year in Hiawatha. Then, shortly after, his family returned to a farm north of Hiawatha and he returned to the same school he left, Hart Country School District #33. It was there that Bowen completed grades six, seven and eight. Bowen's father attended the same Hart District #33 school and completed eight grades with perfect attendance. Bowen still has the certificate his father was presented for that accomplishment.

Bowen attended high school in Hiawatha. His ninth-grade year he wanted to go out for the football team but his parents would not allow him to play. The year prior his brother, Hillis, had broken his wrist playing football one week into that season. The broken wrist was upsetting enough, but what may have upset his folks even more was this. They had purchased a clarinet for Hillis to play one week before he broke his wrist playing football which prematurely ended his ability to learn the instrument.

They did allow Ron to go out for basketball as a freshman, but his career was one year in the making. He was 5'8" and he had three classmates over 6'0" tall and one eighth grader who eventually grew to be 6'8".

His sophomore year Bowen took it upon himself to take his physical card to a doctor who did not charge for the sport physicals that consisted of the doctor listening to your heart and then having you take some deep breaths. Without his parent's blessing, Bowen stayed after school for football practice. After the first practice, he began the eight-mile walk to his home from his high school. About half-way home his brother Delayne met him in the family's 1950 Ford sedan. He fully expected that, when they got home, he was in for a stern scolding from his parents. All his father said was, "if you get hurt, don't come whining home."

Bowen continued to attend football practices and right before the first scheduled football game, he came down with an excruciating headache. He could barely open his eyes. He was so weak he could barely stand up. His brother Delayne had the same symptoms. And when his parents found Delayne crawling to the restroom in the middle of the night, an ambulance came and took his brother to the KU Medical Center where he spent time in the hospital. The diagnosis was polio.

According to Bowen, even though he was not nearly as bad off as his brother was, he also had polio and was extremely weak for a long period of time. He remembered milking their cows by hand and he tried to run with the cows one day and fell. No football for Ron that sophomore year. The doctor's felt that his football conditioning during early during preseason practices may have helped him overcome polio. However, Bowen said he went from the third fastest individual in his class to the third from the slowest in his class due to polio.

Eventually Delayne was sent home from KU Med. They sent him with leg braces that went from his feet to his waist. A local chiropractor told his parents that, if he used the braces, he likely would never walk again. So, his dad put the braces in an upstairs closet. His dad also put a bed in the front room of the house and bought the first television the family had ever owned. Delayne began ambling around in a wheelchair but his father was determined to help his son walk again. His dad would work his legs daily while Delayne laid in bed and watched television. His father would exercise each limb and manipulate his son's legs every day. After a while, he would get Delayne out of bed, drape him over his back as Delayne held onto his father with his arms around his neck and his father would drag him around the front room forcing his son to use his legs to the extent that he could. It was painful for his son. That routine was repeated daily until Delayne could stand on his own and move his feet to some degree following his dad around the front room. His father also built a frame for a stationary bike that his brother used to strengthen his legs. He eventually used crutches but many falls ensued. Then he traded the crutches for two canes, then eventually one cane. Then no canes.

According to Ron his brother developed a strange walking gait but walked until late in his life when he needed assistance. Ron said, "He walked because of our dad."

Ron Bowen played football for Hiawatha during his junior and senior years. He was a fullback on offense and a defensive lineman. Bowen played during the time when there were only leather helmets with no face masks. According to Bowen he became proficient with what, at the time, was called a "forearm shiver." Basically, you raised your arm, bent and stiff and applied it to the opponent's chest or face. Bowen said he accidentally broke a teammate's nose during practice.

During Bowen's junior year the coach told the team he had gotten 33 new plastic Riddell helmets and told his players the top 33 players would get the new helmets. He humbly says, "I guess I lucked out and got one." Chances are much better that Bowen earned one of the newer helmets. He was obviously excited to FINALLY get to play football after not being allowed to play and then contracting polio. I'm certain his appreciation for the game grew due to the circumstances he faced.

That junior year his team made a trip to Topeka to play a football game. No buses in those days. Players were transported by cars. Bowen's parents didn't make that trip, so Ron rode with his coach. The opponent was Washburn Rural High School. That year the game was played on the old Seaman High School field just north of the river in Topeka, Kansas. The field had been flooded the summer before and had a layer of silt on it. And Hiawatha was sporting their new white jerseys.

Bowen remembers being on the punt team and was assigned to protect his punter. He believes he made his block because he remembers the opponents knee striking his nose. The blow shattered the bone in Bowen's nose. Bowen remained on all fours and stayed in that position until the punt was blown dead. His coach came onto the field and Bowen was still on all fours. His coach asked, "what are you doing?" Bowen's reply was that he was on all fours so, "I wouldn't get blood on my new white jersey."

A physician who was attending the game came to tend to Bowen's injury. Bowen says he either had an awfully swollen tongue or was "three sheets in the wind" (under the influence of alcohol). Bowen could hear the doctor mumble, "Shunny, does your nose always set over like that?"

Bowen didn't know what he was talking about until he went into the locker room and looked into the mirror. He says the tip of his nose was under his right eye.

After the game was over and they returned to Hiawatha, they took Bowen to a doctor and he recollects his nose felt like it was about four inches wide and was throbbing. He recalls the doctor laying him on his back on a table and the physician sticking two sticks up his nose, moving them around and around attempting to get his nose back straighter. Then the doctor sat him up in front of a mirror and asked Ron if his nose was straight now. Bowen said his nose was so swollen he had to turn side to side to see it clearly. When he told the doctor it wasn't straight like it used to be, the doctor laid him on the table again and did more work with the sticks. Again, he sat him up and asked about the straightness. It was not straight, so back on the table for stick work number three.

It's at that time Bowen said he made up his mind (because of the pain he was experiencing) the next mirror gaze was going to be "straight" whether it was or not. When he showed him the nose, Bowen said, "it's straight" and he remember thinking, "glad that is over."

Not yet. The doctor once again laid him down and packed his nose. Bowen said it felt like he was pushing gauze clear up his nose and settling behind his eyeballs.

And during the next appointment the doctor again repacked the gauze in his nose.

During the next appointment, when the doctor eventually pulled the gauze out of his nose, the nose fell to the side a bit and the doctor repacked it.

Then the doctor put tape across his nose, under his nose and put an X of tape on his forehead to his chin. His dad was waiting for him in the car. It was about 1:00 a.m. Ron said, " I made darn sure I didn't whine."

He spent a miserable night with his eyes blackened and watering, got no sleep experienced terrible pain. Bowen decided that night, if the doctor didn't pull that gauze out of his nose the next day, he would pull it out himself.

Bowen missed exactly one week of football practices and one game. When he returned to practice, he had a leather helmet with a "cage" on the front to protect his nose. The guard resembled a single bar face mask with wrapped leather over it. His first game back was a junior varsity game against Effingham. Their game field was as hard as concrete. Bowen remembers getting tackled and ending up on his back while an opponent grabbed that cage and banged his head on the turf. He said his nose felt like Jello. In fact, he recollects for a time there was a bone fragment in the tip of his nose and if he moved it, for the longest time, it would click.

In the last game of Bowen's junior football season, he was standing on the sideline next to the head coach. The coach for some reason turned to him and said, "you know you are better than (a player who will remain nameless), but he is a senior. That's why he's playing."

It's moments like that you always remember. Moments that can shape you. And, if you become a football coach yourself, you learn from that poor examples of judgement; both the playing of an inferior upper-classmen and also having the audacity to admit it to the player who should likely be playing.

As Bowen contemplated that assessment by his coach, he was thinking to himself that the senior was also the banker's son. And Bowen thought, "I'm a country kid, the son of a farmer."

Bowen says, "Later, when I became a coach, I never forgot that statement from my high school coach. I always told my players that we are going to play the best that show in practice. It won't be based on your name, your grade or what your parents do for a living."

As a high school senior, Bowen was able to play for a new football coach, Les Huber, who was on his second stint as head football coach at Hiawatha. His first game of his senior season Hiawatha beat Topeka-Seaman 19-0.

He also remembers scoring a touchdown against Powhattan and Hiawatha winning the game 33-6. That game had another highlight or low light for Bowen.

Coach Huber had a practice of giving his players a half an orange during halftime of the games. Bowen says he was sitting in the locker room when one of his teammates came up to him and asked him why he was still sitting in his gear in the locker room. Bowen replied, "I'm waiting for my orange."

His astonished teammate looked at him incredulously and said, "The game is over!" Apparently, Bowen had been concussed and didn't realize it. In fact, the last thing he remembered was blocking a defensive end and then asking his own quarterback which way he was supposed to go before each play.

During that senior season, Bowen remembers a solid Effingham team that had over 80 players suit up for the games, handing them their first loss 27-0. Effingham had a 23-game winning streak at that point.

He also remembers Homecoming. It was a game folks predicted would be a loss for Hiawatha to the team from Sabetha. Bowen says for some reason he and Oliver Dickenson were picked by the coach to be co-captains that game. Bowen felt like it was because he and Dickenson were two farm boys who didn't care much about the Homecoming festivities. And Bowen scored a touchdown in the upset, Hiawatha 19 Sabetha 0.

Bowen remembers finishing his last high school football season 5-3.

In the spring he participated in track and field. He laughingly says, "Great track career!" He threw the shot put and the discus. He says if there were three places for medals, he finished fourth. If there were five places and medals, he would finish sixth.

His track coach stuck him in the mile relay once just so they could score some points. There were two teams entered and Bowen's team took second. And he says he never wanted to run a quarter mile race again.

During high school years he was enrolled in vocational agriculture and was a member of the local Future Farmers of America (FFA) group. He was chapter president his senior year. He says there were several interesting stories of his FFA "activities."

He told me one that had to do with there being an overgrowth of starling birds in the area so there were two separate local FFA "teams" competing to see who could shoot the most. He and some of his FFA colleagues killed around 500 birds. All that was required to be turned in to count them was the heads. So once the boys dutifully turned in their five hundred bird-heads they had to do something with the bodies.

In a good-spirited fun prank, the town of Hiawatha woke up the next morning to find over five hundred headless starlings lying around the town square. It made the front page of the local paper.

Another fond memory of Bowen's high school days was his father taking him to St Joseph, Missouri to buy his first car for $125. It was a 1947 Ford coupe. After driving it home Bowen spent time and effort customizing it which is what kids did in those days.

That winter the Hiawatha basketball team went undefeated and played in the state tournament in Hutchinson, Kansas. They got beat in the opening round of the tournament on a last-second shot by a young man who went on to play basketball at Kansas State University.

Bowen graduated from Hiawatha High School in the spring of 1955. His yearbook would say he was a member of the football and basketball teams and was a track and field participant. He was also the president of the school's local Future Farmers of America organization.

But perhaps the biggest lesson of his high school was that remark his football coach said to him on the sideline his junior year. The remark that Bowen was probably better than the kid who the coach chose to play, but he played him because he was a senior. That was something that he carried with him as he became a teacher and a coach. We learn from our experiences. And I believe we learn a lot from our negative experiences.

Bowen originally attended Kansas State University for a semester. Jerry Miller, a high school classmate, called Bowen and asked him to change schools and join him and the football program at Emporia State. Bowen transferred. It was in Emporia when he was sitting in the cafeteria with another friend, that Bowen told the friend that he hadn't had a date for a long while. His friend saw a girl named Mary Lou and two of her friends, all from Effingham, Kansas going through the lunch line and the friend asked Bowen which one he would like to date. He picked Mary Lou. Well, and the rest is history. Sixty-three years to date and will be 64 shortly after this book is published.

Bowen played football at Emporia until suffering a back injury in 1957. He suffered the injury on the second day after he and Mary Lou had wed. This may have ended his playing career but inspired him to pursue his teaching degree and follow his desire to coach.

Bowen graduated with a Bachelor of Science in Education in 1959 from Emporia State (then known as Kansas State Teachers College) in Emporia,

Kansas. Mary Lou also earned a degree in education.

Their first job was the fall of 1959 in tiny Elkhart High School in Elkhart, Kansas. Ron spent 1959 and 1960 there. He taught physical education, industrial arts, and driver education. He coached junior high football, basketball, and track. They lived in the same 26' trailer they had lived in during college after marrying in 1957. His dad pulled the trailer to the edge of town, by the Cimarron River, which was dry.

At that time, in Elkhart there was a "dual grading system." When kids came to school their parents signed one of two papers. If they were college bound, the traditional grading system was in effect. If they signed a vocational intent, you had to pass them whether they did any academic work or not.

Bowen says he taught industrial education. He had a kid who worked the oil fields at night and came to school to sleep. One day this young man "cussed" at Bowen and, by Bowen's own admission, he got a bit aggressive with the young man and had some harsh words for him before he took him to the principal's office. When the young man was brought before the principal, he was informed that he had a choice. He could go to any other school in the state of Kansas that would take him, or he could go back to Mr. Bowen's class and do whatever Coach Bowen deemed appropriate. This was Bowen's first swats for a student. Bowen cut his own paddle with the shop's band saw. All the other students witnessed and there were no further problems. There wasn't much due process, but there was corporal punishment.

All in all, the Bowens made strong ties with several of the Elkhart townspeople and continue the relationships even today.

Friends of the Bowens who attended Emporia Teacher's College with them encouraged them to come to Carbondale for a job. In 1960-61 the Bowen's returned to eastern Kansas and he taught at Carbondale High in Carbondale, Kansas teaching the same subjects at the high school level and was assistant junior high football and a basketball coach.

From 1961-1966, he had a stint at Udall High School in Udall, Kansas. He taught the same subjects – physical education, industrial education and driver education. He was head football and track coach and an assistant in basketball. It was Ron's first head football job. In those days, your school PE teachers coached three seasons, especially in smaller schools. At the time Udall had only been playing 11-man football for three seasons. Prior to that they were an eight-man program. Also, the town was still attempting to recover from the tornado that demolished much of the town in 1955. There was not a family in Udall that was not affected by the tornado. The town, particularly the mothers, were awfully protective of their young kids as a result. There were only 17 football players. Conversely, there were 35 basketball players.

When he taught physical education, he taught a little bit of wrestling as well.

While at Udall the Bowen's experienced a tremendous loss. Their first- born daughter, Cindy Lou, tragically did not survive childbirth. Mary Lou says," The community grieved with us, prayed and cheered when the next year a healthy baby boy named Damon joined our family and the community".

Then Bowen took on a position at Leon (Bluestem) High School in Leon, Kansas. He got a $1,100 raise. He taught physical education and industrial arts. He was also head football, and track coach and he started that school's wrestling program as head coach of that sport.

Mary Lou taught 8th grade American history and substituted. While at Leon their second child, M'Lissa was born.

At Leon Bowen worked for a superintendent who got a little too involved in the football program. There was a young man who was a bit ornery playing for Leon that year and the kid may have had some discipline issues that the superintendent had to become involved with. In a football game the kid evidently made a bad decision on a punt, muffed it, and the opponent scooped up the ball and ran it in for a touchdown.

Bowen said all of the sudden, the superintendent had made his way to his sideline and was raising a bit of a ruckus about the kid, saying over and over, "He shouldn't be playing, what was he doing?" Bowen said he turned to the superintendent and said, "Sir, if you want to coach this team, you're more than welcome, but if you do, I'm going up in the stands to watch the rest of the game." Apparently, the superintendent wheeled around and hurriedly left the sideline. There was almost a whole school year of no communication offered Ron from his superintendent after that incident. Then, in the spring semester, the superintendent called Bowen to his office and offered him a new contract for the next year. This was after a school year of silence by the head administrator. Despite the offer Bowen looked for another position. He was only at Leon one year.

After that series of jobs at smaller schools Bowen landed a job at Valley Center High School in Valley Center, Kansas. It was the largest school he had worked in and once again he taught industrial arts and driver education. He was head football and track coach and started the school's wrestling program. He was at Valley Center from 1968-1975.

I asked Bowen how he landed this position. He said the Valley Center superintendent had seen and watched closely Bowen's practices while he was coaching at Leon and he apparently liked his work ethic. He liked the fact that the kids on Bowen's teams would be tired from the amount of work expected.

While at Valley, Bowen laid claim to the school's first wrestling state champion and coached several successful football teams. One storied season Valley was undefeated. Bowen would have two of those in his entire career.

In fact, between 1968-1974 Bowen's seven years at the helm at Valley Center, there was only ONE losing season. His second year at Valley was a 3-6 season. In 1970 Valley Center was an undefeated 9-0. His seven-year worth of records at Valley were, 6-3, 3-6, 9-0, 6-3, 5-4, 9-1 and 5-4 for a 43-21 overall record. It was a record to be proud of and Valley Center eventually honored the successes he had while coaching football at Valley placing him in their sports Hall of Fame.

The 1970 team was apparently loaded with talent. In a Wichita Beacon article written by Russ Corbitt for the October 15 edition, the headline was "Valley Center Coach Does Know What to Do." It mentions that Bowen started that season with a stable of very good running backs. "You never have too many, but we did have to do a little shuffling," Bowen reflected.

Three of the running backs shared the time and the share of carries. By game four three of the running backs had scored 34 or more points. "Craig Erickson (38 points) and Dale Hayden (36 points) usually alternate at right halfback, with Don Garman (34 points) at left halfback most of the time," Bowen told the reporter. Don Garman's twin, Ron Garman, was the fullback. The Garman twins apparently had a bit of an asthma problem, so they had to be spelled occasionally.

Commenting on senior quarterback, Danny Dundas, Bowen said, "We feel we have to run at people, but Dundas can keep them honest with his passing. He was 9 of 14 passing against Circle High School and his main targets were King Doolen, Randy Brooker and Hayden. Both our ends (Doolen and Brooker) are juniors and both had real good hands". Bowen went on to mention that most of his athletes have to go both ways – offense and defense. Ever one to spread credit for successes, Bowen goes on to mention lineman, Mike Unruh, who was a running back who switched positions in order to get as many good athletes on the field as possible. He mentioned tackles Mark Acuff and Ron Warner when talking about a defense that had only allowed 31 points in four games.

Valley Center was a member of the Chisholm Trail League and their schedule and scores that year were:

1. (Win) Valley Center 42-0 over Maize
2. (Win) Valley Center 26-12 over Chapparal
3. (Win) Valley Center 39-12 over Circle
4. (Win) Valley Center 22-7 over Kingman
5. (Win) Valley Center 14-8 over Augusta
6. (Win) Valley Center 28-11 over Mulvane
7. (Win) Valley Center 36-6 over Goddard
8. (Win) Valley Center 52-0 over Andover
9. (Win) Valley Center 30-22 over Andale

I had the opportunity to visit with George Pearson who was a lineman on that undefeated Valley Center team. I commented to George that there didn't appear to be many close games that year. In fact, Augusta was a six- point win and, traditionally had a very good team.

Pearson recollects boarding the bus for the short ride to Augusta and, once they got to the town, there were a group of Augusta boys that met their team bus and egged the Valley Center player's bus. Of course, that infuriated the Valley Center players and, in football, it is better to leave a sleeping dog lie. All the vandals did was fire up the visiting team and from the opening kickoff came out like gang busters to mount a lead.

Andale had a tradition and a string of consecutive wins against Valley Center that may have been more than 15 straight years of losses. That was the next closest game, an eight-point victory in the last game of the season.

I asked Pearson what was so special about the Valley Center team in 1970. He mentioned, "we had four guys that were exceptionally fast and strong. The juniors also had 3-4 talented kids too." Pearson went on to reflect, "We realized we were going to be good, but by the middle of the year, about week five, we realized we could do something special. We had a exceptional kids, but the role players knew what to do for their jobs."

He also remembers that the philosophy and the confidence with which they played. "At Valley we were going to run the football. It was basic stuff," Pearson commented on Coach Bowen's offensive philosophy and expectations. "Coach's practices were intense. Our senior year they had built a new school. There was a practice football field, no grass growing on it in August.

"We were having a pre-season meeting and we were coming off of a 3-6 season," Pearson remembers. "We lost the last game of the season. In a pre-season meeting Coach Bowen asked us players what the score of the last game was. And nobody knew. So, we did some asphalt and barren turf bear walks and there were some torn-up hands after that little reminder."

I asked Pearson what made Bowen a special coach to Valley Center. "He was hard core, expected you to do what you had to do and he taught us how to deal with adversity," Pearson remembers. "He pushed us to get up when we were down and taught us how to get better. There was a lot of demand and expectations, but we wanted to do well for him."

Times have changed a lot since 1970 and one of the areas of change involved the emphasis on staying hydrated. "I believe it was our senior year and, in the day, drinking water was not very popular. But he sent some of us on an errand and told us to get a NEW Hudson sprayer and then they could have some a water. They were about $28 but one of the hardware stores gave it as a donation to the football team." And the team got properly watered.

In 1973 Valley Center again reeled off nine straight wins and made the playoffs before losing their only game that season at the hands of Wichita Kapaun.

Those Valley years saw Mary Lou substitute teaching and she taught the last two years at the Sedgwick County Extension Service. Two more daughters were born to the Bowens at Valley – Andrea and Heather.

There was an interesting football story that Mary Lou was involved with during that 1970-71 school year and the undefeated season. Bowen remembers that George Pearson, Jr., had an upset stomach prior to the first game. During the school day he came to Bowen and reported his stomach issues. Bowen told him he'd be all right and he went out and bought his player some Pepto-Bismol. George decided to take it. He made it through the first game and, as these things can happen, the Pepto-Bismol became sort of a superstition for Pearson and the team and he would always down a good portion of Pepto-Bismol before each game. He remembers drinking some at a pep rally in front of the student body. Just good fun if nothing else.

Mary Lou Bowen wrote a letter to the pharmacal company, Norwich Products, and they chose to use George's experience as part of their advertising for their product. And at the end of the year Valley Center had an all-sports banquet in which Norwich was sending a representative to the school to present a special "trophy" that featured a Pepto-Bismol bottle. There was a KSHSAA rule that prohibited amateur athletes from being given such awards. So, after the year was over and Pearson graduated, an assistant brought Pearson the trophy and he's kept the keepsake ever since.

Pearson was an offensive lineman that undefeated year and, due to the odd point system KSHSAA had at the time to determine who made the playoffs, Valley was left out. According to Pearson conversations he's had with Ron Bowen since then, Bowen still feels like that team was one of his best and had more than a good chance to compete for a state championship.

Bowen also remembers having a superintendent who attempted to put him on a limited contract because his son didn't play. Bowen says, "the young man didn't even want to play football." Later down the road that same administrator got run out of the state for misappropriation of funds. Maybe a bit of Karma if you believe in that kind of stuff.

In the meantime, in 1973 Bowen had purchased an 80-acre farm near Holton, Kansas so the Bowens were looking to land a job closer to the farm. In 1975 the call came from Auburn-Washburn schools and Washburn Rural High School. It was about a 60-minute drive, one-way from the farm to Washburn Rural. The school was growing and was wanting someone to turn their mediocre football program into something the community could take pride in. Mediocre was a kind term. They were not very good.

INDUSTRIAL EDUCATION CAN BE TAUGHT – AND ALSO ENJOYED BY THE INSTRUCTOR

Ron Bowen had just completed a lengthy stint teaching at several schools. Elkhart, Carbondale, Udall, Leon and Valley Center. He had gained lots of experience in each of those locations and undoubtedly learned a lot about teaching and coaching during those early days. After all, he spent from 1959-1974, a total of sixteen years before he ever got to Topeka and Washburn Rural.

When talking to Ron and Mary Lou, they tell humorous stories about those early days, but they also speak fondly of the countless relationships they made in each of those communities.

Despite losing their first child, their other four children were all born while in these communities and their family grew in those 16 years.

One of the things that very few Washburn Rural students or faculty may know about Coach Bowen who became so near and dear to them in the realm of teaching driver education, health, physical education and strength and conditioning and, of course coaching, was that he gave up something he dearly loved to come to Rural. He gave up teaching industrial education.

Prior to coming to Rural, Bowen taught some drafting and lots of wood shop classes. He speaks fondly of students he had who were able to take their projects to be judged and who won awards for their skilled work.

But a side note to that is, not only did Coach Bowen teach woodworking, he also loved to do his own wood projects. And his only son, Damon Bowen, shared his father's love for woodworking.

When you think about the relationship you can make between woodworking and coaching football it really kind of makes sense how Bowen applied some of the same principles.

Bowen believes in discipline. It takes a lot of discipline to stick to a project like building a desk or turning a wooden bowl. Bowen speaks with pride when he shows you his desk he made. It's walnut wood and looks very professional. He's humble and it is never about "look what I did." But you can tell that there is pride in his work. He has two desks in his office – both heavy as all get out and made with walnut. He built a computer desk that was custom sized to fit in a corner. Complete with a pull-up tray for a keyboard and many cubbies for various office supplies, paper, etc.

Like football to construct something solid, you start with the basics and build it and shape it. Bowen did that very thing with his offenses. Each year he would introduce a handful of plays that were basic to his offense and he would drill and execute countless repetitions until the precision was in his players to run the play correctly. To execute. What good woodworking project doesn't begin with its' base? From there the "frills" are added. As Bowen's players executed the basic plays, he would add more plays to the repertoire.

And when you hear Bowen talk about his woodworking and his offense, you conclude quickly that he takes great pride in the simplicity of things. The fundamentals. The basics. Every good offensive player he ever had started from a proper stance. After all, if you did not start a woodworking project correctly, from the ground up, it probably was not going to be a very good finished product.

So, two crafts that take a lot of patience are coaching and woodworking. Makes perfect sense this relationship.

One sacrifice that Bowen had to give up when coming to Washburn Rural where he was so successful as a teacher and coach, was his woodworking instruction. But you know Bowen never taught subjects. Bowen taught kids. So, all that changed for him was the kids and kids are pretty much the same wherever you go. But one thing is for sure, students who were fortunate enough to have a class with Bowen or were coached by Bowen got a very enjoyable experience and each one knew from his actions that he cared.

What I quickly realized was that Bowen cared about all kids. It's easy to develop relationships with your athletes. But Bowen genuinely cared for all kids and wanted them to find happiness and successes no matter what they did in life. I guarantee you for every athlete who sings his praise, you'll find another non-athlete that speaks of his influence on them as well.

BOWEN TAKES A POSITION AT TOPEKA-WASHBURN RURAL HIGH SCHOOL THE EARLY YEARS 1975-1977

S o just like that Ron Bowen took a new job so he could continue to be a teacher, continue being a football coach and could also be a farmer. Luckily, he had four kids and a wife to help him be a farmer. The farm on which they still reside is located about 10 miles east of Holton, Kansas and about a mile north off the highway. In the early days they raised hogs. Bowen says he did not do farm chores in the mornings. He had four kids who had their chores to do when they got home from junior high and high school. And Mary Lou worked at Effingham High School between 1975-1983 so she too arrived home before Ron did. Many a time Bowen would teach all day in Topeka, coach football at Washburn-Rural and drive the 60- minute commute to his farm THEN do chores or work a field. Sometimes till midnight.

"Thank goodness they make implements with lights," he quipped.

Topeka Capital Journal sportswriter, Allen Quakenbush, featured Bowen's farming job in a 1981 Topeka Capital-Journal article.

"The first time I drove down here (to Washburn Rural) to interview for the job," Bowen said with a wry grin, "I told myself I'd never drive that far again. But here I am in my seventh year."

He and his family could farm the 280 acres, raise hogs, cattle and enjoy the advantages of farm life AND he was able to teach and coach. There may not have been too many coaches with that kind of a "side business."

Bowen said that he was fortunate that the superintendent who hired him for Washburn Rural had previously been at Halstead. So he hired Bowen to be his football coach the same year he started as superintendent in Auburn-Washburn. Being from nearby Halstead, the new superintendent was familiar with Bowen. He knew a bit about Bowen's successes at Valley Center. Despite that knowledge, Bowen said he still was not the first choice to take the position. However, when the other candidate failed to take the position, new Auburn-Washburn superintendent Irvin Myers wanted the Valley Center coach to accompany him, along with a new principal, Dale Smeltzer, to Washburn Rural.

The previous football coach, Mike Reed, had resigned in the spring of 1975 to enter private business. Reed had led the Junior Blues from 1969-1974 and there had been some lean times at Rural since 1962. The last winning record at the school occurred in 1962. Bob Peel was the coach who led the Junior Blues to back-to back undefeated seasons in 1961 and 1962.

When Bowen arrived at Washburn Rural there was also a new assistant principal at the school, Dick Patterson. Patterson was at Topeka High the previous school year. Upon Bowen's first visit to the high school after his hiring, Patterson may have set up the most important meeting to better enable Bowen's chances for rebuilding the Junior Blue program.

Bowen said Patterson knew he was wanting to fill some vacancies on his new coaching staff, so he suggested that Bowen walk over to the gym and meet the new wrestling coach, Ray Glaze. Patterson and Glaze were colleagues at Topeka High the previous year and made the move to Rural that summer. Bowen asked Patterson how he'll know it's Ray Glaze. Patterson said, "He'll be the short, stocky guy with a crew cut and a bottle of Pepsi in his hand."

And, when Bowen crossed the hall to the gym, sure enough Glaze was easy to spot matching that exact description. Bowen had never met Glaze so after some brief conversation and small-talk, Bowen simply asked Glaze if he would consider coaching with him. He said Glaze, in his soft-spoken, unemotional way of speaking said he had one question for him, "Are you the kind of coach that has lots of coach's meetings?"

Bowen told Glaze that he believed that it was only prudent to have a meeting if there was something the staff needed to hear or needed to discuss. Glaze said he'd coach with him. And that inauspicious first meeting was probably one of the most significant hires Bowen would ever make. This duo would go on to become one of the states' most successful tandem of coaches the state of Kansas would ever know. Each complemented each other's style and philosophy. And not only did they make a good pair of coaches ON the football field, they also became great friends off the field and enjoyed each other during the teaching day as well.

Glaze was from Maryland and had come to Kansas State University to attend college and play football and wrestle. Glaze was quite likely as close to an Olympic quality wrestler that never made the Olympics. He had spent years teaching elementary physical education in the Auburn-Washburn district, moved to the Topeka-Seaman district. He was one of many teachers who lost their teaching positions by going on "strike", over negotiations. Kansas law did not allow teacher strikes. Glaze's wife, Cicely, also taught in the Seaman district and, in order for the Glaze's to have an income, she did not go on strike. She stayed and taught in the district her entire career.

Glaze landed on his feet at Topeka High School and, it was there that he may have developed an aversion for coach's meetings. He also saw that the meetings had very little affect on the successes of the team.

Eventually Glaze, who coached football like he was wrestling or playing chess – he would make a move, the opponent would adjust, and Glaze would counter it. I had the privilege of coaching defense with Glaze when I was on the Rural staff. He forgot more defensive football than I ever knew. I learned more about defensive football from that man than anyone. I learned a lot about how to get athletes to play hard, earn their respect and still have fun with them while helping them become good men.

Bowen said early on he had spoken to Glaze about what kind of defense and what kind of philosophy he believed in and then, he just let Glaze take over the defensive side of the ball. This was a critical element for time management sake, because Glaze watched the bulk of the film of the opponents' offenses and mapped out game strategy and defensive plans to take away the things another team did the best. Bowen studied the opponents' defense and game planned what plays would work for our offense. All the coaches were assigned individual positions to coach on both sides of the ball. Bowen took on the defensive ends and he followed Glaze's techniques for ends. They had to be both run stuffers and outside containment on sweeps. Bowen could coach the technique and skills for the defensive ends during practice sessions focusing on individual defensive positions, but it allowed him to focus on the offensive side of the ball and he was a master at setting up opponents with his play calling. He commented, "Glaze and I didn't always agree. But we were pretty good about doing it in private and it was always professional, nothing personal, and we came to an understanding." They also learned from each other.

They developed a respect and a friendship that was unmatched. They genuinely were on the same page about expecting a disciplined football team and insisting their players had self-discipline. But an underemphasized and, often, a little-known fact to folks outside the program, Bowen and Glaze believed in having fun. And fun during the school day often carried over to the football practices.

During the day often Glaze would find his way to the gym and the coaches office. Often time students would bring cinnamon rolls to the duo. I believe they bartered cinnamon rolls in exchange for lighter calisthenics for warmups. They poked good natured fun at each other. They liked to talk about who was the fattest (neither were fat, just short). And the infamous "Butterball" award began. They liked to call each other butterball, chunk, etc. One Thanksgiving Bowen put a phone number in Glaze's school mailbox. When Glaze called the 1-800 number, the recording on the other end said, "Welcome to the Butterball hotline." Bowen and Glaze loved pulling pranks like that on each other.

Annually Glaze would make up a little Butterball of the Year "award" and put it in Bowen's mailbox.

On the football field they expected precision, focus from the players, and there was plenty of repetitions. But each of them also made practices fun and there enthusiasm kept players loving football.

I remember preparing for the 1986 state championship game and we were at practice. My brother-in law was at the practice, the weather was nice. It was the day before the kickoff, which was on a Saturday, the Saturday after Thanksgiving. After the practice I remember my brother-in law commenting that, "if having a relaxed and loose bunch is a good thing going into this game, they will have a very good game." And we did.

I won't go so far as to say there was a switch that we could turn on and off, but the players we had knew how to get ready- and they enjoyed the preparation and repetitions. Our players had a swagger that was more like an expectation to win. They knew if they executed and did their assignments well, we had a very good chance of beating anyone. Everyone. And they trusted each other. It was like a brotherhood. A family. And we all know how no one likes to see their family harmed. That's how we blocked and that's how we played. For each other. It was a special time in Rural football. A mixture of talent, fun and, what everybody strives for, team chemistry. We had it.

But in the first season of 1975 coaching at Washburn Rural, one of Bowen's biggest challenges was to make the players they inherited from a previous coaching staff a whole lot tougher. Remember that Washburn Rural had not registered a winning record for a season since 1962. It was a lot of losses. Losing can become a habit. An expectation. You just show up each Friday and take another "L". It couldn't be a whole lot of fun. What did the program need? According to Bowen, the Junior Blues needed discipline and toughness. A pretty easy observation and statement to make, but what a challenge it is to change a culture of losing.

To this day I am certain that the early years of Bowen's coaching the drills he called, "Blue mountain", the "humper drill" and the "free lick drill" probably still strike a familiar cord and recollection in many of Bowen's players.

One of the first experiences Bowen had was looking over the equipment that was inherited and it was not good. Bowen was informed by the previous coach that he would inherit tough kids. "They weren't tough, I'll guarantee you that."

In the first padded practice he says that they were attempting a linebacker drill and his analogy had something to do with hitting and not crushing a marshmallow. It was about that time Bowen started teaching his players this chant. A coach would start it, "What do you say when you look in the mirror?" And the players would yell, "I'm tough!!!" And the coach would say, "What else?" and the players would say, "I'm a winner." It's surprising what a bit of this reminder repeated multiple times can do for one's mindset and inspire one to work hard at being tough and a winner.

"They weren't tough, but I guarantee you they got tough." Bowen brought some of the drills that helped him be successful at Valley Center. He couldn't believe how "soft" the team was. One of the drills was the "tack hammer" drill – a tackling drill. And the "humper" drill. These drill names have meaning for Washburn Rural alum. Especially during the early days of Coach Bowen establishing expectations.

I think the challenge is that you have some of the same kids for three years – sophomore – senior years. So, if the senior class is content with losing and doesn't conform to your philosophy's it's a challenge to get the underclassmen on board as well. In 1975 Bowen knew he had to be positive with the kids, but also knew he had to instill discipline and toughness. A very hard balance to maintain.

In Bowen's initial season in August of 1975 after several days of two-a day practices, getting to know his players and coaching staff, on September 12 it was the day of the very first game of the Bowen era. Their opponent Holton. Capital Journal sportswriter, Alan Eskew, wrote about the inauguration. He mentioned that Bowen had come from Valley Center and that in 1970 had an undefeated team and in 1973 made the playoffs. But Bowen, like any new coach, knew that the players at Rural didn't care what you did at another school. Hell, most of them likely didn't even know where Valley Center was.

"The opener is real important to get things going," Bowen said. "It gets the momentum going. It's important to win the first time. It starts your season on the right step when you win it."

Eskew wrote that Bowen had the Jr. Blues thinking about winning even though they recorded just two wins the previous season of 1974.

"We don't know what to expect from Holton," Bowen said. "This is a big problem."

That season also started with a decision about who to play at quarterback. Curt Hicks or Steve Schuster.

"Don't say number one because we've got two quarterbacks," Bowen said. "They will split time and we'll see how it goes. They will probably play a series each or possibly by quarters. It just depends. If a kid has a good series, we may not change. We want to see both under game conditions," Bowen commented.

You can bet he had a plan, even though it included variables. But Bowen had a plan. At this point in his career Bowen had been coaching seventeen seasons.

In an earlier pre-season article, also written by Alan Eskew, Bowen laid some "bricks" about his philosophy and his plan for Washburn Rural.

"One thing we have been dwelling on since I've been here is that we are going to be winners," Bowen said. "They have to believe in themselves first." He went on to add, "When a kid starts believing in himself and has the fundamentals, he's a football player,"

What Bowen did not say, but every coach knows, is it's the coaching staffs' efforts and part of their jobs to instill this self-confidence in their players. Every day, every drill, every way possible to build that player's confidence. A critical recipe for coaching success.

In that article Bowen told Eskew that he had looked at last year's game films. But not to evaluate HIS players, but to learn about the opposition's offensive and defensive schemes. And that is so he and his staff could better prepare their players for what to expect, how to attack and what to defend. The better prepared your team is the more confident they can play. The more calculated are their moves. Bowen didn't want anything the other team did to surprise his players.

About the current players Bowen said, "We want to judge a kid on what he does right now. Every kid gets a fresh start with me. We don't even think about last year."

And it might be worth noting that because the culture was changing and the expectations were steep for players, not all of them survived it. According to Bowen he lost seven players who quit because they thought his methods and his drills were too close to "torture." In fact, one group of kids asked to meet with one of the assistant coaches. And they asked this assistant why Bowen was torturing them so. A credit to Bowen's assistant was his loyalty in informing Bowen of the meeting. The only thing that changed was the Rural team entered the season with seven less players. They simply were not accustomed to working so hard. And when you make changes to the culture, not everyone wants to come along or buy-in. Casualties are bound to happen.

The year before Bowen arrived the rushing game was not present. Their leading ground gainer garnered 112 yards. For the whole season.

So, who were some of the players who stuck it out and Bowen planned on using extensively to turn this thing around?

Well, they had a senior quarterback in Hicks who was a 6'3" 185 pounder who also would start at defensive end. Schuster was a fine passer and lettered as a sophomore at defensive back. Both would contribute and Bowen wanted each to get a fair assessment, both in practice reps and in game conditions. Then he would make the decision.

Bowen had a big bruising back in John Myers who was a transfer from tiny Halstead, Kansas and who missed a good portion of the previous season for Halstead with back issues. Myers was a fullback in a three-back offense.

The other halfbacks with promise, who would share two positions in the Rural backfield, were Kevin Jackson, Kevin Henderson, and Larry Rosselot.

Bowen mentioned three offensive lineman who had stood out in the initial practices, Randy Williams, Pat Hale and Tim Christensen.

The two receivers were Illinois transfer David Little and the defensive coordinator's son, Ray Glaze, Jr.

You can bet Bowen got some tips from Ray Glaze about who had stood out on the defensive side of the ball through practices and one inter-squad scrimmage. Kent Taylor returned as a defensive end and recognition in '74 as a second- team all-Centennial pick. Scott Combs was a transfer from Minnesota who Bowen felt would help the team but had been hindered by knee injuries. Matt McFarland also had an excellent scrimmage and was expected to help defensively at end along with Christenson.

He also mentioned Mike Rader as a good hitting linebacker.

A little subtle Bowen humor when he mentioned that Mark Golden, the previous year's punter who led the city with a 40 yard per punt average for 51 punts had graduated, but Phil Hamilton appeared to be a capable replacement. Bowen mentioned he hoped not to punt the ball as often as they had the previous season though.

So how did the opening game go for the Junior Blues? It was a 31-22 loss to Holton. But there were bright spots and signs of improvement. WR was able to run the ball with some success. And that was a huge improvement over the previous year when the top ground gainer had 112 total rushing yards.

And the Junior Blues went on to lose their first five games. But the critical groundwork was being laid and they were making improvements daily. In those five games they were shut out once by a solid Leavenworth squad. But the offense managed to score 14 points twice, 18 points against Highland Park and 22 points in their opener. The Junior Blues were improving whether or not they were posting wins in '75 or not.

Ray Glaze, Jr. had this to say about the initial season, "I was a sophomore at Rural the year before Coach Bowen came. My first year I played for Coach Mike Reed. When Bowen and his staff came, it was a shocker (for players). Very first day of practice with full pads Bowen had us all line up and asked us to deposit our arm and hand pads (he had a derogatory term for those kinds of pads that kind of emasculated it- you can guess) in a pile. You could have filled up several trash bags. He said, 'you can pick them up after practice and take those home or go back to the store and get your money returned because we're not going to use those.' That was shocker number one."

Politically correct was not a term back then, but someone suggested that he might not want to use that word he used for the arm pads while coaching. Bowen pointed out that the abbreviated term was short for the word pusillanimous, which means a little afraid and cowardly. Okay.

Coach Bowen had said that one person carries the ball so you all better learn how to block. Glaze's description of the offense, "We did a lot of running. Bowen would run his offense and we were learning it was run, run, run, three yards and a cloud of dust, which was fine, that was great," Glaze Jr. commented.

He went on to say, "They had me in the back field as a running back and I didn't have the slightest idea what I was doing. I was the slot back and occasionally in the backfield like a fullback. In fact in practice one day, I'm running out of the backfield and, like wrestling, which I knew, you put one hand down to go one direction and the other to go the other direction. And dad caught that. My dad (Ray, Sr.) came up to me and shook my face mask and said, 'Don't you think the defense is going to pick up on that?'"

So, there was a lot of learning to do and it didn't come easy. Glaze, Jr. remembers the coaches trying to instill confidence in the players. But they had to start with toughness drills.

Glaze, Jr. remembers an early drill called the "humper" drill. There would be a line of players and someone would be in the front and try and get all the way through the line. And anything goes. They simply wanted to have man-on man.

Glaze described the Humper Drill, "You'd have 10 guys in a line and they would all come at you. And anything goes. You could hit, kick, throw punches, or anything went when they blew the whistle for a minute."

Knowing what I know about Ray Glaze, Jr. I asked, "You were probably good at that?" Glaze said, "Not initially. They woke us up. They also knew who on the team were buddies so they said, 'if we catch you brother-in lawing it (going easy), we're gonna run sprints until you throw-up. So, you better hit.'

"Hell, there was a time you went through the line of ten players, with a minute with each guy. And there was times we'd go through it twice and you'd be all bruised and bloody. They just wanted to get us mad and toughen us up."

It wasn't until October that Bowen, his staff and most importantly his team, tasted a victory. It was a hard fought 9-6 win over Abilene High School. Despite Bowen's pre-season contention that it was important to start the season with some success it did not come until week six of the high school season. It was the last game before District football games which were designed by the KSHSAA playoff system to determine what eight schools would battle it out for the state championship.

The schools assigned to Washburn Rural's football district that season were Emporia, a perennial power, Atchison and Shawnee Heights. Emporia predictably had their way with WR beating them by a score of 48-14. Rural played Atchison much better dropping a one-point loss, 21-20. And the conclusion of the season ended with the Junior Blues taking down rival Shawnee Heights High by a score of 16-0. A shut out.

Before Bowen's initial season In 1974 Rural was shut out four games out of nine and managed to score only 48 points the entire season – an average of a little over 5 points per game. You don't win many games with that kind of offense. In 1975 it only took four games for their offense to outscore the previous year (50 points).

As a junior quarterback, Steve Schuster led the city in total offense with 476 total yards. He had more rushing yards as a quarterback than the WR leading rusher the year before and threw for 335 yards. By today's standards and a more wide-open offensive scheme, that doesn't appear to be many passing yards. And Coach Bowen is admittedly one who favors the running offense. However, Schuster's passing yards were the most in the city of Topeka that year. And he was selected to the Capital-Journal's all-city football first team that year. His anticipated return in 1976 was something to build upon, something to look forward to for the Washburn Rural faithful.

Two WR receivers, Little and Golden, were second and fourth in the city in receiving yards. Those skeptics of Bowen's propensity to run the ball and not throw it, probably should have taken heed. He knew when to pass.

So, the 1975 Junior Blues ended up with a 2-7 record, identical to 1974. Make no mistake, there were lasting habits instilled as a new face was also being instilled on the Junior Blues program and the team was starting to take shape. The players, who stuck it out, understood that their hard work paid off and hopes were high going into the 1976 season. Players were starting to believe in their coaches. But most critically, players were believing in themselves. And, according to Bowen, "that's when they become football players." Football players to be reckoned with I might add.

YEAR TWO – 1976 A YEAR OF PROMISE

The results of the football season of 1976 could have been viewed as one of the quickest turnarounds in any school in Kansas. For a team who had not had a winning season since 1962, there was anticipation but not assuredness that the new coach could be making strides. During the first five games of the season Rural reeled off four wins. They started the year 4-1. The teams of Holton, Leavenworth, Seaman and Highland Park, that had beaten them in '75, were paid back and defeated that year.

They defeated Holton 14-6 in the opener. That's your quick start and confidence builder.

In the second game Rural defeated Leavenworth 20-13. The same school that had handed them a 14-0 defeat the year prior. These two wins were an excellent start. WR had already matched their winning totals for '74 and '75 in just two games.

Game three was against rival Hayden High and they beat the Junior Blues 24-6.

In the next two games Washburn Rural defeated Seaman 30-14 and Highland Park 22-19. Rural had not beaten Park in the last eight seasons. That kind of a signature win would boost confidence in players. Folks were seeing signs of improvement. There was momentum being built at Washburn Rural.

So much of a high school athletes' performance and their team successes hinge on confidence. And, when the past lent very little success, the athletes had to believe in themselves and trust their coaches were doing all they could to prepare them. And success was starting to set-in.

In game six Rural played Shawnee St. Joseph. And they were a very strong program and handed Rural a 24-0 loss. But this still was a measuring stick for a team looking for positives to hang their hats on.

Going into district play they lost to Emporia 28-11. In game two against Atchison WR lost an overtime game 22-16.

The last game of district secured the first winning season for Rural in thirteen years with a 22-0 drubbing of Shawnee Heights.

In 1976 there was a solid foundation laid. The school community was elated with a winning season. They were encouraged by the character that was instilled in their young men. It was a priority. Football, once again, became fun for Washburn Rural kids. They had something to look forward to and build towards going into the next school year. Weights became a priority and strength became a trademark at Rural. Strength and conditioning became important to the athletes.

CAN 1977 BE A
TURNING POINT?

After two solid years of rebuilding, instilling confidence and toughening up players, it appeared that the renewed interest in football at Rural was about to pay dividends. Coaches bought into the formula and players were buying into what kind of preparation they had to do in the off-season to be winners. Despite losing their senior quarterback, Steve Schuster, who went on to attend and play football at Kansas State University, there were some solid returning lettermen ready to make their mark on the school's improving program.

In an August 30, 1977 Topeka Capital-Journal sports article written by Stan Wilson, he talks about the difference a couple of inaugural seasons made for the Junior Blues. He called Bowen a "man of few words" but also said, "he gets a sparkle in his eye when he talks about the upcoming season."

"We know we've got some hitters," Bowen said. "We're getting back to the kind of game I like."

In 1976 the Junior Blues started the season 4-1 when quarterback Schuster wrecked his knee, but still finished 5-4. Jim Speake, now a senior, got lots of experience as the replacement quarterback and was ready to lead the team his senior year.

Also returning was a stronger Steve Stallard, running back-linebacker, who put on 20 pounds of muscle between seasons.

Of the increased muscle of Stallard and some of his teammates Bowen said, "That builds confidence. He knows he's strong and he's able to handle it. And he's not the only one."

In fact, Bowen hesitantly predicted that this season the Junior Blues might have four college prospects. Joining Stallard would be tight end-defensive end Will Cokeley, a 6'2" 195-pound senior. Also on the team were two linemen, Ed Linquist, 5'11" 211-pounds and Fred Palenske, 6'2" 223-pounder. Add another six returning starters from the previous season and it was easy to see where Bowen's optimism came from.

When asked how much better Rural would be in '77 Bowen cautiously said, "We're stronger. I know we're stronger. But I imagine everybody in our league is stronger too. The competition is there. We're either going to have to rise to it or we're not going to win." Bowen was good with the media. Kind of a "we could be good" approach, never one to tip his poker hand.

Ottawa High School was the opening game and there was anticipation. In a hard-fought game Rural won 8-6 and all scoring occurred in the first half. Bowen, undoubtedly, was happy with the win, but probably not too pleased with fumbling seven times. They lost three of those fumbles for turnovers. It was the second year in a row that Rural started the season with a win though.

They went to Leavenworth and pulled out a 12-7 victory. This was a school that, just two years prior, shut them out. To start 2-0 was a big step, but league rival Hayden, whom Rural had not beaten in the two previous years, awaited.

The close games with Ottawa and Leavenworth may have paid dividends. Mentally the athletes were not intimidated by close contests. This one was more than close. Playing the second half in a torrential rain, Rural had to go three overtimes to defeat Hayden 18-12. Somehow Rural was able to knot up the game at 6-6 on a third-quarter touchdown pass, Speake to Brett Holtom on a fourth-and-nine play that netted a 13-yard score. Both teams scored in the first overtime. Rural's score came on a two-yard plunge by quarterback Speake. In the second overtime neither team scored, but in the third overtime Rural stopped Hayden and was able to score on a Stallard four-yard touchdown run to win the game. It was Rural's best start at 3-0 under Bowen.

After three wins the Capital-Journal had Washburn Rural ranked number nine in 4A. Nice recognition, but rankings are mostly for fans. Still, it was good to hear

Washburn Rural's name amongst the best football schools in their classification.

In their fourth game they met a very good Seaman team who was coming off losses to Emporia and Hayden. And this would be Rural's homecoming game. Seaman was a team that Rural had handled the previous two seasons beating the Vikings. But funny how high school seasons differ. Seaman scored on Rural's first possession when the Junior Blues fumbled the ball and the Seaman defender scooped the football and scored from 62-yards out. Seaman never relinquished that early lead. Rural scored a touchdown in the second quarter on a five-yard Chris Tantillo run, but missed their extra point. And opening the second half Seaman returned the kickoff to the Rural three-yard line before scoring the second touchdown and led 13-6. Seaman scored a third time and made the extra point which widened the lead to 20-6. Long-time Seaman coach, Bill Mosley, told the sportswriter, Stan Wilson of the Capital-Journal, "I don't think Washburn Rural will lose another game." That statement would end up being pretty prophetic, but Seaman handed the Junior Blues their first loss of the season 20-12. It was an opportunity to learn from your mistakes or it could be a turning point if there was a lack of confidence because of the loss they suffered.

In game five the Junior Blues fought tooth and nail to scratch out a 12-7 victory over a talented Highland Park team. Park had some excellent young players and their program was on the rise. It was a good bounce-back win for WR. The soggy field conditions probably held down the offenses and the scoring a bit. Rural had to rely on a late comeback after Highland Park took the lead 7-6 in the fourth quarter. Immediately after Park scored the go-ahead touchdown, Rural, on their first offensive play following the kickoff, gave the ball to Brett Holtom on a dive play and he ran the distance, 66-yards for the go-ahead score making the final 12-7 Washburn Rural. Each of Rural's four wins had been by less than a touchdown and they stood 4-1.

In their final regular season game before entering district to determine playoff teams Washburn Rural gained some momentum with their best offensive showing in three years by drubbing Holton 41-0. Washburn Rural scored almost every way imaginable and scored often. Between Tantillo and Holtom the duo combined for nearly 200 yards rushing. Five different Junior Blues scored touchdowns during this game. This could either be a momentum builder for district play or it could be detrimental if the athletes became too confident. Bowen always had a pretty good idea of the pulse of his teams. This team was proving to be resilient, could win close games and the offense was improving each week.

Ron Bowen had a very sound, fundamental premise for all his teams. He kept the offense simple. Every player had a good grasp of each play. He introduced a minimal number of plays and schemes and only expanded the offense once the team could show they had mastered the existing plays. He wasn't a gadget guy that tried to fool the opposing team or their coaches. He moved players to positions that they could play and where they could contribute to team successes. Then they applied practice repetitions to improve the execution of the simple offensive plays until they became habit and second nature. Timing and precision would consistently be terms that you could apply to Washburn Rural offenses.

Waiting for Rural in the first round of district play was longtime nemesis and league rival Emporia which had just come off a loss to Leavenworth but was still ranked third in 4A classification. In the previous two seasons Emporia's combined score against Rural would have been 25 points allowed and they scored 70. Pretty lopsided and not a confidence booster. There had to be preparation for what Emporia did as a team and the Rural kids would have to be playing their best in this one.

One thing defensive coordinator, Ray Glaze preached about defense was keep it simple as well. He also tried to take away the one, two or preferably three things an opponent's offense did the best. Emporia was no exception to that rule. He would absolutely make certain his personnel were solid where it needed to be solid and he would make certain the scout team ran Emporia's three best plays so his defense knew what it would take to defend them. And example was Emporia's fullback trap.

In 1977 a major milestone was achieved when Rural defeated Emporia 22-14. Washburn Rural amassed 318 yards on the ground against the Spartans. And Emporia lost two fumbles to set up short Junior Blue drives for touchdowns. It was a close contest right up to the end and it took an interception by sophomore

Kerry Golden to preserve the win and give Rural sole possession of first place in the Centennial League. Rural's defense held Emporia to two scores and 266 yards of total offense. Emporia had nine first downs compared to Rural's 16. Funny thing about district play. You win your first game you look at game two as a real opportunity.

The next two district games were two league rivals Atchison and Shawnee Heights. Washburn Rural defeated Atchison in a hard-fought game 16-0 and the defense again was dominant in that win. And Washburn Rural entered that game as the fifth-ranked team in 4A.

What was on the line in week number nine against Shawnee Heights, was a chance for the first time ever for Washburn Rural to earn a playoff game. Standing in their way was league rival Shawnee Heights. Rural had shut out Heights 22-0 the previous season and this year Rural beat the Thunderbirds (some Rural faithful referred to them as the "Dirty birds"- origin unknown) 24-0. Two solid shutouts to earn the school's first playoff appearance. And Washburn Rural grounded out 382 rushing yards to Heights' 95 yards. There wasn't a single passing yard by either team. The game was also the first time since the KSHSAA had implemented the playoffs in 1969 that Rural earned a playoff berth. It capped the second straight winning season (5-4 in 1976) but this time the Junior Blues were 8-1.

As successful as Washburn Rural was on the muddy field Friday night, the team could only get Coach Bowen in the showers to celebrate which sort of parallels the current tradition of the winning teams dousing their head coach with a Gatorade bath from the water cooler. The remaining assistant coaches took refuge in their coach's office and fought off player's attempts to get them into the showers. Bowen told Capital-Journal sportswriter, Stan Wilson, "I was trapped on the field." So, it was Bowen that paid the price of getting doused by his team. "I'd like to pay it (the price) every year," Bowen told Wilson.

Pittsburg High had won its district and were awaiting the Junior Blues. The Dragons had established a solid reputation in southeast Kansas but very little was known about the opponent. What was known was that Pittsburg had made the playoffs five of the last nine years. They also had played for one state championship in 1970 against Dodge City.

Another thing worth noting is the transformation of Washburn Rural's football program and the transformation of the school culture seemed to go hand-in hand. In an article from the Topeka Daily Capital from November 11, 1977, staff writer Don Skinner wrote an article called "Washburn Rural exudes new spirit." In that article there was acknowledgements from school officials that stated school absences were down and students were generally taking more interest in their classroom work.

How much of this could be attributed to football or how much the renewed spirit inspired the football team was not able to be measured. But a resurgence in both was present. As an example, Dick Patterson, who was in charge of student activities and who came to Rural the same year Bowen started coaching there in 1975 said, "When I first came here the attendance bulletin (listing of school daily absences) ran three pages most days. Now we're down to one page. And that includes students who have excused absences. We have about one student a day absent on an unexcused basis."

Washburn Rural took approximately 250 students to Pittsburg. Football players, cheerleaders and band students were included in this count. The team chartered a bus, and there were five school bus loads of students who made the trip. And numerous cars drove independently to the game which made even more fans cheering for Rural.

Washburn Rural's close games earlier in the year may have paid off. Washburn Rural capitalized on three of the six Pittsburg turnovers as they defeated Pittsburg 26-23. Rural's poise played a big part in this game as Pittsburg scored on its first possession, a 55-yard nine play drive and a touchdown. But Rural came back and scored on their first possession as well and then scored twice more in the first quarter to take a 20-7 lead. The three touchdowns were made by Steve Stallard. His first was on a 57-yard run, his second on a fumble he scooped and scored from 37 yards and the third on a 32-yard pass from Jim Speake.

After halftime, the Junior Blues finished their scoring on a Chris Tantillo four-yard run for a 26-7 lead. And then it was hang-on as Pittsburg scored twice to draw to 26-23 with about three and one-half minutes left in the game.

This set up a tough semi-final assignment with traditionally powerful Bishop Miege, a private school from the Kansas City area. The winner would advance to the state championship game. Washburn Rural fought tooth and nail as did Miege. The game went to overtime and Rural suffered only their second loss of the 1977 season. Bishop Miege 20 Washburn Rural 14.

Miege was a team who already had two state titles under their belt. They had to come to Washburn Rural who had to bring in extra bleachers to accommodate the over 3,000 fans anticipated (their stadium had seating for 1,000 spectators).

Washburn Rural came out strong and had a 14-3 halftime lead on Miege, but Miege came out with a renewed energy and scored the second half's only points to ruin Rural's chance to be the first Topeka football school to play for a state championship. But the entire second half was played on the Junior Blues side of the field and turnovers, penalties and miscues uncharacteristically allowed a good Miege team to come back to tie it. Miege had a chance to win it in regulation on a field goal from 22-yards, but Bill Holtom blocked the kick to send the game to overtime.

Miege won the coin toss and elected to take the ball second so they would know whether they had to score a touchdown or a field goal. Washburn Rural stalled at the two-yard line. Miege scored a touchdown on their possession on a 3-yard run to end the overtime game 14-20.

Miege Coach Len Mohlman after the game said, "This is the finest football team I've seen in Topeka since the Levi Lee era at Topeka High." Mohlman added, "They're the best we faced this year. We were scared of them all week." Quite a compliment considering Rural's lengthy accumulation of losing records dating back to 1962. Miege went on to defeat Winfield for the state championship a week later.

That year, in addition to winning the Centennial League title, Rural took seven of the 23 positions on the All-Centennial League team. Fred Palenske, Ed Linquist and Steve Stallard were first team offensive selections. Will Cokeley, Brett Holtom, Chris Tantillo and Palenske were recognized on the defensive side of the ball.

Palenske, Cokeley and Stallard were selected to the 4A all-state team. Linquist, Holtom and Tantillo were honorable mention 4A all-state. And Palenske was chosen for the all-state all-class team and Will Cokeley was honorable mention all-state all classes.

Despite the loss to Bishop Miege, in a short three-year period Rural went from 2-7 in 1975 and a perennial losing team for 13 years to back-to back winning seasons (1976 and 1977) and their first ever playoff appearance. They came within an eyelash of playing for a state championship in 1977. Spirits were riding high in the little country school called Rural. And I was about to become a part of that tradition.

MY STUDENT
TEACHING
EXPERIENCE- FALL
OF 1978

As a young, impressionable college student, nearing graduation, I was asked to choose a Topeka, Kansas school for my upcoming student teaching experience. At the conclusion of my course work at Washburn University the final step of student teaching was like an internship which is the culminating part of many other college degrees. As a student teacher, I would work in a school for a semester, under the supervision and watchful eye of an experienced instructor. And just like my random, thoughtless choice four years prior of where I would attend college, I also did little to no research about where I should student teach. Yet it would be the high school in Topeka where I would spend a semester learning the nuances of instruction and it would be a very important step in my attempts to become an effective educator. I didn't think of the decision that way when I was twenty-two. Few prospective teachers do I would imagine. But the experience I gained and the connections I made lead me to eventually spending my entire teaching career in one school district.

I was from a small town, Baldwin City, Kansas, where in 1974 I and 59 other graduates received our high school diplomas. I thought what might be best would be to choose a Topeka high school which might most be like my high school experience. No public school in Topeka was nearly that small. I spent a couple of weeks observing at Topeka-Seaman (which was considered rural) and I also spent two weeks at an urban junior high school, Eisenhower. They called these short experiences a "practicum." I even got to spend some time observing at Topeka West High School and enjoyed being around their football coach, Frank Walton. Coach Walton who is now a Topeka West Hall of Famer was a well- respected professional at the time and had a wonderful coaching record while leading their football team. He was also a very competent physical education instructor.

So, having observed at Seaman, the other two remaining rural high schools to choose from were Shawnee Heights and Washburn Rural. During my college days, I was an avid reader of the Topeka Capital-Journal sports page, so I knew the local high school sports scene from 1975-1977. And I knew that Washburn Rural had the good fortune of making the Kansas High School (KSHSAA) football playoffs in 1977. At that time, the football playoffs were relatively new and certainly exciting. In 1969 the KSHSAA created a system where schools of common size could qualify and advance through a playoff system to determine a state champion in football. Rural's recent successes in both basketball and football caught my attention. When I found I would be working at that school, I wanted to volunteer as a football coach while student teaching. I student taught in the fall of 1978. The school year and the high school football season began in August. So, I chose, what appeared to me, to be a successful school, at least in the sports realm. Washburn Rural High School was strong in football and basketball. Little did I know that the school also had outstanding academics as well as successful activities like debate. In addition to those positives Auburn-Washburn schools had such a supportive school community and was not too large in enrollment.

Now, the next step, after checking the student teaching box for Washburn University's education department, was to contact the gentleman with whom they assigned me to student teach. It just so happened that the school's physical education teacher was also their head football coach, Ron Bowen. I might have seen a photo of Coach Bowen in the local newspaper but I'd never met him. So, in early August, I called Coach Bowen and set up a meeting.

The day we met I was nervous. After all, I wanted to make a decent first impression. This was the gentleman who would oversee the start of what, I hoped, would be my long career in education. He would be my first mentor and teach me what he knew about instructing classes, teaching kids and maybe teach me a little about coaching football. I admittedly knew relatively little about any of those. I don't remember what I wore that day. Probably some workout type clothing. Maybe a sweatsuit. And I took the long trip south on Burlingame Road, which coincidentally turns into 61st Street without any turns (I know that is difficult to understand) and I thought I was way out in the boonies. After all, the school was called Rural. And in those days, it was in a rural area at the intersection of 61st and Wanamaker. Lots of farmland between the city of Topeka and Washburn Rural High School.

Rural was the high school of attendance for the kids of the men and women stationed at Forbes Air Force Base. Children of Air Force families attended Rural schools. Enrollment in the Auburn-Washburn district boomed in the 70s partly because of the Air Base. There was some transiency associated with Rural back then, and the school enrollment teetered between 3A and 4A. Kansas schools are classified by the size of their enrollments. The largest 16 schools were 5A at that time, the largest enrollment classification at that time. The Manhattan, Lawrence, the KC Shawnee Missions and Wichita schools comprised the largest 5A classification at that time. Eventually they would expand the classifications to 1A-6A attempting to reduce the enrollment disparities a bit more.

Auburn-Washburn schools were a mixture of military kids, farmers' kids and some folks who chose to live on the outskirts of town in newly formed suburban housing developments. It was the time of urban flight in Topeka. There was a new subdivision of homes surrounding Lake Sherwood. More about the school later.

So, on the day of Coach Bowen's and my meeting, I entered the back door of the locker room, as per Coach Bowen's instructions. His office was just off the locker room. There was a glass window in his office where he could view and supervise the locker's dressing area. I made my way through the door and called out, "Coach Bowen?" A gruff voice responded, "Right here." And that began what would be a lifetime friendship that took on many shapes professionally. I couldn't predict that day how our lives would continue to be intertwined professionally and personally for so many wonderful years. More about that later.

Coach Bowen stood to shake my hand and I introduced myself. He was not a tall man, but he had a firm handshake and a warm smile. I would have described him as a positive, assertive individual. We sat down and I do not remember exactly what the conversation consisted of. I believe he asked me a lot of questions about my background. Where did I grow up, what did my family do for a living, what had my life experiences been like up to this point? I am certain I talked too much and probably babbled on a bit too long about this and that. He happened to know my former high school football coach. In fact, Coach Bowen attended Kansas State Teachers College-Emporia with my coach during their days as college students. That brought about numerous stories about Merle Venable. My stories and Coach Bowen's recollections as well.

I remember Coach Bowen mentioning that Venable's reputation and his antics were something the Emporia football squad found about. And before Venable joined them at Emporia, they were wondering what kind of a character was coming to their campus.

As Bowen and I talked, he told me that he would welcome my help on his coaching staff. He thought I could be most useful to his program helping the two coaches assigned to the sophomore team. Rural, at the time, consisted of three grades 10-12. They had one junior high feeder program so sophomore football was their athletes' first exposure to the high school programs. He emphasized how important the sophomore football experience was. He gave me every indication that my work with those kids would be extremely important. Coach Bowen had a way of making you feel like you had just been assigned the most important position on the coaching staff. He treated his assistants like he thought WE would determine the amount of success he and the Rural football teams would have. He believed in us and he treated us assistants with reverence and respect. Always.

So began my journey into what would eventually become a 36-year career in education, all at Auburn-Washburn. After I elected to take early retirement in the summer of 2015, I was asked to coach for Steve Buhler's football staff at Washburn Rural High School. I've been coaching freshman football ever since so my running total is 41 years. I guess Coach Bowen's first impression of me was decent. My first impression of him was fantastic. Like all great head coaches, he had a presence. He was a difference maker. He was a leader. It was not hard to recognize. It didn't take long to figure out.

MY STUDENT TEACHING EXPERIENCE AT WASHBURN RURAL HIGH SCHOOL

I was thrilled with the prospect of student teaching and having an opportunity to coach football at Washburn Rural. At that time the high school included grades 10-12. The high school had a sophomore football schedule, a Junior varsity schedule and varsity schedule.

Coach Bowen asked if I, being the newbie, would assist the two coaches assigned to sophomores. Of course, I was in no position to bargain about my assignment on the football staff and, for me, I felt I was needing the lowest level (sophomores) possible to try to develop and hone some coaching skills. I really felt like I knew very little about the game of football, let alone knowing how to coach the game.

The sophomore coach at the time was a young math teacher named Steve McDermeit. He had an assistant coach, at the time, who knew very little about football, and had never coached, so McDermeit was happy having me around helping. The three of us got along well and, although we had a limited number of sophomores in 1978, I felt like we got the most out of them. At least at the time we felt like we did.

We had a couple of kids capable of playing the position of quarterback, Kevin Crow and Ron Gifford. Crow played varsity secondary, so we made the best of having two QB's. I don't remember much about that season, but I remember very vividly a play that I drew up for our kickoff return team.

Since we had two quarterbacks, I told them that whoever caught the ball on the kickoff, allow the opponents to converge on you. I instructed that the other QB stay behind the QB that caught the kickoff which would allow the one who catches the ball to set-up and throw back across the field to the other QB positioned clear on the other side of the field

Fortunately, Gifford received the kick, as we had wanted, and he quickly turned to toss the football back behind him, constituting a lateral and made Crow, a faster athletic kid, eligible to advance the football.

And we fooled the kickoff team so badly. Crow literally jogged the length of the field for a touchdown. Those were fun football days. We weren't smart enough to be afraid to try something. I do think back and regret that we didn't play players more liberally. Of course, we didn't have many substitutes that year. Years later, as a sub varsity coach, I learned that you didn't have to have your best athletes on the field every play to be a successful team. And playing more kids kept player interest higher and helped encourage more kids to stay out for football during their high school attendance.

In those days the sophomores played on Thursdays. Varsity team, of course, played Friday nights. Junior Varsity played the following Monday. We had a kid (Crow) who started on offense for sophomore games but was a starting defensive back for varsity. During those years he got to play offense for the sophomores and defense for the varsity on Friday nights. `

Ron had a philosophy that I still respect today. He would not put a sophomore up against an upperclassman in a contact drill unless he deemed the younger player was mentally and physically ready for the physicality of high school football. I think this is a very key part of his success. He wanted to make certain a player was ready physically. Boys mature at vastly different rates. If a player was not ready, Ron wanted to make certain that when they were asked to hit and be hit by strong athletes, it would be an experience they could handle. No sense rushing it and causing a player to get "stung" before he was ready, which might result in him quitting football. I've seen it happen.

Another aspect related to Ron Bowen's coaching was he knew the importance of having a dedicated group of players who backed up the starting players on offense and defense. He called these scout team players, who wore yellow penny targets to identify themselves, the "Golden Goodies." On more than one occasion he stressed to his players how important having a good scout team was to the varsity's successes. The harder the substitute players made it on the first teamers, the better prepared the varsity was for a Friday night game. Makes perfect sense.

In 1978 the Washburn Rural Junior Blues finished 4-2 in the Centennial League and were 6-3 overall but did not make the playoffs losing in district play to Emporia. Rural was classified as 5A as the state classification boasted SIX classifications by then. Emporia made the playoffs that year and were first- round losers to Great Bend 31-21.

Lineman Kevin Heideman was selected first-team all-class 5A and running back/ linebacker Chris Tantillo was a second-team selection.

That school year Washburn Rural graduated 204 seniors.

1979 Football Season Bowen's Fifth at the Washburn Rural Helm

Washburn Rural started the 1979 campaign with two wins over Ottawa and Leavenworth, holding each opponent to just six points each.

After losing to Hayden by a narrow margin in week three, 6-0, the Junior Blues went on a pattern of win, lose, win, lose, win and lose. They finished the season with a 5-4 record for their fourth straight winning season but failed to make the playoffs, losing to district and league foes Emporia and Shawnee Heights.

In three of the four losses to finish the season they were shut out three times (Hayden, Highland Park and Emporia) and scored just once in the final game losing 9-7 to Shawnee Heights.

Backs Kerry Golden and Andre Dillard were selected to the Topeka all-city first team. Lineman Tim Wagner was chosen as a second team all-city selection. Dillard led the city in rushing yardage with 837 yards averaging 7.9 yards per carry. As the quarterback, Golden used his quickness to run the option effectively and was credited for making good decisions about when to pitch the ball to Dillard.

Bowen's five-year record at Washburn Rural was 27-20. The program was showing signs of stability.

BOWEN TURNS A HAPLESS WASHBURN RURAL FOOTBALL PROGRAM INTO A WINNER

Coach Bowen had come to Washburn Rural in 1975 at a time when WR football was not very good. He, along with Ray Glaze, a defensive football genius, and some solid, longtime coaching staff members turned Washburn Rural into one of the most consistent, successful, winning programs in the state. In fact, in Bowen's second year Rural had a 5-4 record and it was the first winning football record the school had had since 1962, ending a thirteen-season drought with only losing seasons.

And the biggest advantage, one he recognized, was he had numerous great athletes and hard-working kids who played football at Washburn Rural during those years. In the early going Bowen and his staff had to overcome a losing mind set. And they had to make kids a little tougher. In 1985, just ten years after taking over a program that was in shambles, Washburn Rural became the first Topeka school to win a state football championship. We repeated that feat in 1986 and had a near miss in 1987. Another state championship added in 1989, all of these in the 5A classification (next to biggest schools in the state because there were now six classification sizes). It was an incredible time for the football program. WR made another state championship appearance in 1992 losing to Lawrence in the 6A state championship in one of the best games I have ever witnessed. I was the school's athletic director by then.

How effective was Ron Bowen as a leader, a coach, a mentor to student-athletes as well as an influence on the non-football playing students that he taught? I can tell you that, as great a football coach he was, he was even a better teacher. He spent time teaching Health classes to Rural sophomores, but he was primarily the school's Strength and Conditioning teacher. In September 1998 the Auburn-Washburn school district named the football stadium "Bowen-Glaze Stadium." Ron Bowen and Ray Glaze were a coaching tandem perhaps the best duo in the state. Both had retired at the end of the 1997-98 school year as coaches. Glaze had retired as a teacher a few years prior to 1997 but, at the request of Bowen stayed on the football staff. They were two of the most technically sound football men of their time. And they happened to be on the same coaching staff. In 2008 Bowen was selected for the Kansas State High School Activities Association's Hall of Fame. I am proud to say I nominated him for that distinction. He was also selected to be inducted into the Washburn Rural High School's Hall of Fame in 2009. In 2019 he was selected for the Shawnee County Hall of Fame AND was placed into the Valley Center Hall of Fame. He also was selected to be a HOF member for the Kansas Shrine Bowl.

Prior to coming to Topeka and Washburn Rural, Bowen also led a Valley Center team to the 1973 playoffs. At Washburn Rural playoff appearances occurred in 1977, 1981, 1985, 1986, 1987, 1988, 1989, 1990, 1991 and 1992. Washburn Rural won 3 state 5A championships in '85, '86 and '89. They were state runners-up in 6A in 1992. They won 10 Centennial League football championships. His teams captured two Chisholm Trail championships while at Valley Center. He was selected Topeka City Coach of the Year six years, Centennial Coach of the Year four years, and in 1989 was selected as Kansas state coach of the year by the Topeka Capita-Journal and the Wichita Eagle Beacon and the Kansas State High School Activities Association. Also, in 1989 Ray Glaze was selected as the Topeka City Coach of the Year, the first and only time an assistant coach ever received that recognition. Bowen has been an assistant coach and a head coach for the annual Kansas Shrine Bowl (a senior all-star benefit game) and has continued his association with that organization's annual event by serving as co-chairman of their alumni committee. The proceeds benefit the Shriner's Hospital efforts.

Ron Bowen's overall record in football was 220-127-3, a .630 winning percentage. At Washburn Rural his record was 156—73, a .681 winning percentage. He was a leader. He could coach football. But more importantly, I was most impressed with the relationships Coach Bowen developed with non-football playing students. Every young person in his classes were important to him and he treated them as such. You will be able to read several accounts provided in this book to really tell these stories and those accounts will best represent what he meant to students. Accounts and recollections from family, colleagues, former football players, opposing coaches AND non-football playing former students who will best tell that part of Ron Bowen's story. They will say it best, the kind of mentor Ron Bowen was. I was simply glad to have had the opportunity to student teach under Ron. It was a different time back in the fall of 1978 when my association with Ron Bowen began. I soon learned that it was great to be a Junior Blue.

WASHBURN RURAL HIGH SCHOOL- TOPEKA HISTORY

T he high school was founded in 1918 when the Washburn University preparatory academy and its neighbors south and west came together to form Washburn High School in Topeka, Kansas. Classes were held in the basement of the university's Macvicar Chapel from 1918-1939. Students enjoyed the privileges of using the college library, gymnasium, and science laboratories. Since the high school was located on the college campus, the same colors of the blue and white, and the college mascot, Ichabod Washburn, were adopted by the high school. Students from Washburn High School became known as the Junior Ichabods and later adapted the mascot Junior Blues.

By 1939, the crowded conditions on the campus forced Washburn High School to build its own building located at the intersection of 19th and Hope street. In 1946 the school became officially known as Washburn Rural High School. For many years the high school enjoyed its own building which, at the time was considered in a rural setting between the streets of Gage and Fairlawn. However, by 1953, the city had expanded surrounding the school and forcing it to a new location on southwest Wanamaker Road in the 4900 block.

Within 10 years the school outgrew this location and fall of 1964 a new school was opened at SW 61st street and Wanamaker Road (the current location). The old building at 4900 Wanamaker was transformed into Jay Shideler Junior High School and eventually was converted into Jay Shideler Elementary School.

Over 100 students were enrolled at the new WRHS in 1964. Many of those students were third generation Junior Ichabods. This was the fifth building that had housed the high school since 1918. Since opening, the current school has undergone expansions and numerous renovations. In 2020 it was one of the largest high schools in Kansas with a grade 9-12 enrollment of over 1,900 students. It is also one of the highest performing schools in Kansas. (1)

(1)   Taken from Auburn-Washburn's current web site from a section written in 2018 commemorating the 100th anniversary of the high school.)

In the 1970s Washburn Rural High School was a school on the outskirts of Topeka in the rural southwest part of the city. It served a large segment of a rural farming community and also was school for Forbes Air Force Base at the time. The growing population of the Air Force Base was largely responsible for the school district's decision to build a larger facility and move south from what is now known as Jay Shideler Elementary. In 1964 the original building was constructed at 61st and Wanamaker. With all the additions to the facility, the original building was surrounded by additions and even added a second story section.

There was a large influx of urban flight in the mid-1960's and 1970's. The housing addition known as Lake Sherwood was a popular, growing neighborhood. Additionally, when the district made the decision to close Auburn High School, Washburn Rural High School absorbed that population of its' students. Thus, the name of the district, Auburn-Washburn School District #437.

When there were only five classifications of schools in Kansas, WRHS quickly grew from 3A to 4A and eventually became a 5A school when classification expanded to six divisions (1A-6A). Back in the day WRHS won their first and the city's first ever basketball state championship in 1960. At the time the state had two classification of schools, A and B. WRHS won the 1960 Class B classification with a couple of players who went on to play at Kansas State University (Ron Paradis) and Kansas University (Delvy Lewis). They were surrounded by a host of good high school athletes as well and, under the coaching of Bryce Stallard, captured the school's third state title. The first two were in the early 1950s in baseball.

When the next basketball state championship was won in 1982 the school was a mixture of socio-economic groups. But the school, by name, Rural, was generalized and largely looked upon by the city and state as a school for cowboys and farmers. That 1982 basketball team thought it would be great fun to dress up for their trip to the state basketball tournament in Emporia, Kansas in cowboy hats and cowboy boots. They had a lot of fun with the stigma and generalization others assigned to their school.

Ron Bowen came to Washburn Rural High School in 1975 and took over a football program that was in abysmal shape. The football program was not successful. Winning football was not yet considered very possible.

When Bowen arrived, he took over a Washburn Rural football program that last had a winning season in 1962. That was a dozen years of losing records. One colleague that Bowen called to ask when considering the Rural coaching job told him, "that place is a career ender, you can't win there." Ironically, Bowen did end up ending his career there. On his terms, he retired in 1997.

Previously, Bowen had coached in several smaller schools, even a junior high school. He had been able to be successful at Valley Center, making the playoffs. But Rural was a tougher challenge. Bowen felt good about the location and what he heard from Washburn Rural folks and took the job.

WASHBURN RURAL BOWEN-LED ENTERS THE DECADE OF THE 1980'S

T he Junior Blues opened the '80s with a 13-0 win over Ottawa on a windy night. Rural outgained Ottawa in total offense by about 100 yards. Rural's quarterback, Kevin Crow, rushed for 101-yards and threw for another 81-yards but unfortunately twisted his ankle in the fourth quarter.

John Hughes took over as quarterback in week two and Rural ran into a stubborn and talented Leavenworth team and was beaten 21-7 to even their record at 1-1. Rural's only score came on a swing pass, Hughes to Greg Golden.

In week number three the Junior Blues hosted rival Hayden and Kevin Crow returned to quarterback for most of the game. What got Rural the winning score was a 92-yard opening kickoff return for a touchdown by Greg Golden. After Hayden scored and drew to 7-6 it was right before half and Crow re-injured his ankle. In came Hughes and found Lyndall Yarnell with a 10-yard touchdown with just 15 seconds remaining in the first half to push the score to 13-6. Hayden had more total yards and more first downs but hurt themselves with turnovers and the kickoff return was all Rural really needed. There was no scoring in the second half and Rural won 13-6 and now was 2-1.

In game four the Junior Blues handed Seaman its first defeat and moved to 3-1 with a 14-0 victory. Rural's defense was dominant in this game. Seaman only got into Rural territory once in the game and the Junior Blues held the Vikings to 37 yards rushing for the game.

Highland Park was too much for Rural in week number five defeating the Junior Blues by the narrowest of margins, 8-7. Highland Park was led by Melvin Douglas, who later would become an Olympic wrestler. Washburn Rural was now 3-2.

In a rare meeting between Topeka High and Rural in week number six Washburn Rural found some offense that had been lacking and defeated the Trojans 30-21. Both teams compiled over 300 yards of offense and, once again, John Hughes had to take over for Crow due to an injury. Hughes threw two touchdowns and ran for a short 1-yard touchdown. Ironically with the score 24-21 it was a 14-yard defensive interception for a pick six by Danny Larson that sealed the victory for Rural 30-21.

Washburn Rural lost their first district game to Emporia 22-7 and despite ending the season with district victories over Bonner Springs 14-6 and Shawnee Heights 14-12 the Junior Blues did not make the playoffs but finished 6-3.

Bryant Combs and Tom Dultmeier were selected all-city first team. Dultmeier was also chosen to the All-City team. Danny Larson and Larry Cox were selected second-team all-city. Honorable mention selections were Greg Campbell, Kevin Crow, Greg Golden, Robert House, John Hughes, Barry Hutton and Kevin McCarter.

The stage was set and the pieces in place for a really good 1981 season.

1981 the Second Year for the Junior Blues to Make the Playoffs

There was a lot of optimism in the fall of 1981. But no one would likely have predicted the success that the Junior Blues would have on the gridiron that year. How could one be so bold?

The Capital-Journal wrote a pre-season article. Sportswriter Allen Quakenbush predicted that Topeka West and Washburn Rural would be the class of the city programs. Rural had turned a perennial loser into five consecutive seasons a winner, with one playoff appearance. The Capital-Journal placed Rural as the fifth ranked team in Class 5A before there were any snaps.

Rural had eight defensive starters, their entire defensive backfield returning from a city leading defensive unit that only allowed 96 points in nine games. With two strong running backs, Jack Kelly and Greg Golden, accompanying quarterback John Hughes, who was more of a throwing quarterback, Coach Bowen was considering scrapping the wishbone offense for a more traditional power I formation. This would make the best use of a blocking fullback and a throwing quarterback.

Bowen's comment to sportswriter Allen Quakenbush about John Hughes spoke volumes. "John's not real fast," said Bowen, "but he makes up for it by being ahead in thought. He's always ahead in the thinking game and he's gotten quicker and bigger than he was last season."

Two additional backs were mentioned-Robert Steele and Danny Larson-who would spell the other backs. Steele was coming off of a knee injury so his productivity was unknown.

The line had four returning starters, tackle Greg Campbell, center Gary Tucker and two good tight ends in Lyndall Yarnell and Tim Stallard. Tim Filburn would be a wide receiver and Richard Bishop and Chris Toner would anchor other positions on the offensive line.

On defense Stallard, Tucker and Campbell were returning starters and would be joined by Ron Allen, Joel Warkentine as well as Bishop. Larson, Toner and Yarnell would man the linebacker slots along with Kelly.

All the secondary returned from a year ago with Rob Kaelin, Filburn and Golden.

Washburn Rural's first opponent that year was Atchison-Maur Hill. Within the first three minutes of the game Washburn Rural scored on a 28-yard Greg Golden run for, what would be the only score needed. But Rural added three more scores- two on the ground, another Golden run of 12-yards and Jack Kelly added a short four-yard touchdown run. The scoring was complete in the third quarter as John Hughes hit Tim Filburn on a 21-yard pass play. Royce Reed added the extra point-kick and the Junior Blues had a 25-0 shutout to start the season.

Next up was non-league and traditional powerhouse Manhattan. In a hard fought first half that saw the only scores be a Manhattan field goal and a one-yard Golden touchdown run, Washburn Rural found itself with just 40 seconds remaining, with the ball on the 49-yard line. Most thought Bowen would be content to take a three-point lead into halftime and regroup. Wrong.

John Hughes dropped back and hit a streaking Tim Filburn down the field for 48-yards. All that was left was Hughes to run the quarterback sneak and the Junior Blues had a 12-3 halftime lead that their defense made hold up. Final score Washburn Rural 12 Manhattan 3. Manhattan racked-up more offense than the Junior Blues, but Rural refused to let the Indians in the end zone. Rural made some big plays. Manhattan was 12-yards from the end zone on a fourth down-play, the back made the first down, but the defense caused a fumble that Richard Bishop fell on.

Later Manhattan drove again to the 12-yard line, but got a costly penalty moving them back to the 27-yard line and they tried a pass that Lyndall Yarnell intercepted with just a little over seven minutes remaining. Then Manhattan got the ball to the 13-yard line, but Danny Larson, Greg Golden and Yarnell stopped plays and Gary Tucker batted down a pass attempt. The victory was a big confidence boost for the Junior Blues as they started the year 2-0.

In the third game a very good Highland Park team took the Junior Blues to overtime before Rural prevailed 20-14. John Hughes hit Lyndall Yarnell with a 10-yard pass to seal the overtime victory. Once again Rural was outgained on the ground but won the passing game. And the game. They were 3-0.

Next on the schedule the rival league school Hayden but they were no match for the Junior Blues. Washburn Rural 25 Hayden 7. The offense was beginning to click on all cylinders and the defense was its annual stingy bunch. 4-0.

Emporia looked to be a stiff test going into the week five and the game did not disappoint. Even though it was Homecoming, which always made Coach Bowen a little nervous about the potential for distraction to the main event, Friday night football. By this time the Junior Blues were getting a lot of respect from the media. They went into the game as the third ranked team in 5A.

Emporia put the first touchdown in the books early with a first quarter six-yard pass and a made extra point kick. They held a 7-0 lead to halftime. But

Washburn Rural scored on a bit of trickery, a half-back pass from Greg Golden to Tim Filburn to move the score to 7-6. The two-point conversion attempt failed and there was not another score until Emporia kicked an impressive 38-yard field goal to go up 10-6.

Rural had one last chance, but the odds looked steep. They were 79 yards from their end zone with just 36 seconds remaining. And no timeouts. Rural used the clock and the sideline well. Two passes from Hughes to Filburn netted 24 yards. Then Hughes connected with Bob Steele for 20-yards over the middle and the Junior Blues had a new set of downs on the Emporia 15-yard line. Hughes only incompletion on the series stopped the clock with 6 seconds left. Then lightning struck.

In a post-game interview Bob Steele said, "I was running a post pattern (as time ran out). John rolled out to the right and everybody else started rolling with him. I just faded back to where nobody was, and he just laid it in there." Final score Washburn Rural 12 Emporia 10. Steele went on to say, "I think we had some help from the man upstairs tonight," as Rural ran its' undefeated record to 5-0.

They did get some help from Emporia. Four times the Spartans drove deep into Rural territory in the first half. Greg Campbell, a Rural defensive lineman, recovered fumbles at the 30, 10 and 11-yard lines. And Golden stepped in front of a pass at the Emporia 15-yard line for an interception. Lineman Gary Tucker caused three of the fumbles and managed to intercept a pass himself, as Emporia committed five turnovers. Linebacker Danny Larson told the Capital-Journal sportswriter Allen Quakenbush, "It's a dream. We've dreamed about this all week."

Quarterback John Hughes was the only person who didn't see the touchdown reception. He was flat on his back with the wind knocked out of him as he was hit as he released. "All I heard," Hughes said after the game, "was the roar of the crowd. But I didn't know who it was because Emporia had so many people there." Still on the ground Hughes found out that Rural had scored the game winning touchdown from the sideline chain gang, who came running onto the field in jubilation.

"Coach Bowen and I were talking on the sidelines," Hughes said, "and we thought we had a chance. We had two plays called and we just kept running the same two." About the last score Hughes said, "I rolled out and saw Golden in front of me, but there were just too many of them – four or five (Emporia defenders) so I just decided to hold up and throw. I saw Filburn waving his arms, and Steele was behind him and I knew I was getting pursued. I just figured, if I'd just get the ball to Bobby Steele it'd be easier."

The only error Hughes made was thinking there was anything easy about this miraculous drive. He earned City Player of the Week of course.

In the last regular season game before district play Rural had to face Seaman. In a thick fog that night John Hughes continued his air assault. In the first half he hit Lyndall Yarnell six times and hit Tim Filburn for a 24-yard score. For the half he had 130-yards passing and Rural tacked on a short run for a touchdown by fullback Jack Kelly to go to halftime set-up by a Chris Toner interception and 20-yard return. Rural was up 13-0 at halftime.

Rural managed only one more score on a short two-yard run by Bob Steele. Defender Greg Hanna ended the only Seaman threat to score by sacking their quarterback. The Junior Blues proudly went home with a 19-0 shutout. Seaman couldn't get untracked against the stingy Junior Blue defense putting up 147-yards of total offense and the Junior Blues were 6-0 and rolling.

Washburn Rural had tough district opponents with Bonner Springs and Atchison both 4-2 and losses coming at the hands of some quality opponents. League rival Shawnee Heights was the last opponent and were a respectable 3-3.

Bonner Springs proved not to be too stiff of a district opening opponent as Washburn Rural rolled over them 34-0 to move to 7-0 and, most importantly getting that first district victory.

Washburn Rural traveled to Atchison for their second district game. Atchison, despite being held to few yards, took a 7-0 lead into halftime. This was not a good start for the Junior Blues. But, as was often the case, some halftime adjustments were made and the Junior Blues came out with a vengeance and scored all of the 27-points of the second half. And it didn't hurt that Atchison recorded just 55 yards of total offense. Rural relied on a rejuvenated ground game picking up 148 rushing yards, almost all in the second half and three Bob Steele short rushing touchdowns of 8, 1 and 2-yards were plenty. Substitute Brien Brown tacked on a fourth touchdown on a one-yard dive play. In all Rural scored 21 points in the final quarter to get that all-important district win and move to 8-0.

The only thing standing between Washburn Rural and its second playoff appearance during Coach Bowen's tenure was league rival Shawnee Heights T-Birds. Heights had posted a 3-3 regular season record but stubbed their toe a bit in district play. That misfortune continued against Rural.

The first quarter was scoreless and, once again, the Junior Blues would have to come from behind when Shawnee Heights put the first score on the board with a nine play 45-yard drive that culminated with a short one-yard plunge. Shawnee Heights 7- Washburn Rural 0.

That drive must have woken Washburn Rural up. Starting on their own 12-yard line they completed an 88-yard drive with a touchdown. John Hughes had a 27-yard keeper and connected on two passes totaling 52 yards. Greg Golden banged one in from three-yards out and then carried the ball another three for the two-point conversion. Washburn Rural 8 Shawnee Heights 7. That would be all the scoring needed to win the district championship.

But, for good measure, the Junior Blues put up 25 points in the second half. On the second play after the second half kickoff, Golden carried the ball five yards for another touchdown, WR 14 SH 7.

The defense stiffened in the second half holding Heights to just 41-yards on the ground, never allowed Heights any closer than the 36-yard line and forced two turnovers.

But the offense was not done and the aerial show continued. Hughes needed just 147-yards passing to become the city's first passer to surpass 1,000 yards since Rural's Steve Schuster did it in 1975. He hit the city's top receiver, Tim Filburn, with three touchdown passes of 12, 37 and 59 yards. And Hughes finished the season with 1,018 yards for the regular season. But most importantly, Washburn Rural got a 33-7 district win over Shawnee Heights and finished the season 9-0 which was the first undefeated team in Topeka since 1962. Ironically, the last city team to go undefeated was the 1962 edition of the Junior Blues led by star running back Dave Hupp. That 1962 team outscored their opponents for the year by a count of 332-33 and had five shutouts.

In a Capital-Journal article by sportswriter Allen Quakenbush, he talked about the similarities and the differences between the 1962 team and the 1981 team. "We're just pretty level all the way across as far as ability," Coach Bowen told Quakenbush. "They all do a good job at their position. I'd like to have 22 or more stars, then I wouldn't have to worry. But this team just works well together."

Quakenbush himself probably captured the essence of the 1981 Junior Blues when he said, "But there's something intangible about Washburn Rural's football team, a togetherness, an esprit de corps. The Junior Blues may not be overwhelming, but they're certainly a group of winners." Man, Quakenbush had a way with words.

Waiting for them in the first round of the playoffs was Olathe South who was 7-2. In 1981 South had lost their opening football game to KC Harmon 7-0. Their only other loss was to Bonner Springs in week five by a score of 14-6. Bonner was a team that Washburn Rural defeated 34-0 in week number eight. It's never safe to look at comparative scores in any kind of football, but especially high school football.

Optimism, however, ran high at Washburn Rural and in the city of Topeka. This team had proven to be resilient. Their defense was always going to be able to keep them in games even if the offense sputtered. In nine games the Junior Blue defense allowed only 54 points, averaging about six points per game. Only one team had scored two touchdowns on them (Highland Park). They gave up only 10 points to 6A playoff bound Manhattan and third ranked Emporia in 5A as well.

And their offense was a great balance of rushing and passing. Plus, the first playoff game in the quarterfinals was going to be on Rural's home field.

Olathe South had been almost as consistently impressive. They only allowed 68 points or just over seven points per game. And to get to this game South defeated Bishop Miege 16-15. This was the first year of South's existence as a high school when Olathe High split into two schools, North and South. Olathe South's coach was Bud Wheeler who coached at Olathe for several years prior to the district's move to split into two high schools. They were a veer team and moved the ball well on the ground. It promised to be a good game.

The game was a bit of a downer for the Junior Blues and their faithful. Olathe

South scored twice for a 12-0 victory to move to the semifinals only to be eliminated a week later by Emporia in a lopsided 53-22 loss. Emporia, the team that Rural beat on a last-second touchdown pass, would end up losing to Wichita Kapaun, 37-7 in the 5A state championship game.

Ron Bowen was selected Topeka city coach of the year by the Capital Journal. Junior Blues joining Coach Bowen on first team all-city were John Hughes, Lyndall Yarnell, Greg Campbell and Greg Golden. Yarnell was chosen defensive player of the year in the city. Gary Tucker and Tim Filburn were selected second team all-city. Honorable mention selections were Richard Bishop, Greg Hiebert, Robert Kaelin, Jack Kelly, Tim Stallard, Robert Steele and Chris Toner. That's 13 Junior Blues garnering honors along with their Coach.

The Junior Blues had one fine season, but likely wondered what could have been had they been able to beat Olathe South and meet Emporia in the semifinals.

Bowen's Service in Kansas National Guard

As you might guess I wanted as much input from Coach Bowen as possible concerning "his story." After all it was HIS story I was telling and along the way was able to mention a lot of good folks that helped him along the way.

When I told him I wanted to interject different phases from his life between the football summations, he very readily asked, "Would you like some information about my Kansas National Guard service?"

Of course. And I think this is a very important and significant part of Ron Bowen's life. I think the experience tells a lot about the man. And I felt it would be best to exemplify the humility, the simple, hard-working values he has through his own words. I took his text verbatim and in his voice, because his voice demonstrates qualities that he showed us everyday as people who had the good fortune of working with him and listening to him.

So, here is Coach Bowen's story, as told by him, about his experiences serving in the Kansas National Guard.

As told by Coach Bowen- "Hiawatha was home of headquarters and headquarters battery of the 154th field artillery battalion of the 35th Infantry Division. Housed in the same building where the Hiawatha High School basketball team played all their home games.

At 17 1/2 years- of age my parents signed so that I could enlist in the Guards. Many of my fellow classmates also enlisted at the same time. I enlisted April of 1955. It was common for many young kids to do so in Hiawatha.

One of my first experiences was to spend a night in Fort Leavenworth for the next day small arms qualifying. Of the three levels of qualification, Sharpshooter, Expert and Marksman, I was fortunate to be one of two in our outfit to earn a Sharpshooter medal.

In the year I enlisted you did your basic training the two weeks you went to your first camp. Later on enlistees spent six months of basic.

My first year we rode the troop train from Hiawatha to Camp McCoy in Wisconsin. All of the other years of my eight, except for one year at Camp Guernsey in Wyoming, were spent at Camp Ripley in Minnesota.

All years, except the first, we traveled by convoy in 6 by 6's, ¾ ton trucks and jeeps. It took two days at speeds, a lot of the time, at 40 mph.

A few of my experiences.

I was driving a jeep as we convoyed through Omaha, Nebraska. They always ran the 6 by 6's, known as deuces and half tons in front, followed by ¾ tons, then jeeps. They ordered us to close-up the convoy with a motorcycle cop leading us through Omaha. Well, jeeps didn't have very good brakes. So, when the convoy came to a sudden stop, I turned and braked to miss the jeep in front of us. The jeep behind us ran into us. Only did a little damage to our right front fender. Can't say that much for the one behind us.

One year, at camp, I was the driver for our first Sergeant Gene Shorb. We were out in the field and were supposed to have dug fox holes. Sgt. Shorb had me just dig down and throw a ridge up instead of a deep hole. A Major in our outfit, who was not the most liked, came by and he let the Sergeant know, in no uncertain terms, that the foxhole was not good. After the major left I asked the Sergeant if I needed to dig it deeper. He said no. He had served in World War II and in Korea in some tough situations. He said if you were down in a foxhole and a tank crew knew you were down in a fox hole they would spin around on it and bury you. In a shallow one you could roll out between the tracks to avoid them.

Every year in Camp Ripley the MPs would put on boxing matches. Well, when my brother Delayne and I were kids we got boxing gloves for Christmas. We did a lot of "boxing" with each other and with some neighbor kids. I didn't enter the MPs fights but one of our guard members did and wanted me to spar with him the night before his match. So, I did in front of our twelve-man tents in the Minnesota sand.

I saw him later in the week and asked him how he did in his match. He said he couldn't fight because I had broken his rib. I never knew for sure if that was true.

One night in Wyoming, I was getting ready to put my sleeping bag on the ground. On a rattlesnake. Since I was in the medic section and drove the jeep-ambulance I slept in it on a stretcher. The ambulance tire did the snake in.

One year I took one of our members to the doctor's tent out in the field with a bad case of poison ivy. The howitzers were firing overhead down range. All of the sudden there was a loud whistling sound and noise in the trees. Two doctors jumped down on the ground. Then we heard someone yelling cease fire. The doctors asked us why we just stood there. Well, we didn't know what was going on. We got out of there as soon as possible.

One year as we were getting lined-up to go to camp an eastern news reporter said the 35th Infantry Division was going to be activated and sent to Iran. Our First Sergeant Shorb was excited and ready to go. We later found out the situation was resolved and the 35th wasn't going to be activated.

One year in Camp Ripley I was selected to be a part of the color guard when the whole 35th Infantry Division was assembled on the parade grounds to stand in review for President Harry S. Truman. The color guard, being in front of our outfit, gave us a great view of President Truman as he rode by in the back of the jeep. The President was a former officer in the 35th.

I served eight years reaching the rank of Sergeant E5 commonly known as a "buck sergeant."

At my honorable discharge in 1963 the Guards had reorganized and with Hiawatha the headquarters and Headquarters Battery Second Howitzer Battalion 130th Artillery."

My commentary on this is simply a sincere thank you for your service Coach Bowen. But I think the text above, in his own words, shows his matter-of fact approach to any, and all duties and obligations he signed up for. He was humble about his service and it was something he chose so he was going to do it responsibly and to the best of his abilities. Whether he was teaching, coaching, serving his country, farming, he gives his all and is very prideful, in an inner-self sort of way. You didn't often hear his pride, but you saw it in his face, in his smile.

1982-1984 Building for that Championship Run

Attrition and graduation hit Washburn Rural hard in 1982. Many of the athletes that were leaders on the football team also played basketball like John Hughes, Marc Lowe, Lyndall Yarnell, Greg Golden and in the winter of the 1981-82 school year they won the 5A basketball state championship. And then they graduated taking with them a ton of leadership and ability.

The next football season Washburn Rural had a very respectable 6-3 record but Bonner Springs won the playoff spot from their district.

That year the Junior Blues started optimistically, returning four offensive starters from the 9-0 regular season '81 team along with six defensive starters. As usual in years following significant senior graduation, Bowen and his staff would look to move as many players into positions of need, even if it meant learning a new position for some kids. Not only did it help the team win and helped kids get more playing time. And those are both good things.

Bowen's staff consistently looked for athletes returning and looked at position moves to get the most athletes on the field at the same time. An example even existed of a starter from '81, Tim Stallard who moved from defensive end and tight end to linebacker and fullback.

And 1982 marked the second year in a row that Bowen abandoned the wishbone style of offense for the slot-I offense that was so successful in '81. The Junior Blues may not have had a proven quarterback with experience, nor a thrower like John Hughes, but they had an athlete who could make something happen if the play broke down. Rob Kaelin was the senior battling for the position against junior Brett Davis. And there were plenty of horses to carry the ball – Stallard, Rob Steele and Brien Brown. Players with some experience would back them up – Steve Pope, Darin Conklin and Scott Willis.

Linemen candidates were returning linemen Richard Bishop, Chris Toner and Doug Combes along with Darrin McCall, and Brian Madeira. Also expected to compete for playing time were centers Travis Smiley and Doug Hamilton.

The receiving corps of Todd May, David Marple, Brad Swearingen and Todd Yeagley were all good skill players.

On defense the Junior Blues brought back several good starters and if they could fill the void in their line, they could be very good. Stallard, Toner and Combes all started on defense the year before. And the secondary of Kaelin and Conklin was solid while Brown, Willis and Pope could all handle the position.

As per usual Glaze had a sophomore learning the linebacker position and this year would be sophomore Greg Edson.

The Junior Blues finished 6-3 with their only losses coming at the hands of Manhattan 21-6, Hayden 12-0 and Bonner Springs 23-6 in district play that prevented Rural from returning to the playoffs. Washburn Rural finished second in the city of Topeka for team defense allowing just 164 yards per game and only 11 points per game. The offense was a little suspect, however they finished in a tie for the Centennial League championship with Hayden, both with 4-1 records.

Bonner had an identical record as the Junior Blues going into the playoffs but had impressive wins over Olathe South (who beat Rural in the '81 playoffs) and perennial power Bishop Miege, 20-0. It proved to be Bonner's year to advance.

Richard Bishop, Tim Stallard, Rob Kaelin all were selected for the Capital-Journal's Topeka all-city team. Chris Toner was 2nd team and Darin Conklin and Brad Swearingen were honorable mention. Tim Stallard was also selected honorable mention all-class 5A team by the Capital Journal.

Entering 1983 there was a trademark of Bowen's practice philosophy about to emerge. The year before the "scout squad" used to run the opponents plays weekly produced a running back. Converted lineman, Robert Henderson, played his way from the "scout squad" to a potential starting offensive back as a fullback. Not surprisingly, when he was a freshman, we also played Henderson in the backfield. He was simply a hard-nose runner and an excellent blocker.

The Junior Blues returned 13 players who saw the field for varsity play in '82. Brett Davis had to fill in at quarterback the year before and was now prepared to run the offense. The tailback would be junior Greg Edson who, as a sophomore, earned the running back position by game five and gained 195 yards on the ground. Scott Willis looked to be the slot-back. Anthony Dulan, Darin Conklin and Joe Bleidissel would be competing for backfield carries.

The receivers were an inexperienced bunch with Kelly Oliphint, Mike Wilson. David Marple was coming back with some experience. Also competing for playing time would be Roland Trahoon and Troy McMaster.

The linemen would be Darin McCall, Travis Smiley, Mike Adams, Jeff Wools and Bruce Wanamaker. Mark Davenport, Pat Fraenza, Joel Pasley and Rance Craig were expected to compete for playing time on the line of scrimmage.

The defense looked to be respectable with McCall and Davenport with line experience. Edson and Henderson returned as linebackers. Conklin (a three-year starter in the secondary), Davis and Willis round out the defensive secondary.

In 1983 there was a bit of a dip when Rural went 4-5, but they dropped two very close district games 3-0 to Olathe South in overtime and a 10-6 loss to Bonner Springs. And they started the season with three straight wins over KC Harmon, Shawnee Heights and Highland Park. In the fourth game of the season, they lost a heart breaker to Hayden in four overtimes. In games 5, 6 and 7 they were shut out by Emporia, Seaman and Olathe South in the first district game that went to overtime and South won 0-3 in overtime. There was a narrow loss in district game two 6-10 to Bonner Springs and the Junior Blues defeated KC Turner 27-6 to complete their season.

Mark Davenport was selected as a first team all-Centennial league selection as a lineman. On the second- team Darrin McCall, Phil Wilson and Greg Edson received recognition.

In the August 29. 1984 Capital-Journal article by sportswriter Allen Quakenbush, he and Bowen talked about the upcoming season. Quakenbush writes that Bowen pulled out a roster from last season and clicked off 24 names of returning players who had experience. A good starting point. He also mentioned that, based on last year's sub-par record, Rural had something to prove. It ended a seven- year streak of winning seasons while Bowen was guiding the Junior Blues.

"We didn't like that," noted Bowen. "We didn't like that one bit. This is a competitive bunch. They don't like to lose. And that's not all bad." Bowen went on to say, "I think we came back in a little better shape than we've seen in the past. I think the kids have worked harder in the summer than some we've had."

On offense the Junior Blues returned two quarterbacks, Beau (Huscher) Brown (senior) and Jared Peterson (junior). A decision about who would win that position was up-in the air. They also returned the two top rushers from a year ago, Greg Edson (senior) and Fredrick Williams (junior).

As a junior Williams was third in the city in rushing the prior season with 470 yards and Edson added 270 yards in seven games. Edson moved to fullback to take advantage of his blocking skills.

Whoever was named quarterback would have several capable pass catchers at their disposal Joe Bleidissel (senior), Anthony Dulan (senior), Derrick Watts (junior) and Arnie Bazemore (senior). David Trupp (junior) and Eric Olmo (senior) were veteran tight ends.

The line returned starting tackle Mike Adams (senior), but lost Todd Rosetta (junior) to a season ending knee injury. Tim Huston (junior) was battling a hip injury but was expected to play. Brad Brunton (senior), Tom Bruno (junior), Mark Burnheide (senior), Joel Pasley (senior), Jeff Wools (senior), Bruce Wanamaker (senior) and John Haggard (senior) were expected to anchor the line positions.

On defense three returned with experience, Bleidissel, Trupp and Wilson. At the nose guard Bobby Glaze returned. Edson would be a three-year starter back at linebacker. The secondary was loaded with skill as Rick Wendland returns. Either Brown or Peterson, whoever isn't the number one quarterback, will play defensive back. Dulan, Watts, Jeff Combs and Mike Wilson would also vie for playing time in the secondary.

Rural used two key interceptions and overcame six fumbles to win their opener against KC Harmon 27-8. Four different Junior Blues scored. Greg Edson, Jared Peterson (who won the quarterback spot), David Anbari, a senior running back, and Phil Wilson all found the end zone in the opening victory.

Washburn Rural also defeated Shawnee Heights in week #2 a 20-6 victory. Derrick Watts showed his prowess as a punt returner with a 79-yard return and Bleidissel added two touchdowns.

The next week Rural shut-out Highland Park 20-0 and won their third consecutive game. Rural's defense blocked two punts – one for a touchdown-intercepted three passes and recovered two fumbles. Anbari scored two touchdowns and Edson one. Rural was on a roll. But three wins was the way they started the season before and then lost five straight games, getting shut-out in three games.

This season game #4 against Hayden was different. Two Fredrick Williams touchdowns with runs of 90-yards and four-yards, plus a Richard Yohr field goal lead Rural to a 17-6 win over the Hayden Wildcats.

Rural finally met defeat in Emporia at the hands of the Spartans losing one in the final minutes of the game. With five minutes left in the game Rural held a 7-6 lead and had the ball. But a costly fumble and a wild Emporia touchdown run gave them a shot at a short touchdown run and they capitalized for a 12-7 victory, the first loss for the Junior Blues in game #5.

Rural bounced back to defeat Seaman in the last regular season game before district play. The majority of Rural's scoring occurred in a 55 second spurt in the second quarter. Derrick Watts returned a punt 77 yards for a touchdown and then Phil Wilson scooped a fumble that led to Joe Bieidissel's 13-yard touchdown run. Those two scores stacked on Richard Yohr's 26-yard field goal produced a 17-6 victory over the Vikings.

So Rural entered district 5-1 but had to face a traditionally tough Olathe South who beat them 25-14 loss that kept them out of the playoffs. Their only other loss that year was a 12-7 loss to Emporia. They defeated their other two district opponents Bonner Springs and KC Turner to finish the year with a 7-2 record. With a large contingency of skilled juniors and excellent sophomores, the future looked bright at Washburn Rural.

Greg Edson and Bobby Glaze were selected by the Capital Journal as all-city performers. Edson was also selected to the All-Class 5A team on defense and Glaze was honorable mention as a defensive lineman. Fredrick Williams was chosen second team all-city. Honorable mention all-city were Mike Adams, Joe Bleidissel, Beau Brown, Brad Brunton, Jared Peterson, Mark Schumacher, Derrick Watts, Phil Wilson, Tony Winslow, and Richard Yohr. Six of those players would return for the 1985 season.

Washburn Rural looked like they were just upon the cusp of greatness and the off-season was full of optimism and weights. The Junior Blues all recognized the advantages of being stronger than their opponents.

BOWEN OFFERS ME A COACHING POSITION ON HIS STAFF

There are things that happen in your life that you don't forget. You even remember where you were when it happened. One such thing was the phone call I got from Ron Bowen in which he offered me a coaching position on his Washburn Rural varsity coaching staff.

I had spent five years coaching junior high football at Jay Shideler. At that time, the freshman did not attend the high school, they were part of the junior high. I had coached eighth grade and coached ninth grade and was enjoying those experiences immensely.

Then, as I was sitting on my couch, I got the call. In the spring of 1985, I get a phone call and I hear the distinct, unmistakable voice of Coach Bowen on the other end of the line. I don't remember exactly what he said, but I am certain he started out with, "Rid? Ron Bowen." It was unusual, to the say the least, to get many calls at home from Coach Bowen. He was a man who felt very strongly that football and coaching should not take precedence over family. My oldest son was born in March of 1985 so, during that period of adjustment, I was not thinking much about making any changes concerning my job and my duties. But here was a call asking me to consider making a change.

To paraphrase it went something like this-

Bowen: "Rid, I have an opening on the varsity staff. I've talked to my other assistant coaches and they all feel like you'd fit in well. Would you like to be on the varsity staff?"

Me: "Well that's an exciting offer and, of course I'd love to work with you and your staff. I would need to have a conversation with Mr. Paul (Principal Lester Paul of Jay Shideler at the time) and let him know my intentions."

Bowen: "I would have you coach defensive linemen and help Glaze with the defense. You also would help Austin with offensive linemen and he would help you with defensive linemen. Only one condition."

Me: "Condition?"

Bowen: "Yeah, you would have to give up chewing tobacco at practices and games."

I was a leaf tobacco guy at the time.

Me:" I can do that Coach Bowen. Let me talk with Mr. Paul and I'll get back to you, okay?"

Mr. Lester Paul ran a tight ship at Jay Shideler. With all due respect he looked a lot like the character that played Sergeant Vince Carter on the Gomer Pyle television show. Same gruff demeanor and same hair style. In truth I didn't know how he'd feel about losing a coach at the junior high and me continuing to teach there. I was so pleased that Mr. Paul, a staunch supporter of athletics and, scorebook person for the Washburn Rural varsity football program, considered what I was asking to do was an advancement and an opportunity for me personally. I would officially become a part of the Washburn Rural varsity coaching staff. And I had previously coached next year's sophomores, juniors and seniors when they were ninth graders. I knew all the kids that would comprise the varsity football program. And the senior class was poised to make a successful run that season with good coaching. I felt I could help.

As a 29 year-old, teacher, coach and new father, I felt like I had it made. And then the trepidation sets in. Irrational thoughts of inadequacy. I know very little about their system. Will I be able to learn all I need to know about their defense? Will I be able to teach the defensive lineman the techniques necessary to make the defense effective? What the hell am I getting into in the fall of 1985?

Washburn Rural was coming off a 1984 season that saw them post a 7-2 record, 4-1 in the Centennial League for a second- place league finish. The year before, in 1983, they posted a 4-5 overall record. They were getting better and the senior class was a great one. I know because I had coached them at Jay Shideler and we only lost one game, a close one, to Lawrence South junior high. The expectations of the school community and the city were high. As coaches that can be a challenge to deal with but that is a good problem to have. It can be a bit daunting too.

I spent several hours that summer with Sam Austin who explained to me the nuances associated with Washburn Rural's defensive scheme and I felt a little better about going into the season as a "newbie." It was also an easier transition for me because all the players knew who I was.

It was immediately noticeable to me how organized Coach Bowen's practice schedules were, how routine they were. And it became apparent that he simplified his offense by focusing on effectively executing a small number of plays. Learn those and run them correctly. One reason that philosophy was beneficial was he would work those few plays until they were precise and crisply run. To this day I credit a lot of the success to Coach Bowen's recognition of the fact that athletes play better when the system is familiar to them. A habit. When things are less complicated players play with more confidence. Quality over quantity. He would rather run 10 plays correctly than have 20 and ten plays were not run very well.

I learned that, depending on the capabilities of EACH year's team, it determined how much the offense was expanded. The 1985 group proved capable of running a lot of plays well, but they got the plays in small doses. He might add a wrinkle or two each week. If they could run the new play effectively, it became a part of the offense. I think more teams would find this recipe for success a lot simpler than trying to run a ton of different offensive plays in a mediocre or less than average way.

One thing that was apparent with the 1985 team was we had speed. A lot of it. We had outstanding speed at tailback, slot receiver, quarterback, and wide receiver. We had above average speed at tight end and on defense. Combine that with big offensive linemen (we had two tackles that weighed better than 230 pounds) who could move well and were coachable, and the makings of a really great team were in place.

The most interesting aspect of Washburn Rural's success may have been the defensive scheme and philosophy. We ran a defense with three down lineman and a couple of defensive ends. Defensive coordinator, Ray Glaze, was also the wrestling coach. He found value in quick down linemen. Their job was to slant and control a gap and attempt to keep the opponents off our linebackers so the linebackers could make the tackles. And the down lineman had to have a couple of qualities. Quickness and toughness. It did not matter if they weighed a lot. In fact, Coach Glaze paid no attention to weight. Often, we would need a nose guard and he would go find a secondary player who was not going to play much at corner or safety and he'd "recruit" them as linemen. He measured the defensive lineman's value by their quickness, their toughness and their hearts. We had plenty of those kids. My job was to sell the defensive linemen on the importance of their inglorious jobs.

I referred to the number one priority of our down linemen, as "destroying the offensive lineman's legs." Not in the literal sense, just by not allowing them to get off the line of scrimmage, out of their stance, so they couldn't block the linebackers at the second level. And every day, in every way, I coached that premise. It became habit. And numerous kids, when recognizing how they keyed the defensive successes, took a great deal of pride in perfecting their jobs. Coach Glaze gave me a lot of levity while I was teaching. He also appropriately watched over the personnel and he helped me make certain we got the most effective kids in the right positions.

Many a year I coached with Glaze I would see him talk to a young man who may have been playing linebacker or even defensive back and attempt to convince them there may be a position for them to start and play more if they could learn defensive line technique. He didn't sell kids "snake oil." He sold them on an opportunity to be on the field more and play a game they loved.

Possible placement of photo #33 and #34 – Austin, Glaze and Ridley on the sidelines

Coach Ron Bowen took over the Washburn Rural football program in 1975. There's a funny story associated with that hiring. According to Coach Bowen the school also hired, the same year, a football coach named Mike Englebrake a former Kansas University offensive lineman. The story goes something like this from Ron's recollection.

The superintendent of school district #437 hired Ron Bowen from Valley Center to be Rural's next football coach. During the same spring hiring period, the principal at Washburn Rural, District #437, hired Mike Engelbrake to be the head football coach.

When the fall school year began it was prior to the start of football season. Bowen and Engelbrake were having a conversation, both knowing they were on the Washburn Rural coaching staff, each thinking they were hired to be the head coach.

In a civil and productive conversation, both men were sitting outside the front of the building, once they discovered the other thought they were the new head coach, Engelbrake politely conceded saying, "You've got more years in education and experience coaching. Why don't you be the head coach and I'll be the assistant?" You wonder if, in today's world that would be so easily worked out by the two educators.

What became an easy and voluntary shift of duties really started a quick three-year turnaround and success. It helped establish the first critical ten years of the Bowen era. They racked up 60 wins in 10 seasons after taking over a 2-7 team in 1974. In 1975, Bowen and Glaze's first years at the helm the team had the same 2-7 record. The most impressive thing about the first ten years was that there were only two losing records in that span of 1975 and 1983. No doubt the groundwork was laid in those first ten seasons to help prepare to take the next step in 1985. And I was going to be a part of that next ten years.

In looking at the 1984 league records it was easy to see that Emporia posed our biggest league threat. They had had Rural's number for several years. It was not a game on the schedule the players looked forward to at that time in history. Emporia was a school with a bigger enrollment and a ton of confidence based on their past successes.

1985- A State Championship Season- First Ever by a Topeka Football Team

That 1985 season had two new schools on the front side of the schedule. Two non-league teams. Both schools from the Kansas City Kansas League.

We opened with Washington and, without knowing much about them, we defeated them in the opener 20-0. With a shutout to our credit the defense was feeling pretty good. Offense was showing signs of jelling. Next opponent was Kansas City Schlagle. We may have looked past them. Schlagle hung a 28-14 loss on us. Instead of being shell-shocked a veteran staff helped this new coach understand that adjustments may need to be made. Personnel was evaluated and some changes were made. We had already, unfortunately, lost our senior nose guard, Todd Rosetta, to a season ending knee injury, which is what occurred with knee injuries in those days. Coincidentally, Todd went on to become a physical therapist. Even without that senior year, football undoubtedly played a part in his career path.

There is nothing more disappointing than a football player, one who has put in years training and preparing for their moment and who dedicated themselves to the program and to a sport they love, suffering a career ending injury. My heart breaks for Todd and any football player who has experienced that disappointment. I am also optimistic enough to believe that most, like Todd, turned that into something positive. What doesn't kill you..........

We won our next two games. A 35-7 win over Highland Park. A close game with a very good Hayden team, 26-20 who at that time was a heated rivalry game and Hayden was getting better just like us.

Then came Emporia week. I remember the mindset back in the day. It was difficult to beat Emporia. They had an advantage before we kicked off. They also ran a pretty good inside counter play every year. We had a 3-1 record and knew this would be a pivotal game for our league standings. They also had a slotback named Ginivan. They lined him up all over their offensive sets and he was as good as he was confident. A few of our players may admitted to being a little too focused on him and his game to focus on our game. We lost 34-14 and it may not have been that close.

But as resilient Bowen led teams did, we focused our attention on our last regular season game with Seaman. I felt a bit sorry for them because we would have been a tough matchup for anyone that week following the Emporia loss.

The players focused on their responsibilities, focused on what they needed to do instead of worrying much about what Seaman could do. Seaman was a better team that year than the score indicated. We won 35-0.

In Kansas there were pre-determined football districts. Everyone played three games for an opportunity to get into the playoffs. Our opponents were DeSoto, Bonner Springs and league rival Shawnee Heights.

Judging by the scores our district looked incredibly weak. We hung a 52-20 on DeSoto. The following week we beat Bonner Springs 27-6 and finished unblemished and moved to the state playoffs with a

35-6 victory over league rival Shawnee Heights. The path looked easy, but we practiced with a purpose.

We had a healthy respect for a traditionally strong private school, Bishop Miege out of Kansas City. After a bit of a rough start, particularly on defense, we beat Miege 31-7. I distinctly remember Miege's attempt to block our inside linebackers with tight ends. When I pointed this out to Coach Glaze, he asked what I thought we should do about it, I suggested shading the tight ends towards their middle and having the ends not allow them to cross their face or go around them without first being stood up by the defensive ends. To my absolute delight Coach Glaze agreed and, for one of the first times I felt validated that I was a coaching contributor.

I should also mention that Ron Bowen was a masterful pre-game, half time and post-game speaker. His pep talks were legendary. But what impressed me the most was at halftime, Bowen would walk slowly to the locker room with Ray Glaze, Sam Austin and myself and we would talk about what adjustments we needed to make. The final decisions laid with Bowen on offense and Glaze on defense. That's the way it should be, but they valued our quick assessment of the first half and what adjustments we suggested. I felt Washburn Rural's ability to adjust at halftime won us many games. Football, to Bowen and Glaze, was truly a chess game. The other team decided what they wanted to take away from you and you adjusted. Not all coaches, nor coaching staffs, were that proficient at making the in-game adjustments and getting athletes to understand and carry out instructions.

We were now in the 1985 semifinals of the Kansas football playoffs. We were to play against host Pittsburg in southeast Kansas, not a familiar opponent for us. But film of their games was obtained by us and we began the process of making an offensive and defensive game plan. On film, Pittsburg looked very good. They were talented and looked capable of matching our size and our speed. As a new coach this playoff football had me on a euphoric high, the likes of which I had never experienced before. We were truly having success that the school had never experienced. I think we were too unfamiliar with it to be scared or nervous. We had young men who understood their roles and accepted them. They truly were a family of brothers. I believe that, had this been war, our troops would have defended each other to the bloody end. Maybe an exaggerated analogy, maybe not.

These young men had grown up competing alongside each other in a variety of sport competitions. They truly liked, or at least, respected each other. If not as personalities, they respected each other's abilities. When this occurs today, you simply call it chemistry. Call it what you will, but when the game got close they wanted to win for each other. They really were like a brotherhood.

As Derrick Watts described his class of 1986 seniors as they were growing up, "Early indications of having a strong senior class goes back to our 6th grade year in Optimist flag football. Much of our class was divided into two teams. Both teams competed very well." Relationships and respect were developed as far back as 1980 at least in the realm of sports and competition. This class, as freshman, lost one football game and won their Eastern Kansas League (EKL) basketball tournament. I was fortunate enough to have coached both football and basketball when they were freshman. This class had special written all over it."

He went on to say, "We defeated Pittsburg by a score of 19-10. It was unbelievable to think we had just played our way into the 5A state championship game and won the biggest road game of the season. We had a pretty good idea who would be waiting for us," concluded Watts.

Wichita-Kapaun Mt. Carmel High was a football power, a private school with, perhaps, one of the best winning traditions in all of Kansas football. Just in Ron

Bowen's first 10 years beginning in 1975 Kapaun won five state championships (1975,76,77, 1981, 82). Very few, if any, knowledgeable high school football folks in the state of Kansas were giving Washburn Rural any chance of defeating Kapaun. I'm certain that there were even doubters in our school community. I'm certain some of our more knowledgeable parents knew what odds we were up against. That's why you play the game to see if the outcome might be different than the predictions.

On the day of the game, the Saturday after Thanksgiving, the Kansas weather turned awfully bad. No, it was more than bad. For our team, who relied on speed, the last thing we wanted to see was a freezing drizzle. But football is a sport that is played in any kind of weather except in the event of lightning. And both schools probably would have welcomed some lightning, and a postponement to play another day.

The game was to be played in Lawrence, Kansas on the University of Kansas (KU) stadium and field. KU had the old, traditional astro-turf, hard as a rock synthetic surface. Ice would make that field treacherous.

Except for Coach Bowen, the coaching staff rode to the games in a separate suburban vehicle and it was loaded to the gills with players bags and equipment. We laid on top of the equipment bags. No regard for seat belts in those days. And we were all commenting on the weather in a not so positive fashion. We could hear the ice pelts bouncing off the vehicle's roof. This was concerning. Coach Bowen always rode on the team bus.

We got even more concerned when we stepped on the field for the first time and the field was so frozen, a good number of our players could not get any traction at all. Their cleats were too long. We as coaches hurriedly exchanged our turf shoes with players who had the long-cleated shoes. One of our defensive players, Darren Caster, was looking awfully downtrodden and disappointed. We asked what was wrong and dejectedly he said, "Nobody will have shoes that will fit me." Bowen piped up and said, "What size shoe do you wear?" Caster dejectedly mumbled "Size eight." Bowen proudly said, "I've got your shoes." Took them off and handed them to a surprised Caster. Bowen had polio as a youth and his feet failed to grow.

Washburn Rural alumni, Will Cokeley, who played football at Kansas State and was also a member of the Michigan Panthers who won the first USFL championship, was at the state championship game. Michigan was known for weather similar to what occurred in Lawrence, Kansas that day. A new phenomenon just beginning to be used were football gloves. Cokeley brought a supply for many of the starters to wear.

After that shoe disaster was diverted and many players fitted with gloves, the game could not have possibly started any worse for Rural. Well, actually it could have and would have. I'll get to that in a bit.

Kapaun jumped out to a 13-0 lead. We helped them with a couple of poor special team efforts giving them a short field. They scored the first two touchdowns. They were driving inside our 10-yard line for what would be potentially be a third score.

And this is where it could have gotten worse. But Kapaun helped us out. They decided to try a pass inside the 10- yard line. Our defensive back, Richard Yohr, read it perfectly and stepped in front of the route. He picked off the pass and had clear sailing to the end zone. One of our players, no fault of his, but a result of hustle and the field conditions, inadvertently knocked his teammate, Yohr, out of bounds negating a potential pick six. As I say, no fault of our player.

The momentum swung our way after that play and for the remainder of the game.

We decided to try and increase our offensive line splits to see how far Kapaun would spread out with us. I swear, on the video from the game, it looks like the two opposing lines almost stretched from sideline to sideline. A slight exaggeration, but that created holes for us and all our linemen had to do was put a body on the side of the defender. And with those angles, we had no problem doing that. The defense got stubborn and we managed to score the next two touchdowns, plus a two-point conversion.

Legend has it, but it's hard to substantiate that our place kick holder, senior, Tony Winslow, a converted fullback, decided to scrap the kick and attempt to score the two-point conversion. And he did just that which allowed us to take a slight lead, 14-13. With time dwindling down and us controlling things, Kapaun had one last gasp. They had the ball near the 50-yard line and, again, attempted a pass that Antoine Dulan picked off and took in for another touchdown, giving us a cushion of a touchdown and a two-point conversion, 21-13. There was not enough time and Kapaun hadn't scored in what seemed like months. Washburn Rural defied all odds, defeating the tradition laden Wichita Kapaun Mt. Carmel.

Defensive back, senior Derrick Watts described his view of the game winning play, "Midway through quarter four Kapaun was on their own side of the 50-yard line and they were in a third and long situation. They were fancy with their motions and schemes and they did just that on the third down play. They motioned a couple of guys away from their left (our right). I happened to be the cornerback on the right side so I went from 2-3 receivers on my side to just a one-on one situation. The receiver I was covering ran me off on a fly route. They moved their blue chip running back into the flat where their receiver was and I was and then prepared to throw him a screen pass. Our safety, Antoine Dulan, saw the play developing apparently and moved up to step right in front of their back making a pick six from over fifty yards out. The Kapaun quarterback was athletic and fast so he gave chase and had a slight shot at Dulan around the 10- yard line, but Dulan was simply too athletic and too motivated to score. And Richard Yohr made the extra point allowing us to go ahead 21-13."

And on that frozen field all was forgotten except our victory.

Now It's hard to say Coach Bowen's pregame speech was effective since, in the early going, Kapaun put up the first two scores. But the overall theme of the day was set when Coach Bowen chose to address the weather conditions. He talked a lot about how hard we had worked to get here. How, no matter what the odds, this team overcame them. And in a direct commentary that was supposed to help our players mindset about playing in a frozen state championship game he spoke the legendary words, "I've never seen a finer day to play some football." Bowen gives credit for that quote to one of his first assistant coaches, Mike Engelbrake, the guy who thought he was hired as Rural's head coach.

1985 POST SEASON HONORS

You don't win state championships without good leadership. Leadership on the sideline with coaches and on the field with your players.

And with state titles come many post-season honors. The 1985 champions had 16 seniors on the roster. Most of them had starting positions and some played both offense and defense. Of the seniors there were five who received post-season recognition as 5A all-state player selections by the Capital-Journal newspaper.

Most notable was Rick Wendland who not only garnered 5A defensive recognition but was selected as an all-state, all-class selection. Wendland caught nine touchdowns his senior year but was most notably one of the fiercest defensive players in the state prowling the secondary and making hard hitting tackles. In addition to his touchdown catching ability, Wendland was a crushing blocker in the open field. He went on to sign with the University of Nebraska.

Running back in the Rural system got to carry the ball for the majority of the offensive plays. Fredrick Williams, another senior, was named all 5A first team offensive selection as the result of his work in that offense. Williams played four games his senior year on a sprained ankle. In the 5A state title game, on the frozen KU turf, Williams rushed for 117 yards. For his career Williams amassed 2,018 yards rushing which at that time placed him as the third all-time rushing leader for the city of Topeka. Williams wbsws up playing football for Benedictine College.

Quarterback Jared Peterson was unquestionably the offensive leader who could run and throw with equal success. Peterson was selected honorable mention 5A all-state by the Capital-Journal. Peterson was not only a state football champion in 1985, the winter prior, as a junior he quarterbacked the basketball team to a 5A state championship as well. Pete was unquestionably a winner. In his senior year he threw for 633 passing yards, 13 touchdowns and only five interceptions. He also rushed for an additional 324 yards and 10 rushing touchdowns. His combined yards passing and rushing accounted for 957 total yards placed him third on the city statistical leaders. His playmaking ability made him a dual threat. He was one of the most efficient quarterbacks and ran the option better than anyone. Pete had huge hands, and even on the icy field, would fake a pitch out with one hand, then bring it back in to himself to keep the ball on the option. Peterson could have played college football but chose to play basketball at Pittsburg State in Kansas. PSU football coach asked him to join the football team. He declined.

Derrick Watts was a speedster selected 5A all-state honorable mention as a slot back/ receiver. His senior year he led the city in receiving yards with 20 catches for 284 yards. At 5'5" and 152 pounds he also had big gains when rushing the football from the slot position. He was notably dangerous as a kickoff and punt returner. Ironically, Watts remembers, as a sophomore, winning the punt returner role. In the third game of the season he muffed a punt and suffered all there is that goes along with that mistake. Watts went on to receive punts for three years in high school and four years in college and NEVER muffed another punt. His 85-yard kick return in the playoffs against Bishop Miege turned the momentum in that game in Rural's favor. He also had a 100-yard kick return against DeSoto in the district game. In addition to being one of the Junior Blues best defensive backs, he also was one of the state's best half-milers in track and field. Watts went on to have a fantastic football career at Baker University and was selected to the school's Hall of Fame.

Defensive standout Phil Wilson was also selected as 5A all-state honorable mention. Wilson doubled as a defensive end and fullback. In Coach Bowen's power

I offense the fullback is a critical lead blocker for the tailback. Wilson accepted his role well and can be credited for protecting Peterson so he could throw and was extremely important helping Williams gain so many rushing yards. Wilson scored a critical two-point conversion in the state title game. And remember how we coaches gave our turf shoes to some of the players. Mine went to Phil Wilson and found their way into the end zone for a two-point conversion. Forever connected I'll be to Phil Wilson. I wish I had kept those shoes. Trophy case material.

All five of these seniors were also recognized as first team Topeka all city players. Quarterback Jared Peterson was named Topeka City Player of the Year.

Joining these five on the all-city second team were also seniors Brad Elder an offensive lineman, and Tony Winslow, a converted fullback who unselfishly played center on offense and anchored one of the best offensive lines.

Seniors recognized as all-city honorable mention that year were Richard Yohr, defensive back and place kicker, David Trupp who played end on both sides of the ball, along with linemen Doug Campbell, Tom Bruno and Tim Huston.

Also selected as a second team all-city performer was junior Antoine Dulan most noted that year for being a more than capable replacement when Fredrick Williams was hurt. He had many highlights during that season but he had a pick six for Rural when they held a slim lead in the state championship game against Wichita Kapaun to seal the victory.

Sophomore lineman, Mike Herzog, was also selected as all-city honorable mention for his work on the defensive line.

Having five players receiving state recognition for their efforts, with an additional 12 receiving recognition as all city players makes coaching a lot easier. But don't underestimate the work Ron Bowen put in that year. He was selected as Topeka's Coach of the year. Awards for coaches and players are always subjective because any of the state coaches from the six classifications could garner the recognition as state coach of the year. Coaches realize this and are appreciative of the efforts and the efforts of other coaches.

That particular year Marc Juhl from tiny school Midway Denton was recognized. But all coaches of the state champions realize that they all were deserving of "coach of the year" honors. Most, like Bowen, give credit to their athletes and their coaching staffs. Ron Bowen always took opportunity to recognize his staff for the successes of the team.

In the article Pam Clark wrote for the Capital-Journal about the All-City team, she noted that Ron Bowen gave his assistants credit saying, "I always have thought what made a good head coach was good assistants." He named Ray Glaze, Sam Austin, Jerry Beardslee, Bill Edwards, Dick Evans and yours truly, Chris Ridley in that article. That kind of recognition makes the journey so worthwhile. Bowen never missed a chance to thank his staff for their hard work. We noticed.

He also was quick to point out the obvious reason for success. Quality players. He compared this 1985 squad to the 1977 playoff team and the 1981 team saying, "We had the intelligent type of kids, athletically oriented types."

So how does a team replace those losses of personnel? Next man up with 1985 juniors and sophomores who wanted to continue to build a winning tradition at Washburn Rural. It's our turn.

In addition to Dulan and Herzog in 1986 there were several outstanding returning players waiting for their opportunities to contribute and hopefully make a run in the playoffs.

REFLECTION OF A FORMER PLAYER:

Quarterback Jared Peterson 1983-1986---------- "I watched Coach Bowen coach and teach PE for three years while I was at WRHS. While most people will likely bring up the positive attitude he brought everyday emphasized by his famous, "I've never seen a finer day" slogan, an equally positive impression Coach left on me was his humility. He didn't care for notoriety or attentions. He looked at ever day just like any other day; get up and go do your job the best you can. Keep it simple and don't complicate things by getting distracted. It's because it takes a level of self-discipline and mental strength that most of us don't possess, but it's a great way to approach your life and it was a great way to approach coaching football. That's why his teams were fundamentally sound and disciplined. If you can't do the simple things, like run the football on offense and not fumble it, then you don't do things more complicated. Coach used to say, "Pete, there's three things that can happen when you throw the football and two of them are bad." He believed this to a degree, but he was also smart. Smart enough to know that you needed to keep a defense off-balance so they couldn't load the box. Smart enough to know you need to use your talent in order to win a championship. A balanced offense is one of the reasons we won a state title in 1985.

Another very positive impression Coach made on me was how he showed interest in everyone. It didn't matter if you were a first-string player or a third-string player. In PE class, it didn't matter if you were an athlete or someone who was there because it was a required class. It was because he wanted to help young people any way he could. I'm sure there are many special stories he could tell us where he did just that. And I'm sure there are many others that he doesn't even know about."

REFLECTION OF A FORMER PLAYER:

Slot back/ defensive back Derrick Watts 1983-1986--------"It was an exciting time for the school and for this class. In 1984 WRHS won a state track championship and I was a sophomore and personally was part of that scoring team. In the winter season of 1985 we were juniors and won the state basketball championship. Then, in the same calendar year, yet the next school year (fall) we pull off a major upset winning the state championship in football as seniors. That is a lot of state titles for one class in a short amount of time. Does a state championship make a student's life? Hard to say, but likely no. However, you can't takeaway how special it is. There are approximately 450 high schools in the state of Kansas, which means about 20,000 high school football players. Each year only about 300 of those 20,000 players can say they are state champions. That is about one percent of annual participants. In 1985 we were part of the one percent and these Junior Blue football players get to carry that championship mentality with pride the rest of their born days. One of the only things we should want as human beings is to leave something or someone a little better off than when you found it or found them. I feel the senior class of 1985, with the help of special coaches like

Bowen, Glaze, Austin, Ridley, Edwards, Beardslee, Evans and others along with Principal Smeltzer, and Assistant Principal Bruce Thezan did just that – a legacy that left it better!"

BOWEN'S ASSOCIATION WITH THE KANSAS SHRINE BOWL

When you coach football, and coach it well, there seems to be accolades, awards, and opportunities that present themselves to you. Just one of those opportunities happened to be Coach Bowen's association with The Kansas Shrine Bowl, an association that continues and is an important part of his life.

When Rural played in the 5A state championship game in 1985 this cemented Bowen's prospect of being selected as an assistant for the summer's all-star, Shrine Bowl football game.

The executive director at the time, Mr. David Mize, offered Bowen his position for that summer Shrine Bowl event. There is a five-year wait for an individual's next opportunity to assist in the game. However, the assistants can select a head coach and after the 1986 championship, did just that. Bowen was selected as the head coach for the summer of 1987's East all-star game.

The Kansas Shrine Bowl is an all-star high school senior, East vs. West, football game put on each year in Kansas by the Kansas Shriners. The event is a non-profit charity and proceeds are used to benefit Shriners Hospitals. To date the event has allowed the Kansas Shriners to send over $2 million to Shriners Hospitals to benefit children.

The actual game has been hosted in various Kansas cities including Lawrence, Manhattan, Wichita, Topeka, Hays, Emporia, Pittsburg and Dodge City. The East squad currently utilizes Ottawa University facilities for their practice camp prior to the game, the West squad utilizes Kansas Wesleyan University in Salina for their pre-game camp and practices.

The game has been conducted since 1974 and there have been a wide array of notable Kansas high school seniors who have participated. Among them are NFL Hall of Famer Barry Sanders, All-Pro Wide Receiver Jordy Nelson, former Kansas State and Kansas City Chief Linebacker Gary Spani and Super Bowl champion Linebacker and former Kansas Stater Mark Simoneau along with many others.

The weekend activities include a banquet, the state's largest Shrine Parade, Shriner's Hospitals for Children Free Screening Clinic, Strong Legs Run 5K, junior all-star challenge (ages 5-14), High School Football Combine/ Clinic and a 4-man golf scramble.

Coach Bowen's association with the Shrine Bowl all-star game dates back to its inception. In 1974, while Head Coach at Valley Center, one of his seniors was selected to participate in the game, Gerald Lawrence.

Since then, Bowen has participated as an assistant and as a head coach of the East all-star squads. In 1986 and 1992 Coach Bowen was selected to be an assistant coach for the annual all-star game. And in 1987 he was selected to be the head coach of the East squad.

Bowen has served in the capacity as game rules consultant to the Shrine Bowl Director and spent time as the co-chair of the Shrine Bowl Alumni.

So, on the years that Bowen was not coaching, Mize would have him standing on the sideline alongside him as his unofficial official, so if there was a question pertaining to a rule, Mize would turn and ask Bowen his thoughts. Mize described having Bowen on the sideline to help him interpret rules with the calm demeanor Bowen possessed helped put everybody at ease. He explained that to establish some balance between the all-star's offense and the defense, there are restrictions that help avoid a defensive dominated game. Offenses tend to struggle a bit and defenses come together easier.

Mize reflects, "My wife was executive secretary for the Shrine Bowl for 32 years and I was the director for 31 years. And during those years we had the opportunity to meet many high school coaches. I have no doubt after all those years Ron Bowen possessed the most class of any of them."

And on January 6, 2007 Ron Bowen was inducted into the Kansas Shrine Bowl's Hall of Fame.

Washburn Rural has a lengthy list of participants who played for Coach Bowen dating back to 1978.

Washburn Rural Shrine Bowl Participants:

1978 – Fred Palenske and Steve Stallard, 1982 – Lyndall Yarnell, 1986 – Derrick Watts, Rick Wendland, Fredrick Williams, 1987 – Antoine Dulan, Jeff Cowan, Matt Marple, 1988 – Jeff Hughes, Todd Scott, 1990- Mark Chrisco, Dusty Zander, 1992 – Luke Yarnell, 1993 – Mark Longhofer, Todd McKinnon, 1994 – Michael Atha, Justin Howe, 1997 – Cody Snyder, 1998 – Eric Johnson.

Being selected as a coach or a participant for the all-star game is quite an honor. But the real rewarding part of this selection is the opportunity to visit the Shriner Hospital in St. Louis, Missouri. Unless you are leery of flying. Which Coach Bowen is indeed leery. However, he masks personal concern for the good of the cause. He has made several trips and each one is rewarding. In recent years some of the patients have been brought to the games instead of flying teams and coaches to the hospital.

Prior to kids being brought to the games, the players got to visit with the children in the hospital and spend time talking with each of them and learning their individual stories. Some stories are more gut wrenching than others, but all have stories. The players walk away from that experience with a whole new perspective. And an appreciation for health and well-being.

WHAT WILL BE THE PRESSURE TO REPEAT FOR THE 1986 TEAM

There were 13 juniors who contributed to the 1985 Washburn Rural offense, defense and special teams. And an additional nine sophomores who completed the roster that state championship season were ready to contribute in 1986 as well.

The season began with two quarterbacks competing for the starter's role, both capable of running Coach Bowen's offense. One would be a senior, Kraig Burough. The other was a junior, Jeff Hamilton. Coach Bowen sat both down and told them they would each get an equal look with equal reps in practice, prior to the start of the season. But, ultimately, he told them he would have to select one to lead the offense in '86.

Not only did this say a lot for the kind of leader Ron Bowen was, but it spoke volumes about the value of having a competition for starting roles. We seemed to have a lot of competition that year for many spots. Talent does that for you.

After the evaluation period Bowen sat down with both Burough and Hamilton and gave them his most honest assessment. He said something to this affect- things being pretty much equal, he would select Hamilton since he would likely get two years as the quarterback. He was matter of fact, but spoke in a caring manner as this was a big decision, not only for the team, but each individual player.

He also made it very clear to Burough that his role on the team as a backup quarterback and a starting defensive back was as vital to the team as Hamilton's being selected the starting quarterback.

I will never forget the kind of class Burough demonstrated. He basically said he just wanted to be the best contributor to another successful season. And he was content with whatever role Coach Bowen thought he could provide the most value to the team. Burough could have been a selfish athlete, but he was not. I think that speaks volumes about the kind of person Kraig Burough was / is. I think we had numerous athletes with the same commitment and that was crucial to the chemistry of the 1986 team. That may have been a turning point, either good or bad, depending on how Burough handled that decision. It could have divided the team. Coaches respect that kind of selfless, team first attitude. Kraig Burough and his unselfish attitude quite likely, in my opinion, was the first step towards defending the state title in 1986.

Our schedule included the same schools we played in 1985. Kansas City Washington was much improved from the previous year and we lost many starters from the year before. So, when the first game was a 34-27 victory, although it was a little too close for comfort, we felt like we had some answers on offense. Hamilton was going to learn with each game and get better as a quarterback. He had good leadership qualities and seldom got rattled. He was not the runner that Peterson was from the year before, but he was a very skilled passer. And kids believed in him just as they had Peterson.

Antoine Dulan was ready to take over the running back chores and was a perfect I-formation running back. He was super quick out of his two-point stance and lightning fast once he got up steam. He also had uncanny vision for seeing the slightest crease and hitting it explosively. He was tough to tackle too. You never knew when or which way Dulan was going to make a cut. Defenders didn't know either.

He was especially tough running behind the lead blocking of Kirk Cerny and eventually powerful fullback, Jeff Cowan. Cerny was injured late in the season. Cerny had the experience and was very sure with his blocking efficiency. He had some foot speed when he occasionally got a carry. If you were a WR fullback you were essentially an occasionally rewarded offensive guard. Cowan grew so much between his sophomore and senior season he was not remotely the same kid physique wise. He was a short slot back and grew into a tall, solid, punishing blocker, capable ball carrier and a bruising tackler on defense.

Add a potential scoring threat carrying or receiving the ball out of the slot back position in Todd Scott and Hamilton had plenty of weapons. Scott was just a junior and he was shifty, fast and ran good pass routes.

In addition to the above-mentioned players that garnered All Centennial League post-season honors so did linemen Matt Marple (senior) and Mike Herzog (junior). They lead a group of linemen on both sides of the ball that were capable of opening holes for the backfield and were very stingy on defense. The above mentioned Burough also received first team honors as a defensive back.

Despite how much progress and confidence we had from 1985 and an opening win against KC Washington, the second game of the season was once again KC Schlagle. They managed to win the game in 1985 and managed to have a losing record. So, once again, they were a team we didn't matchup well against in 1986 also. Or perhaps we were over-confident. At any rate, Schlagle came to Rural's stadium, McElroy field at the time, and defeated us 12-7. After this many years I think all of us coaches and players still wondered what happened in those second games of both seasons. Any given night. That's why they play the games.

In the third game of the season we played Centennial League foe Highland Park. The local paper picked us to win that game by six points. We managed to put both sides of the ball together and won that game 41-0. Coincidentally, that game started with a false tornado siren that interrupted kickoff for 15 minutes, a lightning storm that also delayed the game and eventually a torrential rain that affected the field conditions, but didn't slow down the Junior Blues.

The Blue's defense forced 10 three down and outs in 12 Highland Park possessions. The Highland Park offense only had 87 yards of total offense. They never advanced further than the Rural 44-yard line all night. This was dominance and just what the young team needed for their confidence.

On the first offensive play for Rural we scored on a 49-yard pass play Hamilton to Scott. Hamilton was 6 of 8 passing, four touchdowns. The first to Todd Scott who also caught another 36-yarder. He also threw two touchdowns to Tailback Antoine Dulan of 37 and 56 yards. Scott added a 12-yard carry for a touchdown. And late in the game, Dusty Palmer scored on his first varsity carry, a 34-yard run.

This game seemed to spring-board the young players' confidence level. As good as the seniors were the juniors were equally capable of filling starting positions. These two classes complimented each other well. Defensively we were once again, not very big, but the quickness was obvious in the 5-2 monster we played. The defensive line relied on quickness and their job was to keep the offensive linemen from getting to the second level so the linebackers could make the majority of the tackles. James Walker was a small, quick and aggressive nose guard. Herzog was a slightly larger tackle, but equally capable of destroying offensive linemen and pursuing and making tackles himself.

Jeff Hughes, Mike Evans, and Trey McPherson anchored the defensive end positions. In the 5-2 defense they had a lot of responsibility by defending the sweep plays and shutting off the edge. Technically sound at doing just that, the line of scrimmage was well protected.

The two inside linebackers were Cowan and Darren Caster and Sean Conly also saw action. Dulan was the 'monster linebacker" often matching up with the opposition's tight end or strong side of their offense. The secondary was a cast of Chris Walker, Scott and Burough. There was not a weak link on defense. There was not a good way to attack this unit.

The fourth game of the season we shut out rival Hayden High School 28-0 for the Homecoming game. Coach Bowen never cared too much for the Homecoming game. It was an added distraction, something he felt could take the players' minds off football. Not this bunch.

Dulan broke a tackle after a two-yard gain and scored after completing a 52-yard run on the first play from scrimmage. By halftime Dulan had 106 rushing yards on 12 carries and added 40 yards receiving as we built a 21-0 halftime lead.

The defense held Hayden to 57 total offensive yards on 44 plays. Scott picked off a pass and Hughes, Herzog, McPherson and Dulan made fumble recoveries. We scored on three of those turnovers. Two shutouts in a row should have given us confidence going into the Emporia game.

Just as was the case in the 1985 season Emporia over the years had established a mental advantage over Washburn Rural. The games were often tense and the team that handled the pressure and made the least mistakes often won. Emporia again had our number. They handed us our second loss of the season a 17-7 loss.

The 1986 season saw a couple of early losses and a 3-2 start for the defending state champions. This kind of adversity could have had a bearing on the remainder of the season. Washburn Rural didn't panic. The coaches stayed with the plan which was a simple system. Stay with what you do the best. Don't make the offense too complicated. Simply line up and run over your opponents as much as possible and use the pass to effectively keep defenses on their heels.

I remember many words that Coach Bowen offered. He made no excuses. He said it was up to the coaches to prepare the team and the players were to learn their technique and skills so those become habit and second nature for them.

Our final regular season game was with a conference rival, Seaman Vikings. Seaman always, and continues the tradition, had a lot of tough, hard working athletes. At the time their enrollment placed them at the top of 5A schools or one of the smaller 6A schools. They were well coached by Dale Sample and a staff that had consistently helped develop Seaman kids into tough, hard-nose football players. This year they looked up to the task and we knew, going in, the game would be a tough, hard fought game. We were correct in that assumption.

What some assumed might be an offensive battle turned into a defensive dominated game on both sides. There was no score until a little over four minutes remained in the game. We started the winning drive on the Seaman 40-yard line. In four plays, which included a 34-yard screen pass from Hamilton to Dulan and three Dulan carries for an additional 12 yards, we found ourselves on the five-yard line. We were penalized, once again, (we had 9 penalties for 74 yards) for illegal procedure and were pushed back to the 10-yard line. Hamilton's attempt to hit Scott Stroth in the end zone on 3rd down was overthrown.

Coach Bowen elected to bring on place kicker, Clint Thezan, for his second attempt at a field goal. Early in the game he hooked a 25-yard attempt. There was less than five minutes left in the game, This time it was not pretty, almost blocked, but cleared the cross bar for a 3-0 lead that stood up and we had a hard fought victory to improve to 4-2. As I was writing this book, Thezan and I texted about that kick. He said, "If I remember right, it just barely cleared the upright." My comment to him was there were about 2,000 Seaman players and faithful who remember that the kick barely cleared the upright. I am certain their coach, Dale Sample, one of the really good guys in the coaching arena at the time, definitely remembers that kick and that game. He shares his thoughts on Bowen later in the book.

In that game our defense held Seaman to just five first downs and 50-yards of offense. Both defenses had three interceptions. In a Topeka Capital-Journal article Seaman Coach Sample said, "The whole ballgame we couldn't move the ball. I'm proud of the way we played, but, offensively, we couldn't get anything going. That's a credit to their defense. They lined up and played tough."

Dulan had 123 yards rushing on 25 carries and added the 34 yards on a screen pass. He got dinged up early in the game when we were threatening to score and had to sit out 2 offensive plays and we stalled.

Bowen commented about Thezan and the decision to attempt a field goal, "The ball was in the middle of the field and in practice he can put them through. He had tried one earlier – I felt like he was due to hit one. It doesn't have to be pretty as long as long as it's good. He said he hit his toe on the turf as he kicked."

In those days the KSHSAA had a pre-determined geographical assignment for District play. There were four teams in each of the eight districts in 5A classifications. Our district consisted of us along with DeSoto, Bonner Springs and Shawnee Heights (a Centennial League rival).

I have spent many years coaching and during the '85 and '86 seasons we were developing a confident swagger. We knew we were a talented football team. We knew we had dedicated athletes who wanted to be successful. We knew that the chemistry of the team was special.

I'm asked by coaches now, "how did you develop such good chemistry." A lot of times its circumstantial. Other times, it's based on the makeup of your school community. Back in the '80s we had several groups of athletes, a long string of kids who grew-up playing all sports together, hanging out together and, in a sense, were very much like family. They didn't always get along, but try and hurt one of their teammates, on or off the field, and they got really stubborn, very competitive and defensive in a good way. To put it in perspective, it was a little like the military. They defended you if you put on the blue jersey for Rural.

This team entered the district playoffs with that same dogged attitude. We had swagger which translates to confidence. We had chemistry which brought out that group-protective mind set that serves you well in football. Those athletes would do anything to help each other.

Our first district opponent was De Soto. All we knew about them was what we were able to obtain through film. In those days it was truly film. Reel to reel. You threaded it and re-threaded it and ran it back and forth for preparation purposes. We wanted out athletes to know what to expect. We wanted them aware of certain opponent's players. We wanted them to be ready for their offensive scheme. We wanted to know how to block their defense based on their alignment. Yep, we had smart coaches. Bowen and Glaze over prepared. Every week.

We went to De Soto knowing how important it was to win all three of our district games. You can't win them all unless you win the first one. Pretty prophetic, eh? We may have been a little tight in the first half. And they may have been a very decent football team.

The score at halftime was WR 0 and De Soto 0. We moved the ball up and down the field, but they never gave up the end zone and we didn't capitalize on our possessions. Frustrating when you know you likely have to win every district game to make the playoffs. As per usual, our coaches put their collective heads together, listened to our players and came up with a few moves in an attempt to counter what they were doing and hopefully get us in more of an offensive flow and be able to finish drives. Obviously, defensively we were holding our own. But you don't ever win a game 0-0.

A contributing factor to no scoring was likely that it was a rainy, muddy night. That usually translates into whoever runs the ball and can grind it out often wins. It was true that night. Dulan carried the ball 28 times for 170 yards. Todd Scott added another 79 yards rushing and that translated into two scores.

In that offense we made good use of the slot back on misdirection plays.

Obviously, De Soto was trying to key on Dulan. Dulan told Topeka Capital-Journal sportswriter Jeff Cravens in a post-game interview, "I feel almost every game the other team is keying on me." Well, yeah. When you have an I back capable of breaking a touchdown or long run every time he touches the ball, you better defend that.

For our first score Hamilton faked a pitch to Dualn, the defense over committed for the fake assuming Dulan would get the ball and Scott came back on a slot back counter, a mis-direction play. A good fake and a smooth handoff, a gaping hole for a 52-yard touchdown run with 8:19 left in the third quarter. It would be the only score we would need.

But later Dulan took a handoff on a draw play. Hamilton fooled the defense faking a drop back pass and handed the ball to Dulan who broke a 45- yard touchdown run. In the rain and mud a two-touchdown lead is very difficult to overcome.

De Soto had won the opening coin toss, elected to kick off and hoped to pin us in a hole and let the mud help them defend. It was a good strategy. After the game Bowen echoed everyone's thoughts about our collective team speed. He was asked about next week's second district game that would be against Bonner Springs. "We're really looking for a dry field to play on." When you have a "stable" of fast "horses" you'd like to have a dry race-track. Same theory in football. Speed can kill. Give me three fast kids in high school football and you can be tough to defend and hard to stop. We had three speedsters on the field all the time.

That year we had Antoine Dulan who had sprinters speed and so much athleticism to go with it. One of the most explosive, quick starts from a backfield stance I've ever been around. He was recruited by K State just before Snyder took over. I still maintain if he was utilized on the defensive side of the ball instead of beginning as a wideout or a slot receiver, he had the potential to play on Sundays.

Todd Scott was a smaller package of similar speed and had a knack of finding seams, using his eyes to find creases in the defense. He could catch the ball adequately and was an excellent return man. He went onto play college football at a Division one AA school at the time, Southwest Texas State. He was a junior that year and was moved to tailback after Dulan graduated in the spring.

At receiver Bowen ran offensive plays to our offensive huddle with two individuals. Scott Stroth and Chris Walker. Each had great speed and both were excellent route runners with excellent hands. Stroth was more of a baseball standout but was a huge asset on this team and kept defenses honest. Stroth always was in on first down and third down so he had more opportunities to catch passes. We didn't pass as much back then, but we could pass effectively, and Bowen knew we were had both a skilled quarterback and gifted receivers. We were effective with Hamilton, Stroth and Walker. Walker was the second down and fourth down receiver. Bowen wanted Walker on punt coverage if we had to kick the football when a drive stalled. Stroth played first and third downs. These two ran in the plays from the sideline.

With any of those four on the field at the same time, we were hard to defend.

In our second district game against Bonner Springs it was good to be on our home field. Big crowd for us. We defeated Bonner 32-12 on a fast field. Dry. No rain.

And on the fast-track Dulan ran like a thoroughbred race-horse. He scored four touchdowns on runs of 10, 5, 73 and 32 yards respectfully. He rushed 17 times for 204 yards for an average of a little more than eight yards per carry.

In the November 1, 1986 Capital-Journal article by Pam Clark described so well Antoine Dulan's ability to carry the football. She said, "Only in the instant when Antoine Dulan takes a handoff from the quarterback or catches a pass does a Washburn Rural offensive play involving the shifty tailback look exactly the way the coaches draw it on the chalkboard."

She went on to write, "Once the speedy senior hits the line of scrimmage, though, it's all improvisation. He jumps over would-be tacklers, dodges them, runs over them, runs by them."

In the post-game interview Dulan himself said, "Offensively, once I get past the line, I can play with the cornerbacks and safeties. It gives me an advantage. I think I can break a big one."

Coach Bowen told sportswriter Clark, "He (Dulan) played well. Everybody on the offensive line did a great job and he ran hard. You never know, when he gets the ball, what he's going to do. He's one of those athletes that can do a lot for you."

Clark went on to comment on the offensive line in her article. She said, "Dulan got key blocks from offensive linemen on just about every big play- from Jeff Hughes here, Matt Marple there, Pat Stoffel then John Boley." She forgot guards James Walker and Steve Reynolds so I'm giving them their due as well. Offensive linemen live in obscurity and are generally only noticed if they miss a block or jump off- sides. We coaches noticed their solid play and successful assignments.

I grew to appreciate offensive linemen more and more. Because I coached them. Those who know football know that, when a lineman chooses to put their hand in the dirt or they were chosen to play offensive line, they were destined to obscurity. Offensive linemen make that choice and give up any ego, any chance of stardom or much recognition. They take solace in the fact that, without their hard work and good blocking, the offense doesn't go anywhere.

You are taught to protect the quarterback but asked to play violently. And the only way to be successful is to beat the opponents who are in the way of the play design. You have to be meaner, more aggressive, precise and, in, most cases a bit nasty as a human being. Not every individual could play the line, but those that learn to and relish it can survive anything thrown their way.

Sportswriter Clark also had a classic line describing Dulan, "Once he got into the secondary, though, it was Dulan Magic." Yes indeed. But the class act that Dulan was he not only recognized his line's blocking he had another individual to give credit to.

"The line did a great job," Dulan said. "And one guy I'd like to mention is Jeff Cowan. He moved to fullback this week. This was his first time and he did a heckuva job blocking. He's really a hitter. That was one of the things that broke it up for us."

We led the game 25-0 at halftime on three Dulan rushing touchdowns and a 25-yard field goal by Clint Thezan plus a safety by the punt return special team. The punter had to fall on a bad snap in his own end zone.

We scored once more in the second half and then called off the dogs and let lots of reserves see action. Final score 32-12 and a great tune up for our last district game.

We were rolling with one district game left to win against league rival Shawnee

Heights of Topeka.

As if we needed any extra incentive against the T-Birds, rumor has it that, occasionally Coach Bowen, lovingly referred to them as the "Dirty Birds." If you spent enough time on the coaching staff, you kind of memorized most of Coach's pre-game inspirational speeches. His Shawnee Heights speech was a classic. He always referred to a closely contested game with Heights that came down to an extra point conversion.

Coach always referred to the Shawnee Heights "win" as a "theft" because on the play that gave them their one win way back when, they had twelve men on the field. Film confirmed. And that should have resulted in a penalty which would have negated their conversion attempt. We would have won the game. No matter how many times I heard that speech I always felt like I was ready to strap on a helmet and wear shoulder pads and rush onto the field to compete. You'll get Coach Bowen's depiction of that "theft" later in the book.

Once again, we caught some nasty weather. Seemed as if it was every other week for inclement weather. After all it was November in Kansas. But the field at Shawnee Heights had taken a season-worth of beatings and it was slick and without much grass and the wind was brutal and could have been a factor. But it was better than the weather we had in the 1985 state championship game, on the frozen tundra of Kansas University Memorial Stadium. Silver linings if you look hard enough.

The Shawnee Heights defense used the elements and a good defensive scheme to hold Dulan down for three quarters. At halftime they had held the running back to just 10-yards on six carries. That, in and of itself, would be considered a victory in some folks' minds.

We were unable to score in the first quarter. Neither did Heights. Early in the second quarter Todd Scott capped a 13 play 51-yard drive with a seven-yard touchdown on an inside counter play from the slot position to put us up 6-0.

Heights bounced back on their next position and scored to make it 6-6

But Scott scored on our next possession on the same counter trap play that went for 72 yards. Jeff Hamilton converted the two-point conversion on a keeper play. Score at that point was 14-6 Rural at halftime. Not a very comfortable lead considering the weather and the way the Heights defense bottled up Dulan.

It got even tighter when neither team could score in the third quarter.

It proved impossible for Heights to stop Dulan for four quarters though. He took a handoff, ran into a pile at the line of scrimmage and high-stepped it over the pile and outraced everyone to the end zone for a 79-yard touchdown. Clint Thezan made the extra point kick and it was 21-6.

Later in the fourth quarter Scott scored his third touchdown of the game when he took a pitch on an option play for 16 yards. Thezan made this extra point kick as well and it finished off the scoring 28-6 which capped off a 3-0 run through 5A district play.

Scott had three touchdowns and 112 yards rushing on a night that his efforts were needed. On a night when the combine pass yardage for both teams combined was 31 yards, the miserable conditions changed the way the game had to be played. Despite being held for 10-yards rushing in the first half, Dulan did end up with a 127-yard effort. Rural's ground game racked up 281 yards. The offense was powerful and did what was necessary to advance to the sub state playoff game.

Bowen got on the team bus and echoed his statement from last year's state championship game yelling, "I've never seen a finer day!" Funny how the elements can be a competitor's rallying point.

Bowen told Capital-Journal sportswriter, "Todd Scott did a super job. He ran hard. And Dulan and Cowan ran hard. I was glad to see it (the reverse trap with Scott) open up for touchdowns. Sam Austin (offensive line coach) thought we could go inside on them. He's the one who called the play on the long touchdown."

Our defense forced three fumbles and had an interception in holding Shawnee Heights to one score and less than 200 yards of total offense. It was a real team effort and raised our record to 7-2. It was onto the next opponent, likely a team from the Kansas City area.

THE 1986 PLAYOFFS

S o, we ended up traveling to Kansas City- Sumner with good field-conditions to play on. Sumner learned what it was like to turn over the ball to a fast team. On their first two possessions they fumbled the ball away to us. We scored on each turnover for an early 14- point lead.

Our linebacker Darren Caster recovered the ball on their 32- yard line on the first play of the game. Six offensive plays later Dulan scored from 12 on a third-down play. Thezan kicked the extra point and it was on.

On the very next series Sumner went three an out and, on their punt attempt the ball was bobbled by the punter and we tackled him on the Sumner 17-yard line. We drove the ball to the one-yard line and Hamilton kept it for a quarterback sneak for the game's second score and Thezan's extra point made it 14-0 with a couple minutes left in the first quarter. We couldn't have scripted a more perfect start to a game when we had to kick off to the opponent on their home field.

After the game Bowen told Capital-Journal reporter Pam Clark, "That really got us charged up. The fires got to burning." Bowen was brief, but always a good quote. He went on to add, "Well, they were already burning before that (the fumbles), but the kids really took advantage of their opportunities."

We continued to stymie Sumner's offense. Our defense was a definite strength that season.

And early in the second quarter we scored a third time on a nine-yard run by Scott that capped a 55-yard drive highlighted by a 45-yard Hamilton to Scott pass play. The snap to kick the extra point was high, but Hamilton alertly ran it in for a two- point conversion. WR 22 and Sumner 0 at halftime.

In the second half Scott scored our fourth touchdown with a 10-yard run and that capped the scoring making it 28-0.

Sumner scored twice in the second half, but they were the results of long, grind it out series that ate up the clock. Our bend, but not break, defense shut the door on a 28-14 victory that was never very close.

Sumner nearly matched our rushing yardage – 157 to 148 – but we nearly doubled their first downs. Dulan once again gained 143 yards on 23 carries. Hamilton completed 3 of 6 passes. He hit Scott for the 45-yarder, Stroth for 32 and added a nine-yard completion to tight end Mike Evans. Evans was effective on pass plays but, more importantly, was a crushing blocker which gave us another lineman to open holes and make blocks at the second and third levels. Can you imagine a game in which you score 28 points with so few of pass attempts or completions?

Another effective defensive weapon we had all season. The punt. Kraig Borough routinely punted the ball between 35-40 yards each attempt. And Dulan would often be asked to quick kick for the element of surprise. He got off a 39-yard quick kick in the Sumner game with no return opportunity.

With this substate playoff victory we earned the right to host Pittsburg High from southeast Kansas. And this year they would have to play at Rural. Never underestimate the home field advantage. If, for no other reason, you don't have to ride a bus for four hours.

Pittsburg arrived in Topeka and the Junior Blues stadium, McElroy Field, ranked by the media as the number one team in 5A despite Rural capturing the 1985 state championship.

The Pittsburg Dragons, relying on a strong rushing attack, took a 15-7 lead into halftime. In the first half the Junior Blues only made three first downs and had 73 total yards of offense. Rural's only score was set-up by a Jeff Hughes fumble recovery at the 45-yard line and a few plays later Antoine Dulan scampered in from 7-yards for their lone score in the first half.

In the second half it was almost a reversal. The Junior Blues got stingy on defense and held Pitt to just three first downs and only 51 yards of total offense.

Topeka Capital-Journal sportswriter Pam Clark told readers that Antoine Dulan supplied most of the Junior Blues offense rushing for 136 yards on 26 carries. But it was a big play by quarterback Jeff Hamilton that turned the game around.

Again, a Hughes fumble recovery set-up the second Rural score, a run of one yard and a two-point Dulan conversion to tie the game at 15-15.

At the beginning of the fourth quarter Rural marched from the Pittsburg 49 to the 21-yard line and faced a fourth down and seven play. Rural called a timeout. The play was a Hamilton fake to Scott on an inside reverse, then he was to go down the line and preferably pitch it to Dulan, but Pitt took away the pitch. Hamilton headed up field, dodged a couple of would- be tacklers and fought for 16-yards for a first down. A few plays later Hamilton snuck it in from the one and Rural was up 21-15.

On the ensuing kickoff Clint Thezan kicked it low and hard and it bounced off a Pittsburg player on their return team. Rural's Dusty Palmer recovered the muffed kick and nine plays later, using up a lot of clock, the Junior Blues put the decisive touchdown on the board and took a 27-15 victory.

For the second straight year the Junior Blues were going to the 5A championship game. This year's game was to be played at Kansas State University. The opponent would be Ark City who defeated Salina Central 14-0 in the other semifinal game.

I usually went to Coach Ray Glaze's house on Sunday evenings late to watch football film. He had film on Ark City. When I walked into his house and sat down. He said, "I want you to look at something here." After a few minutes of watching Ark City's offense, Glaze asked, "What do you see?" I told Glaze I wasn't exactly sure why, but I felt like I could tell whether they would run a play to the left or to the right.

Glaze chuckled and said, "Watch the fullback's hand."

After several plays it was obvious what he had spotted. The fullback, the lead blocker on most plays would change what hand he put on the ground. If the play was going left, he put his right hand down on the ground for his three- point stance. If the play were to go to the right, he would start with his left hand down.

I said, "Glaze, that's incredible! Does he do that every time?"

Glaze nodded and said, "Uh huh." Ironic how he told his own son, Ray Glaze, Jr. not to do that as our running back.

So that night we decided how we would use that to our advantage. We used three down lineman and we slanted kids into gaps or into offensive lineman in attempts to get double teams so the linebackers could roam free and make tackles. We decided that we would simply make our defensive slant call AFTER they set-up and the fullback put his hand down.

Needless to say, we had a tremendous advantage on defense. Our linemen that were so outsized by the huge Ark City offensive line now had an advantage in knowing what direction the play was going. Do I think that was the lone reason we won the game? Not at all. We were far more talented, and we got out of the gate with a Todd Scott opening kickoff return for a touchdown. And then we never looked back.

The offense scored three times, the special teams on the opening kickoff and the defense scored twice on a Todd Scott interception and a Mike Herzog fumble recovery to destroy Ark City 42-14.

The offense put up 186 yards rushing, 134 by Antoine Dulan. We actually had -3 yards passing, but we had 129 yards of returns by the special teams and the defense held Ark City scoreless UNTIL the score was 42-0.

Something that was personally gratifying for me was that many of our linebackers and secondary gave credit to our defensive line for sacrificing their bodies by continually diving into the enormous offensive lineman's legs and creating piles at the line of scrimmage. And, of course, we knew which sides to make the piles all day long. Thanks for the directional tip.

A player perspective from Antoine Dulan (1985-1987) "Coach was always the best at observing, seeing and understanding the individual person. It's amazing how far you can go when someone believes in you. I learned this lesson from not only Coach Bowen but from most of the coaches at WR in every sport. Head track and field coach Jerry Beardslee was also a very important figure for me during my time at WR. He believed in me more than I believed in myself. The culture at WR was one of support and a family atmosphere. No matter good times or bad you always felt someone had your back, from your peers to the educational staff. WR at the time didn't have many kids of color back in the '80s. I was never treated or made to feel anything but like a Junior Blue!

I would like to thank Coach Bowen for instilling the values of discipline, perseverance and hard work in me- and for making us the state's best. If anyone deserves honor and great respect, it's Ron Bowen and the rest of his staff. I want to let coach know how much I appreciate the investment in our lives. It was an amazing experience from beginning to end. Coach Bowen was our role model and lived as an example of how to persevere and keep pushing towards our goals. I am so lucky to have had a coach who inspired me every day to be better than the day before.

I remember my senior year after a loss to one of our rivals, Emporia High School, many of the guys on the team decided to go to a party after the game which ended in a very bad night for many of our players. I can remember it like it was yesterday. The look of disappointment on coach's face. It was a look that you wish you never had to see and one you would prepare not to ever see again. I think we all learned some great lessons that season and went on to win a second straight championship that year in the fall of 1986. Not a perfect season but, without the leadership of Ron Bowen and his coaching staff, things could have taken a turn for the worst very easily. " – Antoine Dulan

For the record Coach Bowen addressed the "party" that Antoine referred to with a very stern talk after practice the following Monday. In short, he told the entire team that he was aware of the party, was aware that one of our players were injured as a result of being at a party where alcohol was present. He told his troops that there was going to be a "little party" of their own after practice. And his warning was this- "If you were at the party, even briefly, you were expected to stay for this party after practice." Because if you were there, don't stay and Coach were to find out later that you were present, you would be dismissed from the team. "Check it in" as he referred to it. I have no way of knowing for certain, but I believe every player who was present at that wild party also stayed for the party Coach conducted. And a clear message was sent about how this was not acceptable. It was a "gut check" day of grand proportions and no one complained. No parents complained. Maybe that is the character needed to win championships from the coaches, players and parents. Parents trusted that Coach Bowen had the best interest of their sons in mind. They trusted Coach Ron Bowen and his staff to do what was right.

Possible photos for this section: #41 Scott-25 and Walker-21, #42 D linemen listening for the train, #43 Conly and Stofell, #44 Dulan, #45 1986 state champs team, #46 Topeka All-City Team

1987 FOOTBALL SEASON- ONE OF PROMISE

It would be an injustice to not write about the 1987 season. It was my third year as a varsity coach. There were many returning starters coming back for that season, great senior class (Class of 1988), that it almost was an expectation that we would make another run at a state championship. A "threepeat" a word became popular with the Chicago Bulls NBA run of championships.

We had so many kids who started on the '86 team coming back in the fall of 1987, both offensively and defensively. And a good supporting cast of juniors and sophomores.

And there would be many teams in the state of Kansas who, if you told them before the season started, they would win eight games and lose by one touchdown in the semi-finals of the state playoffs would take that fate. Unquestionably. So, it feels like a bit of sour grapes to complain about how the season ended. But when you write a book you can represent your perspective if you do it appropriately and feel the obligation to report facts and factual accounts.

So, at the start of the '87 football season, as per usual, we had a capable replacement for our tailback. And when your offense is run from the Power I formation, a critical member of the offense is the tailback. Todd Scott, (SR) was ready to move from the slot back position and take over the bulk of the carries on offense. Scott had speed and an uncanny way of shifting gears when the situation called for it which helped him garner both a community college and a Division One football scholarship. He would patiently run behind his blockers until a seam was created and then shift into his high gear. And he had one. Once he was able to reach the second and third levels of the defense, he could avoid tacklers with instinctive moves. He had tremendous vision and instinct. You can't coach that. A back either has that ability, or he doesn't. Prior to the season, I remember wondering what life would be like without Antoine Dulan who graduated the spring before. You don't replace all the tools he had. But when I saw Todd Scott jump over a pile of tacklers in the annual soap scrimmage and hit the ground and immediately shift to high gear, I felt like we were going to be fine with Scotty as our feature back. It was his turn, his time up. And he answered the call like so many players before him had. Next man up.

Scotty's lead blocker was his good friend Mike Gomez, (SR). He was equally well-known as a lead blocker which often was the only block Scotty needed, was a quicker than a hiccup nose guard and had a dry, comedic sense of humor. To say he was easy going was fair. But snap the ball and he got after it. GoGo was the energizer bunny way before that commercial's battery bunny was created. And when we needed a quick hitter on a short yardage situation, you could count on Gomez not to fumble and to fight for that first down marker.

Jeff Hamilton, (SR) was more than a capable quarterback with one year of experience under his belt and lots of reps behind center. He had a different center as senior Jeff Hughes (who unselfishly played center as a junior in 1986) moved his skill set to tight end. Hamilton was an excellent passer. He had a propensity for wanting to throw the long ball. So, since I was his former freshman coach, never one to not be assertive with coaching tips if warranted, I reminded him that the short passes to Jeff Hughes, who was a seam-finding route runner and a sure handed tight end, would help increase his completion percentage. Hamilton was coachable and he listened. Of course, Coach Bowen reenforced this premise daily. The long ball was not always going to be there and was harder to connect on.

He had good receivers in slot back, Chris Walker, (SR), Mike Zweiner, (SR) and Clint Thezan, (SR) who doubled as our kicker.

Walker had excellent speed and was sure handed. He caught whatever was thrown his way. The staff had so much confidence in his hands that he was our sure handed punt returner this year, and past years. He was a smart football player. He was as outstanding on offense as he was on defense. In today's pass oriented, spread offenses he would catch plenty of balls. After the catch he was strong enough to break tackles and could outrun most of our opponents' secondary players.

Zweiner, John Patterson, (JR), ran plays in along with Clint Thezan, (SR). Zweiner was the beneficiary of being the first down and third down receiver. He had an uncanny knack of finding the end zone. Even in a run-oriented offense, Coach Bowen knew when he could have closer balance and the power rushing opened-up the passing game. Since Thezan was an integral part of our kicking duties he was used less on offense, but many teams would have loved to have had any of these three receivers to throw the ball to. Patterson was young, had good hands and was an excellent blocker which was important when Scotty broke to the secondary. All three of those wideouts were good downfield blockers. As pass receivers you earned your playing time based on your hands combined with your ability to block.

The linemen were equally competent on both sides of the ball. The offensive line proved strong enough to open consistent holes for Scotty to run through. At center we had John Boley, (SR) who was a tough, hard nosed lineman with long arms and a great frame. He was coachable and did his number one job well. The center-quarterback exchange was crucial. There were no issues there. No fumbles. And Boley played with an attitude. His attitude mirrored those of his unofficial "brothers" Pat Stoffel, (SR) and Mike Herzog, (SR). Those three were fun loving and hard-nose football players. They wrestled and were experienced lineman. We had a lot of tough kids and then we had a level of aggressiveness with Stoffel and Herzog that was so valuable. They were leaders by actions. They could get vocal with their teammates if necessary, but other players wanted to match their competitiveness. Boley played just like his "brothers."

Sean Conley, (SR) and Trey McPherson (JR) completed a tough, aggressive line. Conley was equally valuable on defense as a linebacker. If you played linebacker for a Ray Glaze defense, you had to be able to make tackles and stuff holes at the line of scrimmage. Conly was a tough young man who also was a gifted musician. He currently plays strings professionally. McPherson was more than capable on the offensive line, but he shone as a defensive end.

And on the defensive side of the ball the line was anchored by Stoffel and Herzog at tackles, Gomez at nose guard. We had backups who pushed these guys to play better and who gave them good repetitions in drills. And, since these were the players I was responsible for coaching daily, I took a great deal of pride working on their techniques and on their minds. Defensive linemen in our 5-2 monster linebacker scheme were the original "inglorious bastards." Wasn't that a movie title? The D lineman's job was to lineup head-up on the center and the offensive tackles and slant across one lineman's face with the goal of taking out another offensive lineman's knee. Not to injure, just to keep two linemen off our linebackers. Few noticed their efforts, so it was up to me, Sam Austin, who helped me coach them and Ray Glaze, Defensive coordinator to give them their praises when they did their jobs. Thankless obscurity is where these guys lived. But occasionally and often with this talented trio there was a quarterback sack or a tackle in their efforts. It took a special cat to play defensive line. And I had three capable ones. Tough, relentless and quick. And fun. We had fun basking in what glory we occasionally found.

The defensive ends were critical parts of the defense. Some would say they were lineman. Some called them linebackers. But they played as "stand-up" anchors. And they had to have the ability to defend the off-tackle runs, closing down that hole as well as be able to string out any sweeps and make the back cut back to the middle instead of getting the edge. Hughes and McPherson were physically capable of both responsibilities and without their strong play we would have been more vulnerable defending opponents. Often their number one job was not to make tackles, but each were sure tacklers as well. And they hit hard.

I mentioned Conly playing linebacker and he was more than solid there for us. Additionally, we had John Anderson, (JR) who anchored the other linebacker position. As mentioned, our defense was set-up for our linebackers to make the tackles. So, if you weren't a sure tackler, you did not play linebacker. The middle backers also had to recognize formations, and react to runs as well as drop in pass coverage, so they had to be as mentally tough as they were physically. Conley and Anderson were good all year. Neither were imposing physically, but they would hit you with all they had. And they were good about reading their keys. They knew where they had to get to make a tackle.

Our monster linebacker was who we tried to put on the anticipated play side to give us an extra defender. Patterson was a hard nose versatile player. He essentially played like a strong safety on many occasions. But we used him to blitz too and put pressure on the opposing backfield. Since he was usually on the play side he was involved in many tackles.

Our secondary was extremely versatile. Walker was a capable tackler at cornerback or safety. Scott played some safety as well. Marc Chrisco, (Soph) alongside Walker were excellent cover corners. They had the speed to close on a ball that had too much air under it. Most high school passers don't zip the ball into tight spots. Scott was able to make up for missed coverage or assignments. When we played thirds of the field it was very hard for opposing receivers to find a seam when the linebackers made the correct drops.

In 1987 we started the season with three straight wins. Our opener with Kansas City Washington was close, a 16-13 victory. There was timing issues with different kids in different positions, particularly on offense where timing is critical. Additional reps in practice the following week and a friendly, known Centennial League opponent, Highland Park, helped us to a 28-0 win. The defense was outstanding, but it was good for the confidence to score four times. In our third game, also a League contest, we defeated Hayden 30-0. Back-to back shutouts cure a lot of things.

In the fourth game we had to face a recent League nemesis, a very good Emporia team. They got the best of us and hung a 21-13 loss on us. It was a game of breaks and they made some of theirs' count. We were now 3-1, but we'd been here before losing two of our early games in '86 (3-2 after five games). And in 1985 same 3-2 start.

Well, we dropped game five, a hard-fought rivalry game with non-league, city foe Topeka West. Once again we were 3-2, but we had been here before. And I'm certain Coach Bowen reminded this current squad about that. He had a way of making setbacks be a rallying point. Since the seniors were a part of the two previous seasons, they remembered well how these teams bounced back and won the ultimate prize – a state championship. There wasn't any reason to believe we could NOT win the remaining games on our schedule. And we had one more regular season game before district football play commenced.

Our opponent was Seaman, who we narrowly defeated 3-0, on a fourth quarter field goal the year before. This team went out and got a 24-7 victory which made us a fairly confident team going into district play.

Our pre-assigned geographical district this season consisted of Kansas City Turner, Bonner Springs and Shawnee Heights. We managed to outscore those opponents in those three games by a total of 126-3. This was one of the negative aspects of this type of predetermined district format. But it gave you a geographical representative for each of the eight districts so the playoffs weeded that out. There were years WR would have to compete with three teams with one or two loss records. It truly was a crap shoot. This year we won the crap shoot.

Our first playoff game was a home game against Bishop Miege. They were a talented team, and Miege got up on us early, but was a mixture of our team speed on offense and some defensive scores we won. It wasn't easy and we had to come from behind. In the 3rd quarter we were down 13-25. A Hamilton to Hughes touchdown pass and a short Patterson TD run and a Thezan kicked extra point and we were up 26-25. That last score was a Patterson touchdown set up by a long and dramatic cut back run by Scott of about 80 plus yards to the 3-yard line. Scott went out with leg cramps for the touchdown play but bounced back quickly. So, with very little time left, they had the ball. Walker read a pass route on defense and jumped it for a pick six and a TD from about 30 yards to make it 33-25.

This dramatic win set up another semi-final showdown with Pittsburg, who we had beaten in this game the previous two years. This year was our turn to travel to southeast Kansas. The one humorous story involved with this game was the fact that Bowen had a certain way to make this trip. In 1985 we boarded the bus and drove to Fort Scott, which is less than 30 miles from Pittsburg. We would eat an afternoon meal and then get on the bus for a short trip to the historical Fort Scott site.

It worked so well in 1985 Bowen wanted to do the same thing. Some of the seniors who were sophomores then whined a bit inquiring, "Aw, coach, we've already seen the Fort!?! Do we have to go again?" In typical Bowen fashion he pointed out the "fact" that they probably weren't paying enough attention two years ago and likely missed some of the "high" points. Okay, but who is going to argue with how we played in 1985. Or better yet, who wanted to argue with Bowen. Even we coaches were smart enough to know that would be futile. So, we prepared for a replication of the road trip culminating in a Fort tour. The truth be known, Bowen just wanted the players to walk off their meals and have a short ride into the opponents' stadium. It was a great plan. It did not produce the same results in 1987 but there's a story that goes with this game.

Now I'm not a coach who focuses too much attention on the side of a game called officiating. In fact, I was a basketball referee when I was in college and worked many high school contests as a young man. I have always and still do tell our players that football officials are human, they make mistakes. I also point out that they may make fewer mistakes than the two teams most of the time. I won't let the outcome of a game be blamed on officiating or on a particular call late in the game that didn't favor us. It's just not a good look to whine about a loss blaming someone other than yourself for the outcome.

So, before I go into this part of the 1987 season, this critical game with the outcome of the game determining who got the privilege of playing for the state championship, I want to preface the next part of this story like this.

When you write a book, you are always balancing your perspectives and your biases. This is especially true if, as the author you have the responsibility to report what occurred. History as such. So, what I have chosen to do is simply give the facts as I observed them, or as other players, coaches or film observed them. There will not be a judgement unless it is by you. But I think this warrants the account of the game be reported honestly and accurately. And the aftermath of the game warrants the same consideration.

We arrived at Pittsburg and ran through our normal road-game pre-game routines. The players appeared to be focused and prepared just as they had the previous 10 football games. The stands were full. Pittsburg had a large following of fans and the atmosphere was electric. This is what high school football playoffs are all about. I'm certain Pittsburg was hoping to get some revenge for the previous two years we had beaten them. And, let me be clear, this depiction of the game had nothing to do with the Pittsburg players, nor their coaches.

One interesting pre-1988 playoff oddity was that the KSHSAA assigned the officiating crews and, in this particular game, KSHSAA chose an officiating crew who worked games in Pittsburg's conference. In retrospect this seems like an invitation to skepticism at best.

Being on the sideline I have one account that held true on more than one occasion. There are always occasions for officials to communicate with players. I officiated high school basketball and often either a general warning to a player or players, or a specific communication with a player which was always by uniform number got the player's attention and prevented an abundance of fouls in a contest.

On more than one occasion I could hear the officials call a Pittsburg player by their name. At best this is not professional demeanor and it certainly was unusual. What it represented to us was that the official knew the players and that should never be a part of administering a game if it can be avoided. Did this affect the outcome of the game? You be the judge, but it certainly raised our concern level.

According to one of our coaches, during the very first series of the game when we had the ball on offense, Scott gets tackled and lands out of bounds in front of our bench. Our coach witnessed a Pittsburg player with his forearm across Scott's throat as he laid on his back. He also says the player ran it back and forth across his throat. This coach responded by appealing loudly to the official, "Hey, that's a personal foul, throw the flag!!" I've seen this on film and it is clear that our coach and sideline became upset. The response from the official, according to the coach was, "Quiet down coach, keep it up and you'll get a flag thrown on you!!"

Now, in the heat of a contest, particularly one of this magnitude, both coaches and officials can get pretty testy. However, a coach is going to make every attempt to defend his player. Keep them safe. And officials are human and the coach's demeanor can often dictate their reaction. So, our coach could have waited till calm and said, "Sir, did you see the tackler with his forearm across our player's neck?" Appropriate game administration from an official, would be, no matter how approached, keeping ones cool and talking respectfully to the coach addressing his concerns for safe and sportsmanlike play. Neither happened. But it set the stage for some concern. Especially when, later we hear our opponents being called by their first or last names. And our kids were called by number. Could this cost us a win? By itself, probably not, but it was a prevailing theme that was combined with other situations that caused our overall concern.

One of our players over 30 years later had a recollection that numerous Washburn Rural players could substantiate. Whenever Pittsburg had a good play they celebrated. Not excessively but with normal excitement which is a part of every game. Our player recalls more than once a Washburn Rural celebration and an official saying something to the effect, "You better knock that off" or "calm that celebration down or you're going to be flagged for unsportsmanlike conduct." Would this cost us the game? Probably not, but the discriminate differences of treatment of similar natural emotions was worrisome. Remember, we had already played ten previous games and celebrated the same way without warning or without penalty. Our players were respectful and were aware of what they could and couldn't do. Our seniors had played and been a part of two previous state championships. You don't get to that level if you are considered an unsportsmanlike bunch. Undisciplined. Our players had discipline. In fact we had nurtured self-discipline. They did not celebrate to the degree of taunting the other team. Never had and never would have.

The last piece of game evidence is to go back and watch the film now a DVD. You can see instances where calls were made, were not made, for certain infractions. Now many will say that this is indicative and representative of most football contests. These are not professional referees and even those officials make errors. Now, thanks to slow motion and review, those are evident every week. These were volunteers who are not paid much and always subjecting themselves to scrutiny. Many of the calls/ non-calls occurred at very critical junctures of the Washburn Rural at Pittsburg game. And you could certainly go back and make a score sheet of what you observed if there would be any good to come of it. But we walked away from that game with a 21-14 one score difference. And a season ending loss. You never get do-overs. And if there is a particularly sad side to this game it was the last game for the seniors. They left southeast Kansas wondering. And that shouldn't have occurred. Not the fact that they were beaten. That happens to all but one school in every classification every year. But the fact was that they had doubts about the fairness of it all because of what they heard, saw and observed.

And the only positives to come from a game of this nature with concerns expressed by one school, was to hopefully make the powers to be, the KSHSAA aware of the concerns and show them the film footage of the game.

And to the credit of the leadership of both Bowen and Kaye Pearce, the executive director of the KSHSAA, a process was conducted and reflected upon that resulted in something positive for future playoff games.

In an article written by Topeka Capital-Journal sportswriter, Kevin Haskin, nearly two years after the game in 1989 there was something good that came from a concerning situation. Pearce listened to Ron Bowen's concerns and agreed to view the film footage of the game. According to the article chief among Bowen's complaints were the two personal fouls called on the Junior Blues on the same play, late in the game that set up Pittsburg with the ball on the 14-yard line. The 14-yard touchdown drive proved to be the game winning score.

Haskin writes that after Pearce reviewed the evidence (film) he supported the officials. In his position he had no choice.

Pearce had made the officiating assignments. This showed his confidence in the abilities of that crew to officiate the game from the onset. That year there were 81 playoff games to assign officials to. A daunting task indeed. Officials take enough heat as it is and, if they didn't receive the support from the KSHSAA or the director who assigns them what is left?

Haskin said Bowen supported that premise.

"He's (Pearce) is in a position where he has basically volunteer workers and the pay isn't all that great. I used to referee some wrestling and I know how it goes. One side is going to see it one way and the opposite side sees the complete opposite."

Haskin goes on to write that one of Bowen's beefs was one that Pearce and the KSHSAA could keep in mind for the future. The officials who were authorized and assigned to the 1987 Washburn Rural vs. Pittsburg football game were officials who worked Southeast Kansas League games on a regular basis. And all lived near the community of Pittsburg. Haskins wrote that Bowen contended that an officiating crew that had no ties to the community, nor the Southeast Kansas League would been a better choice to officiate that game.

Haskin quoted Bowen, "I wouldn't want to be on a crew from the local area calling a ballgame with so much at stake. I wouldn't want a Topeka crew working the game either. I think you have a better situation when the officials drive in from a little farther away, outside the area, so no one has any doubts in their minds."

Haskin reported that the points that Bowen made with Pearce were well taken.

On the same day this article appeared in the newspaper in 1989 Washburn Rural once again was going to Pittsburg to play a semifinal playoff football game. This time the KSHSAA and Pearce assigned a Kansas City, Kansas crew of officials. Haskin wrote, "Commend Pearce for listening and making a sound judgement based on past experience."

Later in the book you will find out that Washburn Rural won that football game in 1989. And all that could have been hoped for, by both teams, was that the officiating calls, good or bad, not have a shred of potential bias hanging over the contest. I'm certain you could find good calls and not so good calls in that game, but at least that prospect of bias was not present. And that was fairer to the officials and certainly more-fair to the players and coaches who worked so hard to reach the playoffs.

Another thing that can be safely said is that Ron Bowen and Kaye Pearce always had a great deal of respect for each other. And that is an important fact when considering varying opinions and attempts to make improvements in the system. In December of 2020 we lost Kaye Pearce. I will always respect his leadership and his willingness to make change when change is warranted. He was a class act.

Possible photos #47 Todd Scott and #48 Game celebration "the cockroach."

1988- My Last Year on the Staff

When I was deciding how to write this book, and I'll share my thought process on that, I wanted to include something about each of my years, the short time I had being a varsity assistant on Coach Bowen's staff (1985-1988). The fall of 1987 was my first year of teaching at the high school building. Always before I had taught junior high, which, prior to the fall of 1987 included the grades 6-9 at times. The junior high gradually became eighth and ninth graders, but the district decided to expand the high school to a four-year high school.

Most of the classes I taught at Shideler were freshman level, so I moved up with the 1987 freshmen. I was also assigned the position of part time athletic director and was assigned to teach three freshman literature and composition classes.

Tragically, before the school year of 1987-88 even began the head principal, Dale Smeltzer, was in a battle with cancer. Due to his health issues, he was going to miss the first semester of that year. So, plans for my position changed. They hired a substitute to teach my three freshman literature classes. I was moved to the third administrator's role. I was still allowed to coach due to the generosity of my two administrative colleagues. It was what I wanted to do, and the thought was that this may be temporary. When Mr. Smelter returned, I would resume my teaching assignment.

However, he was unable to return for an entire quarter, so we went back to Plan B. In 1988 I was once again allowed to coach and be the athletic director, but it was a trial basis. There are a lot of game-day duties administering sporting events. I kind of felt like it would be a short-term plan.

In the 1988 football season, we had suffered a big senior graduation of quality athletes. But we had a junior quarterback that appeared ready to lead the team.

Marc Chrisco. There were quality kids returning along with Chrisco and our defensive unit appeared to be just as capable as the 1987 version.

Basically, one of the critical stories associated with the '88 season was Chrisco contracted mono. We obviously made radical changes to how the team drank water to prevent further spreading of mono, but the damage was done. Chrisco missed six weeks and was not the same, physically when he returned. He fatigued so easily it hampered his ability to run with the football and that was an important part of his game.

The abbreviated part of this story was our backup quarterback was just a sophomore and basketball was his best sport. He had no varsity experience and had to step into the offense and learn under fire. We won two of our first six games. We beat KC Washington in the opener 14-7. And we narrowly defeated Hayden in game three, 7-0 as our offense was fairly anemic.

With district play upon us we knew we were not in a particularly tough district. We beat Turner 26-16 in game one. We beat Bonner Springs 16-8 and just had one more game to win. By this time Chrisco was back running the offense and we narrowly won a 14-12 contest over the Thunderbirds. And, to be honest, that may have been one of the most gratifying seasons because we won despite being short-handed.

Our season ended at Bishop Miege in the playoff game by a score of 12-2. Chrisco was not physically 100 percent. Also, one of our stand outs on defense, nose guard Greg McGivern, only played the first half due to a concussion. He was the most dominant and gifted nose guard I had ever coached. He was too quick for opponents to block.

That ended our season at 4-6 and we scratched and clawed to get there.

As I say, I had to make some determinations about how I was going to cover the Bowen years. I was a part of the 1985, 1986 state championship team so they were given a lot of ink. But, as I reflected, how could I NOT write about the 1989 state championship team. And give them equal billing? So, what I decided was that I would give the most attention, the most coverage, to the three state championship years. I decided the state runner-up team of 1992 warranted ample coverage for it's storied season. Theirs was the first and most successful 6A season thus far at Rural.

Then there were a handful of successful years so the most successful years would receive slightly less attention than the state runner ups. But there needed to be mention of every season since this was a book about the Ron Bowen era at Washburn Rural. And many of those years contained stories and they all were about the athletes that chose to sacrifice and play football in high school.

WAS RON BOWEN OLD SCHOOL AND CONSERVATIVE

There are likely no high school coaches, no coaches period, who don't occasionally face the public's scrutiny about their conservatism. There's no arguing that Ron Bowen preferred the running game to the passing game. He reminded all that there were three things that can happen when the ball is passed and two of those are bad outcomes. However, Bowen knew how to use the pass to keep the defense off-guard, to keep them from digging in their heels. That is when and if he had a capable passer. And at Washburn Rural we almost always found a capable passer. And when we had an exceptional passer, Coach Bowen knew how to utilize them even more.

I want to ask you how many high school coaches are willing to take the risks associated with making a piece of football practice equipment and get a patent for it?

Now keep this in mind as well when you are tempted to ONLY look at Bowen's conservative side. Yes, we always had the most conservative uniforms and helmets this side of Penn State University. There was a routine we followed associated with day practices and certainly a consistent way we approached getting ready for the game on a Friday. I wouldn't call it superstition, but it was consistent. There were habits. And to some outsiders, it might have even been viewed as a boring systematic approach. Worked.

So, when in 1989, Coach Bowen was asked if he would participate in a voluntary experiment involving the most significant part of a game, the football, we were shocked when Coach consented. Major League Baseball owner, Charlie O. Finley, had an experimental ball he wanted to try and market to enhance the quality of the game. Finley painted eight neon stripes running across the seams of the football. Thus, Finley created the visually enhanced football. He said he did so because many high schools across the country had poor stadium lighting. This was his attempt to help high school players play the game with a ball that they could see better under the lights.

In 1989 Bowen was leading a very successful team and it was surprising to us that he chose to do something out of the box. Perhaps it helped that it was marketed as something to "help" football players. Bowen was in favor of making the student-athletes job simpler. Perhaps it helped that the director of the KSHSAA at the time, was Kaye Pearce. Pearce was a friend of Bowens and he may have been doing a friend a favor when he agreed to be a participant in the experiment. The experiment was approved by the National Federation of Rules Committee of which Finley was a member.

Like most rules associated with the high school game, there was also a push to get support from college football coaches. Lou Holtz, who was at Notre Dame at the time, gave the football a trial run. To this day Bowen has a notebook full of positive letters (of course) that were sent from coaches who tried the visually enhanced football. The marketing, the media coverage, etc. was very good.

Eventually the ball received mixed reactions from coaches across the country. It was tried in nine states. Finley was known as an innovator in major league baseball as well. He tried very hard to put neon orange baseballs in the major leagues. Which is kind of interesting considering that, eventually, softball went to fluorescent yellowish-green balls for their sport. Finley was also colorful and sometimes this was interpreted by some as being a showman. After all, us Kansans who are of a certain age can remember the Kelly Green and Gold uniforms of the old KC Athletics baseball teams. And the automatic ball dispenser near home plate that was a "rabbit" that popped up with new baseballs for the umpire making calls behind the plate. And he was one of the few owners with a mascot. A mule he boldly called Charlie O. Who is brave enough to name a donkey after themselves?

Now, whether that showmanship quality worked for or against Finley's innovation, you know the rest of the story. There are no visually enhanced footballs in high school. Other than one year of experimentation, there never was.

Bowen allowed his players to be the judge of the football. And he politely wrote a letter to KSHSAA Pearce that said, "In my assessment the present football being used for high school play need not be changed. Our players did not feel that the ball was any better than what we used in our other games."

It wasn't that Bowen was a hard sale, he simply had to be convinced that there were clear and numerous advantages. That ball used in the October, 13, 1989 football game when Rural hosted Highland Park was a fixture in my office while I was the school's athletic director. After all, it was a piece of history. And it made for great stories.

Another interesting story was Bowen's filing for a patent on October 15, 1973 for a "Football Practice Blocking and Tackling Reaction Machine." He filed it officially with the United States Patent and Trademark Office.

The device was designed and built for his practice purposes. For reasons which may have included cost and exceptionally lengthy production time to make the machine, it was never picked up by the numerous equipment companies.

The patent office offered a printed abstract description of the device Bowen invented. "A reaction machine for football practice or the like. An upright is provided supported from its lower portion by a base. A beam is generally mounted with the upright pivotable horizontally around the upright and pivotable vertically. A dummy support arm is vertically pivotally mounted on one end of the beam for mounting a tackle dummy on the like. A brake assembly is mounted between the beam in a fixed, horizontal position. A shock absorber is also mounted between the upright and beam for absorbing shock of a player hitting the dummy. The dummy support arm and beam are provided with latch structure for holding the dummy in a raised position and releasing the dummy to a lowered position."

Fairly innovative, ambitious and creative to build that apparatus.

So, was Ron Bowen conservative? In some ways yes. You might call it efficient, prudent, cautious and disciplined. Was he "old school?" By his own admission yes, but that is not a negative term. His methods were right for the time and, despite how coaching that way today might not be politically correct, he was right for the time. He helped shape an awfully lot of fantastic young men and women. Times change, but basic needs remain the same. Discipline, however you have to instill it, is absolutely a necessity for successful football programs, for the remainder of the participants adult life. Ron Bowen knew this and he used what he knew at the time to help kids become self-disciplined. But don't fool yourself, he could also adjust and adapt when the situation called for it. Ron Bowen may well have preferred the run to the pass, but don't let that fool you either. He was willing to take risks- calculated as they may be, but he would roll the dice with the best of them. And more times than not, he made the right calls.

1989 – ONE FOR THE AGES

The 1989 season was the 15th for Bowen at Washburn Rural and the team was coming off a sub-par year, record wise. And Bowen had some new staff members. But most importantly the KSHSAA had pushed the start of practices up to as early a start as the state high school scene had ever seen. It was the first year for Friday football on Labor Day weekend.

In a pre-season article Bowen indicated that he thought it was not a good change. What he worried about was that the spring sports season moved closer to summer break and fall sports now were also earlier. His concern was a short summer for kids to train, play baseball and vacation with their families.

However, if it was coming earlier, it might as well come with a promising crop of athletes. And Washburn Rural returned some good upperclassmen.

And it wasn't unusual for Rural to make the playoffs the year before. But it was unusual how they made it. The regular season was dim. But they came on to win the district 3-0 and held their own against a very good Bishop Miege team.

And optimism ran rampant when you return eight players who started on offense and five who started on defense. They benefitted greatly by "clawing" their way through district and earning a playoff game.

Back on offense was the team's quarterback, a healthy Marc Chrisco, who was the statistical passing leader despite missing several games in '88.

Also returning was a very capable tailback from a year ago, George Pratt, who as a sophomore had 134 carries for 662 yards and now grew into his 6'2" 191-pound junior frame. In two district games Pratt gained 176 yards against KC

Turner and logged 112 yards against Bonner Springs. Bowen downplayed Pratt's abilities saying, "George has no great moves, but he has a lot of strength." George knew the shortest distance to the first down sticks was a straight line. He ran extremely hard as a sophomore.

Speedy senior slot back, Dusty Zander, who led the team a year before with 11 catches for 164 yards was primed and ready to play a full season with Chrisco heaving the football around.

The fourth back was 6'2" 206-pound junior Aaron Anderson, a capable ball carrier who, if not tackled at the line of scrimmage, actually accelerated into the second and third levels of opponents' defenses.

Tight end Adam Woodward was a 6-0" 180 pounder who had great hands and was primarily a blocker for the Junior Blues powerful off-tackle and sweep plays. He proved to be a good route runner and caught the majority of balls that he could get his hands and body on. Size at the skill position was not a problem. Experience was also in their favor.

In the Capital-Journal sportswriter Kevin Haskin's article, Bowen also mentioned linemen Kevin Burenheide and John Metzger who weighed less than Pratt, Zander, Anderson and Woodward. But they had proven to be excellent blockers. Jason Penrod was mentioned as well and he was a strong 216- pounds.

Defensively Bowen mentioned Zander and Kirk Midkiff at cornerbacks and Chrisco at safety. This was an experienced defensive backfield capable of slowing down passers and protecting the edges with sure tackles. The previous year Rural was number one in pass coverage allowing an average of just 41 yards passing to opponents.

Anderson would start at linebacker again and Woodward would man one defensive end position.

Among the linemen getting a look include defensive ends Pratt and Chris Palmer.

Metzger, Penrod and Lonnie Russell were getting consideration as tackles. Tony Disidore and Greg Harvey were getting repetitions at nose guard.

Mike Robinson, Steven Bane, David Chase and Levi Baucom were getting repetitions as linebackers.

GAME #1

So, on September 2, 1989 Washburn Rural traveled to Kansas City Washington for their season opener. In a Capital-Journal article written by sportswriter Steve Rottinghaus, he notes that Washington got behind Rural by 20 but closed the gap to just a six-point deficit at halftime.

In the second half a very stingy Junior Blue defense limited Washington to a minus 13 total yards and went on to defeat them 34-22.

Two minutes into the game the defense made their presence clear when Aaron Anderson picked off a pass and returned it 43 yards for the touchdown.

After Anderson's pick six, Chrisco hit Noel Roach for a 43-yard TD pass and then hit Dusty Zander for another TD, just two and a half minutes apart. That made the Rural lead 20-0. Washington then hit on their own touchdown pass and, a Washburn Rural fumble was scooped up and they scored to bring Washington within six points.

Anderson opened the scoring with a 41-yard carry for a TD. Then Levi Baucom intercepted a pass and returned it 27 yards for another score. Washington scored late to make the final 34-22 in favor of Rural.

GAME #2

A rainy game against Salina South proved to be a close game marred by mistakes.

In the Capital-Journal article by outdoors writer Jim Ramberg, Bowen said, "We made enough mistakes to lose 14 games tonight."

Washburn Rural's lone score came in the second quarter on a one-yard carry by Aaron Anderson.

At the beginning of the fourth quarter the Junior Blues almost gave the game away. A bad snap on a punt resulted in just an 11-yard kick. This gave Salina the ball on its 34-yard line. South also scored on a one-yard run. Salina was going to settle for a kicked extra point, but the Blues were offsides and that moved the extra point to the 1 ½ yard line and they decided instead to go for a two-point conversion. Rural held on a tough goal line stance and it was 7-6.

Once again facing a punting situation, Midkiff's punt was tipped and South ended up with the ball on the 11-yard line needing just that much to go ahead. They tried a pass and Zander picked it off to preserve the victory. Notice both games were not statistically impressive for Washburn Rural, but they were 2-0.

GAME #3

The third game was a Centennial League game against Shawnee Heights. Rural had beaten Heights nine straight seasons prior and this would make it a decade of wins over their rival. But Rural was a bit dinged up with injury. Both fullback Anderson and tailback Pratt were out with leg injuries.

The first half scoring was only a score by each team in the second quarter. Chrisco scored first on a 12-yard scamper then hit Adam Woodward for the two-point conversion, 8-0 Rural. Shawnee Heights blocked a punt and gave themselves a short two yards needed for a score. It took one carry and Heights was on the board. A two-point conversion was blown dead inadvertently preventing Heights from tying the game. So, a second chance was awarded and they still didn't convert.

In the second half Rural made sure that call was not a critical one towards the outcome when they ran and passed themselves to the one-yard line before Chrisco scored again. Lucas Yarnell made the extra point and Rural had their third straight win 15-6. Once again, the Junior Blue defense held Heights to 33 yards rushing and just 101 passing. They were now 3-0 and the Capital-Journal ranked them number five in the state 5A classification.

GAME #4

The next foe would be rival Hayden. And to make it doubly worse the conditions were windy followed by windier. It was a low-scoring affair and a game where one break could change the outcome.

It was looking like the game could end 0-0 and go to overtime, but with less than six minutes to play the Junior Blues got a break. And it came due to the windy conditions. Hayden's punter could only get a 20- yard punt off from his nine-yard line. Rural took over on the 29.

Chrisco took advantage of having the wind at his back and threw a 19-yard strike to Zander. From the 10-yard line Chrisco ran it in for the game's only score. Lucas Yarnell kicked the extra point and the Junior Blues lead 7-0.

Hayden mounted a drive with time running out and only two timeouts remaining. With 1:03 left they had the ball at the 16-yard line. A botched pitchout was fumbled and recovered by Levi Baucom to preserve the win and move Rural to 4-0.

GAME #5

Washburn Rural was not winning by large margins, posting tremendous offensive numbers, but there had not been but one good night for football and that was the opening game.

And now they had to face Emporia. And Emporia had beaten them the last six seasons, even defeating the two state championship teams of '85 and '86. Coaches had a little mental preparation to do before this Centennial League contest. But this was 1989 and this team had found ways to win last year in district play and this year with two of their best rushers injured and slowed for a couple of games.

And to top it off, possibly make matters worse, it was Washburn Rural's Homecoming. Ron Bowen was more than happy for his players to have great high school experiences when NOT playing football, but he had always been a bit concerned about the team's focus when Homecoming could present a distraction to what the night was all about- football.

Emporia had the only score in the first half when they drove the ball and scored from two yards out and made the extra point kick. 7-0 at halftime. Was this going to be another Emporia win moving the streak to seven years? Was this to be a Homecoming that Coach Bowen would regret?

The game article in the Topeka Capital-Journal written by sportswriter Steve Thompson he mentions the fact that Dusty Zander had very few comments after the game but did mention in the post-game article that Zander had made "several key statements" during the game.

Emporia answered with a 30-yard scoring pass and it was 14-7 Emporia. Zander answered that with a 13-yard inside reverse from the slotback position. Yarnell's kick was good. 14-14.

Then Chrisco scored on a 3-yard run. Zander again scored, his third touchdown of the half on a 54-yard run from scrimmage. Chrisco scored again on a 12-yard run before Emporia scored late in the game. Final score was 34-20 and the Emporia jinx had ended.

Zander had three touchdowns and accounted for 117 yards from scrimmage, run/ pass reception combined and added the 95-yard kickoff return.

In the article both Bowen and Chrisco praised Zander's efforts. "Dusty Zander had one whale of a ballgame," Bowen said.

Chrisco also said of his teammate, "He (Zander) got us back in the game- he kept us in the game." Chrisco also added two TD's and added 135 yards of total offense.

The defense came up big, yet again, when Kirk Midkiff and Ernie Rayton both intercepted second half passes for the Junior Blues. They were now 5-0. In those five games nose guard Greg Harvey led the team with 39 tackles. That's significant when his main job is to occupy gaps and offensive linemen so linebackers can make the tackles.

GAME #6

Two 5-0 Centennial League schools would match-up for the final regular season game and it would likely determine the conference champion. After five games Chrisco led the city in total offense – 234 rushing and 305 passing for a total of 539 yards. Seaman's Shaw had 530 rushing yards to be just nine yards behind him. Seaman's defense was number one in the city allowing an average of 3 points per game. Rural was second allowing just under eleven points per game. Seaman allowed opponents just under 130 total yards per game. Rural was second allowing just 173 yards per game. This looked to be a low-scoring affair. Or at least a game likely won on the defensive side of the ball.

Well, this was partially correct. The offenses of the two schools committed a total of 10 turnovers combined. After 48 minutes of regulation the score was tied and Rural had given up four fumbles and Seaman had thrown five interceptions. So, the game went to overtime at 21-21.

Washburn Rural struck twice in the first quarter when Chrisco threw a short touchdown pass to Adam Woodward and then Chrisco scored on a 36-yard run. Yarnell converted both extra-point kicks for a 14-0 score. The scores were set-up by two interceptions by Aaron Anderson and Ernie Rayton.

In the second quarter Seaman scored on a short run and Rural turned it around with a 74-yard Noel Roach kickoff return and the score was 21-7 at halftime.

In the third and fourth quarter Seaman knotted the game with a touchdown pass and scooped a fumble for a 46-yard fumble recovery for a touchdown. Rural couldn't score in the second half so the game went to overtime.

In the overtime Seaman made a very big mental error. In desperation, to avoid a sack Seaman quarterback threw a pass to his lineman. The lineman caught the pass, but knew he was not an eligible receiver. Without knowing the rule he dropped the ball after the catch, constituting a fumble. Rural alertly recovered the fumble.

In high school football each team gets a possession and whoever has the most points after the shared possessions wins. George Pratt put his head down and bulled his way for a seven-yard touchdown in overtime to end the game 27-21.

If you're going to have a great season, you have to win some close ones. And have some good fortune and luck doesn't hurt either. This was the Junior Blues third game won by only one score.

GAME #7- DISTRICT PLAY

Washburn Rural's pre-determined geographical district to determine who goes to the playoffs was league foe Highland Park, Bonner Springs and Ottawa. One of the criticisms of the KSHSAA district playoff system was, depending on the year, depending on your location in the state, you could experience a district that was loaded with good teams. For instance, the best district, record wise in 5A that year was in southeast Kansas, district number 3. Labette County, Pittsburg and Fort Scott were 5-1 football teams and Parsons was 3-3.

Folks would make the argument that there were multiple teams that should qualify for the playoffs. Eventually the KSHSAA went to four team districts and two schools qualified. Remember, the KSHSAA is a membership organization. This means that the member schools could present and vote on new solutions. If the goal in 1989 was to get the best representative from four schools in close, geographical proximity, this was a good system. After all, you have to be able to beat ALL schools to take the championship.

Washburn Rural held fast to that goal of beating all teams.

Centennial League foe, Highland Park, was the first district win. Rural ended up defeating them 26-2. Their dominant defense continued its stingy ways.

To open the game Washburn Rural capped a 10-play drive that saw Chrisco and Pratt account for all the 54 yards and Pratt scored from 17-yards running it straight up the middle.

Three plays after this first score the Junior Blues got the ball back thanks to a Levi Baucom interception at the 20-yard line. Greg Harvey scored on a short touchdown run of 7 yards.

The Junior Blues capped a 19-point first quarter with a 41-yard pass play, Chrisco to Dusty Zander.

They ended their scoring in the first half with a 34-yard screen pass, Chrisco to Pratt. Highland Park got a safety when Rural punter Kirk Midkiff stepped on the end line of the end zone. Final score was 26-2 and once again Rural outgained their opponent with 201 total yards, holding Park to just 52. Rural emptied the bench as ten people carried the ball for the Junior Blues. It was two games away from another playoff berth.

GAME #8- SECOND DISTRICT GAME

In the second district game they defeated Bonner Springs 34-6. Bonner struck first with a long 74-yard touchdown pass to take a 6-0 lead. That seemed to wake up the Junior Blues as they put three scores on the board in the second quarter. There was only one more pass completion that half by Bonner and two pickoffs, one by Chrisco and one by Zander, set up Rural scores. And Greg Harvey recovered a fumble and Rural also capitalized on that turnover.

Chrisco scored on a short run, as did Aaron Anderson twice to go up 21-6 at halftime.

In the second half George Pratt scored on a 20-yard touchdown run and Chrisco got his second touchdown on a short run to the end zone. Washburn Rural rushed for 248 yards and only threw for 15. Why put the ball in the air unnecessarily? Two things that can happen are bad when you pass- incompletion or interception. Pratt was the beneficiary of this philosophy with 127 rushing yards. Washburn Rural 34 Bonner Springs 6.

GAME #9- THIRD DISTRICT GAME

Washburn Rural's undefeated record was getting them noticed. After this game they were ranked third behind also undefeated Coffeyville and Valley Center. I'm certain Bowen might have enjoyed playing his former Valley Center team for the state championship. But there were two more games to win to qualify for the playoffs. Records didn't matter. And Bowen didn't care who his teams had to play.

Well, maybe they mattered a little. Washburn Rural dismantled Ottawa in a home game in which the muddy conditions and weather delayed the start of the game by an hour. All that did was delay the drubbing Rural gave Ottawa, a 43-0 shutout victory. It was the 100th win of Ron Bowen's storied career at Washburn Rural. It was his 16th year. At this pace he was averaging almost 7 wins per season. Remarkable when you are only guaranteed nine games per year. Of course, two state championships gave the Junior Blues 12 games and, when you win 10, your percentage improves a bunch. Ironically, this would be his ninth victory for 1989.

And it was the fifth straight year Washburn Rural reached the playoffs in 5A classification.

PLAYOFF GAME #1- BISHOP MIEGE

As fate would have it Rural once again opened the playoff with Bishop Miege. The same team that eliminated them and ended their 1977 and their 1988 season. This time around Miege had to come to Washburn Rural McElroy Field to play the undefeated Junior Blues.

In a Topeka Capital-Journal article by sportswriter, Keven Haskin, he posed the question many may have related to the ease with which Washburn Rural made it through district play – a combined three game lopsided score in their favor, 103-8.

Haskin asked Ron Bowen if the lack of a "stern" district test would be a factor? "I think we had some tests back up the line that proved the kids could hold their own in close games," he said. They were tested by Centennial League foes, Hayden, had a comeback win against Emporia and had to beat Seaman in overtime. Those were the three consecutive games prior to district.

And four out of the last five playoff years Rural has opened playing Miege. Rural won three of those games and Miege won the last one in 1988. That still fresh in their mind should motivate this team. Miege had a powerful wishbone offense that averaged 230 yards per game on the ground. Rural's stingy defense consequently allowed only 75 rushing yards per game. This year Miege had a 6-3 record with two of their losses at the hands of bigger schools Olathe North and Blue Valley North. Rural also had forced 32 turnovers, 17 interceptions and 15 fumbles for the 1989 year. Chrisco led the Topeka schools in total offense with nearly 1,000 yards. Pratt, despite his early leg injury, ended the year with nearly 500 yards rushing.

Haskin covered the Friday game at McElroy Stadium as Washburn Rural hosted Miege. One aspect he mentioned in the article was every time Miege made a lengthy drive on offense, defensive coordinator Ray Glaze took a time out and went out and addressed the defense. If you ever had the pleasure of watching one of these trips, there was no yelling. Glaze got his point across in a quiet, stern way that involved lots of finger pointing and much head bobbing. You could see the intensity in his face and his defense paid attention.

The defense held Miege to 136 yards rushing and 143 total yards in a 37-16 playoff victory. The 10-0 start to 1989 was THE best in school history. And it topped the 9-0 season Bowen enjoyed at Valley Center.

Rural jumped out to an early 13-0 lead in the first quarter on a Chrisco to Noel Roach five-yard pass play for a touchdown followed by a Dusty Zander 8 yard run for another score. Miege added a short 4-yard touchdown run in the second quarter to pull within six.

Then to start the half MIege added a 25-yard field goal to draw within three.

After Zander scored on a 35-yard counter play making it 19-10, the defense did what Glaze had asked them to do all game. Chrisco recovered an errant Miege pitch on the 31-yard line. Just moments later it appeared that Chrisco had scored, but a holding call pushed the ball back to the 11-yard line. Chrisco hit Roach for his second touchdown reception in the right corner of the end zone and WR was up 25-10.

"We practiced it all week," Roach told Haskin. "It was a play action deal and if the line does their blocking and Chrisco does his job, we score. He (Chrisco) put the pass right there."

Miege wasn't through. They capitalized by blocking a Kirk Midkiff punt and another Miege defender scooped the ball and returned it 30-yards for a TD with 5:31 left. It made the score 25-16.

Two plays later Chrisco showed his explosiveness and speed when he carried a bootleg 79-yards pushing the lead to 31-16. And then with just two minutes remaining Aaron Anderson ran the ball 14-yards for the final score and it was a 37-16 final. Rural had stopped the powerful Miege run game and put up 301 rushing yards of their own. With 54-yards of passing their total offense discrepancy was Rural 355 to Miege's 142-yard total.

In the last five games of the 10-0 season Washburn Rural averaged 33.4 points per game.

GAME #11

Waiting for the third ranked Junior Blues in the semi-final was, once again, Pittsburg, who Rural had played in the same semi-final game in 1985, 1986, and 1987. This would be the fourth meeting and Washburn Rural had to make the road trip.

Remember this was the same road trip in 1987 when there was concern about having local officials referee the game. This one would be different. The KSHSAA made a sound decision by assigning a Kansas City officiating crew so there would be no concern by either school.

Prior to Friday's big game, Topeka Capital-Journal sportswriter did an article focusing on Rural's hard hitting defense. Ray Glaze who coordinated the defense enjoyed telling this story the most.

Marc Chrisco was a hard-hitting safety on defense but lead the city in total offense. Early in the season, when Rural already had two injured offensive backs, they took Chrisco out of the game. Because he was hitting so hard they were concerned he too might suffer an injury. He begged to go back in the game, so Glaze told him he could, but asked him not to hit so hard and be careful. Not something you normally tell a safety. His first play back on the field he almost ripped a kid's head off and Glaze pulled him and let him stand by him the rest of the game.

"This is the hardest hitting group we've ever had," Glaze said. "They have really played well as a unit."

This was quite a compliment since Glaze had been coaching all of the previous 16 years on the Bowen-lead Washburn Rural staff. And considering the Junior Blues already had two 5A state championships to their credit with pretty good defenses themselves.

Pittsburg and Washburn Rural, once again, looked like an even matchup with similar qualities. Pitt's coach, Larry Garman, singled out the Junior Blue defensive strength saying, "Their strength again is on defense. They chase the ball extremely well."

Almost all the scoring came in the first half. Almost.

The Junior Blues scored on their first possession when fullback Aaron Anderson took a dive play up the middle, ran over two tacklers at the 20-yard line and kept driving for a 29-yard touchdown run. Pittsburg answered with a 64-yard pass play, quarterback Brian Hutchins to tight end Rob Caruso a, 6'5" receiver.

With Pittsburg keying on Chrisco and Pratt, once again Bowen called a dive play to the fullback. 58-yards later Anderson was in the end zone for his second touchdown. Pittsburg answered with a 10-yard quarterback keeper by Hutchins to make the score 13-12 Rural. Four scores in the first quarter.

In the second quarter Hutchins once again found the end zone and the score was 20-13 Pittsburg. But Anderson answered once again with an eight-yard touchdown carry for his third touchdown of the night. A two-point conversion play with Chrisco hitting Zander knotted the wild first half 20-20. This looked like the team that had the ball last might win. An offensive game from kickoff to final buzzer. Not quite.

To their credit both defenses made halftime adjustments. Rural found a way to slow down Hutchens runs and blanketed their receivers. Hutchins did end the game with a respectable 91-yards rushing. And Pittsburg slowed down all the Rural backs, even Anderson who had almost 100 yards in the first half and had three touchdowns. They slowed him down until the last drive.

Rural had the ball on the 1-yard line and had 99 yards to go for a winning score. And on the very first play of what would become known as "the drive" Pittsburg nearly tackled Anderson in the end zone. Perhaps his best carry that night was gaining one yard- enough to avoid a safety. Then Washburn Rural did drive the ball the remaining 99 yards, mixing runs with Anderson, Chrisco and Pratt and a big 16-yard pass to Adam Woodward. That set-up Anderson's fourth touchdown on a final nine-yard run. The long drive also chewed up much of the fourth quarter, almost five minutes, so Pittsburg had to attempt to tie it in the last seven minutes. Rural held and held on for a 28-20 win.

In the game article by Topeka Capital-Journal sportswriter Kevin Haskin, Anderson talked about his 11 carries for 137 yards and all four Rural touchdowns. Well, he talked about it by giving credit to his offensive linemen because that's what smart running backs do. He gave credit for his game to Ryan Roberts, center, to guards John Metzger and Jason Penrod and finally to tackles Lucas Yarnell and Lonnie Russell and tight end Adam Woodward. Once those holes were opened Anderson simply ran through, around and sometimes over Pittsburg secondary players on his way to his biggest night of the season which propelled Washburn Rural into the state championship game for the third time in five years. In the week following Bowen also credited Don Gifford, the offensive line coach.

"Usually, our fullback isn't the big man in our offense, but we kind of liked it tonight," Bowen said. 'He (Anderson) was our second fastest sprinter on the track team last spring. We know he can run- it just takes awhile to get the wheels turning. When he did, he kind of outmanned their defensive backs a couple of times." I'm quite certain there was a big grin on Coach Ron Bowen's face when he made that comment and that assessment.

GAME #12

The only thing standing in the way of Washburn Rural's unblemished, undefeated season and third state championship in the decade was Salina Central. Central was making the first appearance by either Salina school (Salina South) and was coached by Marvin Diener. Diener's rise as a head coach at Central kind of mirrored Bowen's start at Rural 16 years prior. Diener took over the helm at Central and inherited a team who the year prior to his arrival had a losing record. In Deniers first year at Salina Central in 1987, he was 2-7. Same as Bowen's first year at Rural. Bowen had a 5-4 record his year two, Diener a 4-5. So, in his third season, 1989, Diener had his Salina team playing for a championship bringing a 10-1 record into the game. Remember, Bowen's third year, 1977, he had Rural in the semifinals.

In his preview of the 5A state championship game, Topeka Capital-Journal sportswriter Kevin Haskin had a bit of foreshadowing at the end of his article when he said that no matter what color fans wore to this championship- blue or maroon, "fans won't be disappointed in the level of play." He went on to say that the game was too close to predict.

Haskin also wrote a well-deserved article about the offensive line at Rural. Don Gifford replaced me when the decision was made for me to devote full-time duties to athletic director responsibilities. Don was a 1974 graduate of Washburn Rural and an offensive lineman himself.

His linemen were a strong unit lead by the only returning starter from 1988 was tight end Adam Woodward. The line averaged 215 pounds per man which was solid for the time-period.

Anchoring the line, and boosting the largest girth, was center Ryan Roberts at 267 pounds. Despite being their biggest lineman, he was quite possibly the most agile, an adapt tennis player for Rural in the spring. The year prior he had played number one doubles for Rural's tennis team.

At the tackles Rural had a true sophomore, Lucas Yarnell, who himself pushed 270 pounds. At the other tackle was a player who was a senior but was experiencing only his second year of football so was similar, experience wise, to a sophomore, Lonnie Russell.

Russell had to miss the first two games of the season after transferring from Highland Park late. Russell's situation was one of my contributions to this 1989 team. The KSHSAA had a provision and article in their handbook that was the "transfer" rule. Although Russell had not transferred early enough to play in the fall for us, after interviewing him at length, I made the determination that his history and background might warrant a "hardship eligibility" possibility. I notified both his former school and the KSHSAA that we intended to file a hardship for Russell. You have to prepare for these like an attorney. I felt I had a good case and was willing to go to bat for Russell. He was a good kid who had been through a lot, home-wise. He deserved a chance to play football in my opinion. And in Coach Ron Bowen's opinion as well. Fortunately, the KSHSAA felt the same way and their decision allowed Russell to be eligible for week number three of the season. I'm sure this had a bit to do with our football success that fall, but, more importantly, allowed Lonnie Russell to have a very positive experience in his life.

The guards were a couple of characters. John Metzger a 6'0" 176-pound kid and Jason Penrod, a strong, aggressive lineman. In the article Gifford described Metzger. "He's kind of our group outlaw. He's the smallest (lineman) and definitely the wildest and most aggressive."

Gifford said about Penrod, "At least one thing he does a game is usually in the highlight film."

One concern the Rural staff had about the offensive line was lack of depth. Early in the season they lost starting lineman Kevin Burenheide with a vertebrae injury. Gifford said they missed him a bunch.

And Ryan Roberts pointed to the comeback win at Emporia where he felt the linemen stepped up. He also mentioned the games Rural played early without Anderson and Pratt in the backfield. But what he was most proud of was the 99-yard drive, all but 16-yards on the ground, that won the Pittsburg game. The drive was so impressive that the lead official tipped his hat and, after the game, told Rural that he'd seen lots of good high school football team's drives, but he said that was the best one he ever saw. Bill Fenton was a revered Kansas official and, coming from him, that was quite a compliment.

So, Saturday, November 18 will go down as a day all Junior Blue fans will remember. Unless you were a defensive minded individual, a coach or a player- or parent of a player- this game was a grinder and not the wide-open game some expected. The Topeka-Capital Journal headline in the next day's newspaper was "Defense helps Rural nab title." Washburn Rural only mustered 10 points in the championship. But they held Salina Central to just 8 points to capture the 5A championship and complete a 12-0 season.

Two of the most significant things to happen, offensively, for Washburn Rural was a 27-yard field goal by fullback Aaron Anderson and a hit Marc Chrisco took in the first quarter that likely gave him a concussion were story lines. That and the Junior Blue defense that kept Salina Central out of the end zone for three quarters preserving a 3-0 lead most of the game.

The field goal was set up by a fumble deep in Rural territory. Adam Woodward got to the mesh of the handoff in the Central backfield and jarred the ball free. Chrisco recovered it. That made the field goal possible.

Struggling to find any other weapons on offense, Rural relied on George Pratt, who ended the day with 28 carries and 118 yards as Rural stuck to the ground game for 59 carries and only six pass attempts. But it was the pass attempt that caught Salina off-guard that was the key to the game. A play action fake allowed tight end Adam Woodward to get a step on the defender and it was enough for Chrisco to lay a perfectly thrown ball to Woodward, whose momentum caused him to step out of bounds at the five-yard line. Three plays later Rural had the ball at the one-yard line and it was time for Anderson to power his way in behind that offensive line. And he did, giving the Junior Blues a 10-0 lead.

But when Salina Central mounted a seven play 69-yard scoring drive early in the fourth quarter it was still a game, 10-8. And Chrisco was playing on sheer guts with his concussion.

Salina Central had three more opportunities and possessions.

The first possession was snuffed out at the 16-yard line when defensive end, Chris Palmer, snuffed out a screen pass and tackled the Central player for a nine-yard loss. Deep in their own territory Central had to punt.

On its second chance Kirk Midkiff pinned Central at their 8-yard line with an outstanding punt. Two plays later the Junior Blue defense pressured the Central quarterback into throwing an interception by Dusty Zander at the 19-yard line.

Rural, who by this time, was playing without Chrisco, who, late in the game, was knocked unconscious, had backup Ernie Rayton run four keepers and his primary objective was to hang onto the football.

When Central got the ball back they were 80 yards away on the 20 and could manage only six pass plays and advanced the ball no further than the 36-yard line. Game over.

In an article in the Lawrence Journal-World, sportswriter Andrew Hartsock, interviewed Salina Central's coach, Diener and Rural's Bowen.

"It was absolutely a championship game," Diener said, "and there were two championship teams on the field. The bottom line is that it was a championship game. Both defenses were great."

Bowen agreed. "They're a fine ball club," Bowen said. "They're a hard-hitting ball club and they've got an explosive offense. We felt we moved the ball, but you've got to give them credit. The thing of it was, they didn't gain much, but they could have."

The plain and simple fact is that, when your team has a lot of success, the post-season recognition is significant. The exceptionally successful year of 1989 was no exception. The Centennial League recognized 16 players as first team on offense and 16 on defense. Rural was selected and claimed almost a third of those positions. Marc Chrisco was selected as first-team quarterback and first-team defensive back. Dusty Zander was selected as a running back and kickoff returner.

Other first teamers were Ryan Roberts as center, Noel Roach at split end, Greg Harvey as a defensive lineman, Adam Woodward as defensive end and Aaron Anderson as a linebacker. Ron Bowen was named "coach of the year" for the Centennial League.

Second teamers were Adam Woodward, tight end, Aaron Anderson, running back, Chris Palmer, defensive end, Dusty Zander, defensive back.

Chrisco, Zander and Woodward were all selected to the Topeka Capital-

Journal's All-City team. And, in an unprecedented move, Rural assistant coach Ray Glaze was selected "Coach of the Year." The vaunted Rural defense was dominant all year and Glaze was the defensive coordinator. Glaze was the first and ONLY assistant ever to be honored as such.

Anderson, Harvey, Palmer and Roberts were all tabbed second-team all-city. Honorable mention picks were John Metzger, Kirk Midkiff, Jason Penrod, George Pratt, Lonnie Russell and Lucas Yarnell.

Dusty Zander, Marc Chrisco and Adam Woodward were selected to the All-Class 5A mythical team.

In addition to Marc Chrisco being selected All-State, all class second team, Ron Bowen was selected as the State's Coach of the Year.

Washburn Rural football most definitely put Topeka and its school on the map for successful programs. Washburn Rural was in the playoffs 5 of the 10 years and won three state championships. And now, capped an undefeated season, one for the ages.

Bowen brothers

Bowen brothers on the porch of their homestead

Bowen on a horse as a 4th grader in California

Bowen as a kid with a football in his jeans

Bowen as a senior in football jersey (dark) #15

Hiawatha High School team photo from 1950's

Bowen as a junior in football jersey (white) #15

Bowen's family. Back Row: Father Phillip and Mother Edna
and Front Row seated Hillis and son Terry, Ron, Delayne

Bowen's senior picture which was a graduation invite

Bowen with two calves under his arms

Wedding day for Ron and Mary Lou Bowen

Bowen's wedding with cake

Young Bowen family (pre-Heather) with just 3 kids
Valley Center football team photo from 1970

Valley Center George Pearson photo with Pepto-Bismo trophy

Valley Center football reunion and Bowen's VC Hall of Fame induction event

1975 two quarterbacks #13 HIcks and #11 Schuster

1975 Coach Bowen with lineman Willie Long #79

JOE ALLARD
Hayden

DWIGHT STREETER
Seaman

RON NACE
Topeka West

DOUG BOLDT
Hayden

JOHN PRICE
Highland Park

KENT McNORTON
Seaman

MIKE LOOK
Topeka High

CHAD CHERRY
Topeka West

STEVE SCHUSTER
Washburn Rural

LEO RUCKER
Highland Park

ROBIN GOLDEN
Washburn Rural

Topeka State Journal
All-City Football Team
1975 Offense

1975 Topeka All-City football team
(Opposite Page) Newspaper statistics for 1975

Total Offense

Player, School	Rsh.	Pass	Ttl.
Schuster, Washburn Rural	141	335	476
Mueller, Topeka West	235	205	440
Spencer, Topeka West	424	0	424
Stanley, Seaman	358	0	358
Rucker, Highland Park	320	0	320
Toelkes, Shawnee Heights	180	121	301
Williams, Topeka High	295	0	295
Patton, Seaman	17	246	263
Ziegler, Hayden	255	0	255
Boldt, Hayden	226	0	226

Rushing

Player, School	Att.	Yds.	Avg.
Spencer, Topeka West	84	424	5.0
Stanley, Seaman	40	358	9.0
Rucker, Highland Park	75	320	4.3
Williams, Topeka High	62	295	4.8
Ziegler, Hayden	47	255	5.4
Mueller, Topeka West	55	235	4.3
Boldt, Hayden	45	226	5.0
Russell, Shawnee Heights	49	218	4.4
McNorton, Seaman	45	211	4.7
Toelkes, Shawnee Heights	39	180	4.6

Passing

Player, School	Cp.	Att.	Int.	Yds.
Schuster, Washburn Rural	18	33	2	335
Patton, Seaman	11	29	1	246
Mueller, Topeka West	9	26	1	205
Frye, Highland Park	10	27	0	130
Toelkes, Shawnee Heights	7	16	2	121

Receiving

Player, School	Cht.	Yds.
Lolley, Shawnee Heights	9	182
Golden, Washburn Rural	4	152
Warner, Topeka West	5	144
Little, Washburn Rural	3	122
Tenpenny, Seaman	4	92
Slocum, Seaman	3	92

Punting

Player, School	Pnt.	Avg.
Turpin, Seaman	12	38.4
Martin, Topeka High	5	38.2
Reser, Shawnee Heights	2	36.5
Johnson, Topeka High	10	35.0
Neill, Topeka High	4	32.8

Scoring

Player, School	TD	Pat	FG	Ttl.
McNorton, Seaman	5	0	0	30
Spencer, Topeka West	4	2	0	28
Warner, Topeka West	4	0	0	24
Stanley, Seaman	4	0	0	24
Williams, Topeka High	3	0	0	18
Peterson, Topeka West	2	6	0	18
Boldt, Hayden	3	0	0	18
Toelkes, Shawnee Heights	2	1	0	14

Team Offense

School	Rsh.	Pass	Ttl.	Pts.
Seaman	835	246	1081	89
Topeka West	853	205	1058	70
Washburn Rural	490	402	892	50
Shawnee Heights	529	256	785	47
Highland Park	608	130	738	64
Topeka High	660	70	730	40
Hayden	623	80	70	

Coach Mike Engelbrake with hat and black mustache with a lineman

Football player Schuster on crutches staring at the football field

1978 Coaching staff Left to Right is Ray Glaze, Jerry Kramer, Steve McDermeit, Bowen, Mike Englebrake, Mike Naster

Bowen with a white wig on

Coaches office with Austin, Bowen and Glaze

QB Jared Peterson handing the ball to Fredrick Williams

Quarterback Jared Peterson was equally capable running or throwing. This was against Emporia, one of two losses during the 1985 state championship season as the Junior Blues ended 10-2.

Coach Bowen watching Peterson pitch the ball in practice

The Junior Blues coaching staff in 1985. My first year as a varsity coach, 10-2 and 5A state champions. Great coaches, but even finer men. Seated L to R - Sam Austin, Ray Glaze, Chris Ridley. Standing L to R - Ron Bowen, Jerry Beardslee, Dick Evans and Rick Moore.

(NOT IN ORDER) Jared Peterson, Kraig Burough, J. Richard Woodall Jr., Dustin Palmer, Jeff Hughes, Glenn Scamman, Jeff Hamilton, Chris Romine, Shane Cummins, Joe Clifford, Tony Burks, Tim Fritts, Antoine Dulan, Derrick Watts, Todd Scott, Michael Montgomery, Michael Perkins, Dean Harding, Sean Conly, Phil Wilson, Scott Stroth, Shannon Williams, Fredrick Williams, Kirk Cerny, Jeff Cowan, Richard Yohr, Troy Moise, Michael Gomez, Michael Zweiner, Craig Moore, Tony Winslow, Russ Meens, James Walker, Matt Marple, Chris Fink, Darren Caster, Tim Huston, Patrick Stoffel, Gary Douglass, Chris Cushing, Todd Rosetta, Matt Dorrey, Gary Lee, Brad Holmsten, John McGivern, Jeff Bottenberg, Doug Campbell, Randall Starkey, Sam Metzger, Todd Fritz, Steve Reynolds, Brad Elder, Mike Herzog, Scott Berg, Robert Schawo, Ted Frieden, Tod Anderson, David Seidel, John Boley, Tim Dindois, Tom Bruno, Mike Springer, Ed Prekopy, Scott Lee, Rick Wendland, Chris Walker, Trey McPherson, Dustin Carlat, Mark Selbee, Mike Evans, Russ Fieger, Clint Thezan, David Trupp, Troy Lightle.

Topeka's first ever state championship football team, the 1985 Junior Blues. Photo courtesy of *Topeka Capital-Journal*.

Antoine Dulan #22 getting tackled on icy turf

Never Seen a Finer Day

Derrick Watts #24 carrying the ball and dragging tacklers

Bowen giving a pregame talk in the locker room – "Never seen a finer day"

Todd Scott #25 and Chris Walker #21 celebrate the kickoff return for touchdown

Defensive lineman with their heads on the turf "listening for the train"

Blocked punt for a touchdown

Conly #61 and Stoffel #57 celebrate on the sideline

Dulan #22

1986 state champs

1986 All-City

Todd Scott carrying the ball #25

The "cockroach" everyone falls to their back and all legs and arms like cockroaches

Charlie Finley experimental balls

miner—Jerome Schnall
uminer—T. Brown
ent, or Firm—John H. Widdowson

5 Claims, 13 Drawing Figures

one of the
D.

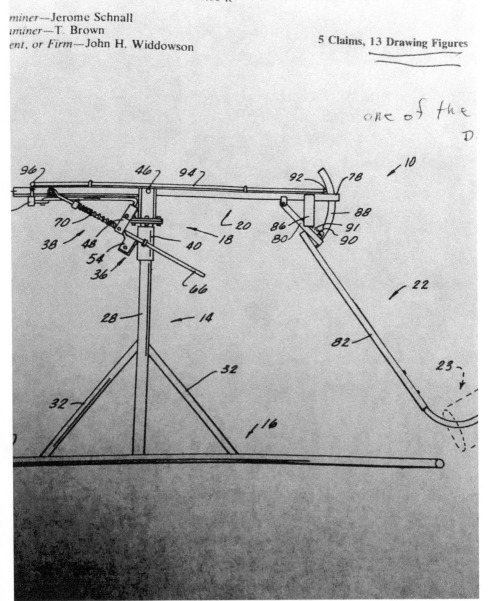

Schematic drawing of Bowen's tackling and blocking invention (patent)

Bowen and Chrisco at football practice

Bowen's 100th Washburn Rural victory

Aaron Anderson #32 runs through the Pittsburg defense

Adam Woodward #86 makes big catches

George Pratt #34 carrying the football against Salina Central

A concussed Marc Chrisco #8 celebrates state championship win

1989 team celebrates undefeated season and third state championship

1992 All-City team

Bowen bundled up on sideline at KU vs. Lawrence

Bowen consoles a dejected QB Mark Longhofer #7 after loss in championship

Coach Bowen holding up the state championship trophy

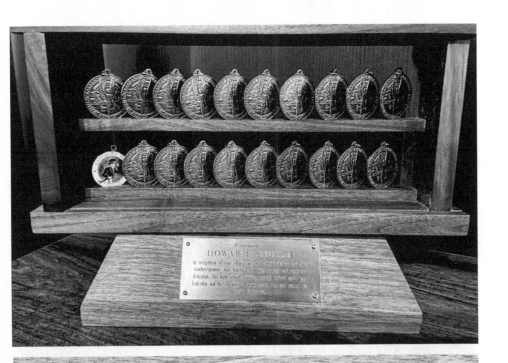

Shuler medal case Bowen made

Inscription Coach Bowen put on the medal award case he built for Mr. Howard Shuler. Says "In recognition of your efforts on behalf of the students and their coaches/sponsors who benefitted from your support and continued dedication. The high schooll activities program thrived under your leadership and the character of the young men and women was greatly influenced." Coach Bowen appreciated effective leadership.

Coach Bowen poses for a photo with 2019 Washburn Rural graduate, Jordan White, who also was recognized at the annual Shawnee County Sports Council's recognition night. Not only players who played for Coach Bowen revere him. Current football players also recognize his sincerity and his accomplishments.

"Washburn Rural alumni at The Shawnee County Hall of Fame ceremony. From L to R- FRONT ROW: Derrick Watts ('86), Head Coach Ron Bowen, Chris Walker ('88) BACKROW: Tim Bisel ("86) former Topeka Capital-Journal Sports Editor, former players, Todd Scott ('88), Mike Longhofer ('88), 18-year football assistant, Sam Austin, Rick Wendland ('86), Jeff Cowan ('87).

In 2013 Washburn Rural alum, Colonel Chris Toner, was inducted into the school's Hall of Fame. Toner, seen here, flanked by Coach Bowen and Glaze gives those two men lotsof credit for helping nuture his leadership skills which he utilized in his over 30 year career in the Army. After he retired, Toner stepped into a leadership role for Wounded Warriors.

The Ron Bowen family. Front Row M'Lissa, Andi, and Heather. Middle Ron and Mary Lou and Back Damon Bowen

Bowen family- Andi- at Mary Lou's Hall of Fame induction

If you can not tell, the Bowen family enjoys life a great deal

ML, Ron and Rocky (dog)

Bowen and Heather dancing

Ray Glaze and Ron Bowen

Bowen in his comfortable place, under the lights leading his players

Farmer/ Coach Bowen in field of sunflowers on the farm

Young Coach Bowen and Ridley on the sideline celebrating 1985

Bowen with Shawnee County Hall of Fame plaque

Ron Bowen's first car was a 1947 Ford Coupe. With the help of his former player, Ed Bozarth, Ron at his first show with his 1948 Couple- same body style.

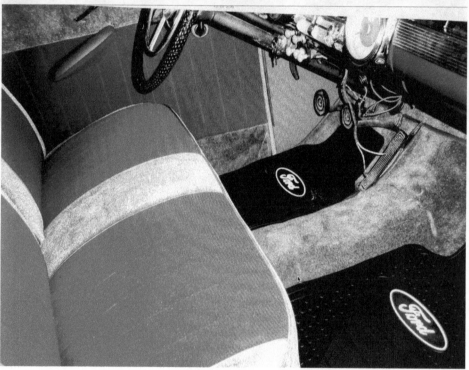

The '48 Ford Coupe restored and returned to the Bowen farmstead.
1948 Ford Coupe refurbished interior with the help of Ed Bozarth, local Topeka car dealer.

Bowen family with kids, grandkids and great grandkids

A PLAYER
PERSPECTIVE,
GEORGE PRATT III,
1988-1991

"Coach is a great role-model, and he was my role-model. As a student at Washburn Rural High School (WRHS) in Topeka, Kansas he was my coach and my educator.

While at WRHS, I thrived to follow his examples and he showed me many examples. However, the ones that have had the most impact on me were Discipline, Focus, Honesty, Humility, Humorous and Strategic.

As my PE teacher, you got to see his lighter side. I remember him laughing and talking 'smack' with buddy and fellow coach Ray Glaze (RIP), during those competitive badminton tournaments.

As one of his former players, I remember he did not over-complicate the game plan. He listened to his assistant coaches, made adjustments as needed and, with the talent that he had, won games because of this. He did this not just for himself or for his coaches and players, but it was for the school and the community. Those were some real Friday Night Lights. During those playoff runs, you couldn't get him to crack a smile on the sidelines, he was that laser focused. As a player, you knew when you screwed up because he would just give you that look, almost Tom Osborne-like (the famed coach of the University of Nebraska). However, his counterpart, Ray Glaze, would let you know when you screwed up because after one of those manly discussions with you, you knew. You either got it right or you would be sitting next to them the next set of downs.

I knew what my mistakes were because we practiced those plays over and over again days before the games. That year our WRHS team went undefeated (1989) and we won the state championship, we were no longer teammates but were brothers. It's one of the highlights that I've experienced and will never forget.

Thanks coach, for not over-complicating the game plans and for giving me those examples. I thrive to lead by those examples even today, as a leader, father and a husband. Thanks Coach, for Paying it Forward." – George Pratt III, WRHS class of 1991

Possible photo #51 Bowen and Chrisco practice, #52 Bowen and Mary Lou celebrating win #100 at WR, #53 O linemen and Line Coach Don Gifford, #54 Aaron Anderson #32 runs through Pittsburg, #55 George Pratt carrying ball in the state championship game, #56 Adam Woodward #86 catches big catch in state championship, #57 Chrisco celebrating through concussion,

Ron Bowen interview with 580 radio talk show before going into the Shawnee County Hall of Fame

On the 1985 state championship with Wichita Kapaun- "I was told by some coaches I called that even some small colleges wouldn't have a chance against Kapaun."

In 1985 and 1986 the key to the two championships were different games. "We were behind Kapaun by 14 points in the first quarter and were playing on a frozen field. My assistant coaches decided we needed to widen our offensive line splits because of the frozen field and the size of the Kapaun team and we blocked angles and came back and beat them on an interception late in the game."

Did you coach the 1986 team differently? "Not necessarily? We coached the same way both years. We ran a slot I offense normally. Blocking and tackling was our key. We had a tough bunch of kids and they played very hard. In 1986 we played Ark City and coach Ray Glaze picked up a real key. Their fullback put his right hand down when the play was going left. When he was going right, he put his left hand down and it was a key for our defense and it was kind of a blow-out game."

What has changed about today's football game? "When we were coaching, you couldn't use your hands to block. Now a days it's all hands blocking. If you did, they would call you for holding. I'm not sure I like the spread, pass first offenses. I'm from the old school. I was always accused of running the football all the time, but I had a couple years when we had 1,000-yard passing."

Was there a favorite game of yours? "In 1989 we were 12-0 for the season and we played Salina Central in the championship. We always had a knock down drag-out battle with Salina Central. Late in the championship game we lost our quarterback to concussion and we had to call plays with a substitute and we managed to hold off Salina Central and won 10-8."

Author's note- That backup quarterback was a starter in our defensive secondary, Ernie Rayton. He was told that all that was needed was for him to take four successful snaps, run over the guard and do not fumble. As were all the Junior Blues players, he was ready and willing to play that role IF it meant the team wins. We had a lot of Ernie Rayton type kids who made the most of their opportunities. He fumbles we may have had a different outcome for 1989.

THE BOWEN ERA
ENTERS THE '90'S

B y this time Ron Bowen was about to begin coaching in his fourth decade. He still was relevant, still had the ability to relate well to kids and had a load of coaching and game experience to rely on. After all, he had just finished an unblemished, undefeated 1989 5A state champion season. Life was very good. But, like always, an awful lot of senior leadership had just graduated. That's part of what makes high school football so great. You must play the hand that's dealt you; kids come in as sophomores, you develop them and in three years they move on. It's a continual cycle, this job of coaching. We love the challenges especially the Coach Bowen types that love the game so much.

In the August 31, 1990 edition of the Capital-Journal sportswriter Kevin Haskin predicted that Washburn Rural would go 8-1. He was correct. And they won a playoff game making it to the semifinal round before dropping their second game to Pittsburg.

Washburn Rural would have gone through the regular season unblemished if it were not for a two- overtime loss to rival Hayden 18-12. The '90 edition of the football program zipped through district play with lopsided wins over Highland Park, 43-6, Bonner Springs 41-6, and Ottawa 33-7. They also handed KC Sumner a 34-14 loss in their first playoff game.

During the regular season their closest game, other than the overtime loss to Hayden, was an 8-6 victory over Salina South in week number two. Emporia held the Junior Blues to 12 points, but Rural beat the Spartans 12-0.

In the opening win against KC Washington six different Junior Blues scored touchdowns. Noel Roach caught a 15-yard pass from Dallas Barth. Then Barth threw a 15-yard pass to Mike Robinson. Running back Aaron Anderson scored on a 19-yard rushing touchdown. Backup quarterback Mark Longhofer scored on a nine-yard run. Jeff Ruediger scored on a 14-yard run. Stanley Quarles rounded out the scoring with a two-yard run. Rural compiled 252 yards rushing and added 68 passing for 310 total yards of offense.

In the second week win 8-6 over Salina South, Rural's defense held South to -1 yard of total offense in the first half and just 121 yards for the game. Rural managed to score on a 26-yard Dallas Barth pass to Noel Roach and Stanley Quarles added the two-point conversion for the narrow victory.

In a 45-0 victory over Shawnee Heights seven different Junior Blues scored – Greg Harvey, George Pratt, Aaron Anderson, Maurice Givens, Allen Evans, Stanley Quarles and Jeff Ruediger.

Then came the overtime loss to Hayden. Then the Junior Blues reeled off six straight wins before Pittsburg ended their season.

Washburn Rural once again demonstrated the vaunted defense that they had been known for and was becoming a tradition. In the October 5, 1990 Capital-Journal article by sportswriter Kevin Haskin he featured the Junior Blue defensive unit's play.

This particular year the size, both height and weight, was impressive. The average height of the defensive players was 6'1" and they had a 6'5" defensive end. "This is probably the biggest unit we've ever had," acknowledged defensive coordinator, Ray Glaze.

Hayden's football coach, Bobby Taul, said, "They're tough. For as big as some of their people are, they're very quick to react to what happens. They just fly to the ball, especially when they see the ball. Once they see the pass, they're coming."

After five games Haskin noted that the Junior Blues were only allowing 123 yards of offense per game. They were only allowing 6.2 points per game as well and had forced 16 turnovers only giving up 10 themselves. Six defensive starters returned from the undefeated state championship game including two key linebackers, Aaron Anderson and Levi Baucom. Greg Harvey moved to the monster linebacker position after he was the leading tackler the year before at the nose guard position.

Mike Robinson and George Pratt anchored the defensive end spots. Luke Yarnell and Jason Penrod were a couple of big tackles and Hank Profitt was a tough nose guard.

The defensive backfield was largely full of newcomers. Noel Roach played safety. He was supported at corners by Maurice Givens, Stanely Quarles and Mark Longhofer.

"We don't want to let down anybody," Mike Robinson explained. "And we especially don't want to let down the people who played last year because they built on what has been a pretty good tradition."

The final season rankings in the Capital-Journal had Washburn Rural ranked number two and Pittsburg number one. Pretty accurate rankings too. Pittsburg defeated Rural in the semifinals and went on to win the 5A state championship defeating Buhler 28-10.

The Capital-Journal tapped Aaron Anderson for the All-Class All State team, picked Lucas Yarnell second team all-class all-state and also tapped three Junior Blues for all-city, Yarnell, Aaron Anderson and Greg Harvey. All three were also selected as all-class 5A selections as well. Jason Penrod was honorable mention all-class 5A.

1991 SEASON
MARRED BY
CONTROVERSY

I will give a little more information about the 1991 season, but there was a story that was too good to not tell.

The team had a very good season ending at 9-2, and a semi-final appearance against a very good Garden City team ended their season one game short of the state championship game.

Let's see, where to start this tale?

The 1991 Junior Blues reeled off six straight wins out of the gate to enter district play 6-0. At that time both Topeka West and Washburn Rural were in the 6A classification of schools based on enrollment. Both were in the top 32 schools for enrollment.

As fate would have it the geographical method of pre-determining district opponents pitted us against Topeka West. It was a good match-up but the Chargers got the best of us 16-7. Any coach will tell you that losing the first district game is not a good start. It means, to have a chance you must win your next two games and would have to hope someone beats West. That's not being in charge of your own fate. And it's especially difficult when your next two opponents are Junction City and Manhattan. To have any hopes of advancing to the playoffs you have to win both games and hope that one of those schools beats Topeka West.

So, week two of the districts was a must win for Washburn Rural. And Junction City. The Blue Jays came into district play 5-1 but lost their first-round district game to Manhattan 7-16. The game appeared to be between two evenly matched teams. The only advantage was the Junior Blues got to host the game on their home turf.

Well, also that year there was a lack of moisture in the fall. The field was worn, dry and hard as a rock. In fact, several teams, including Rural, had injuries to hands and wrists and there were teams complaining about the hard turf they had to play on at Rural's stadium. The decision of the high school administration and the district maintenance folks was to attempt to water the field that week in hopes that field was more playable and player friendly. In the old days, out in the rural part of the county where Washburn Rural sits, there was not a great deal of water pressure at times.

What occurred was part of the field, the portion that had to be watered with a water wheel that moved across the middle of the game field, relied on constant, heavy water pressure to propel it. When the system lost pressure due to the water tower that feeds it, the wheel got stuck in one place and over-watered a portion of the grass. The same could have happened to the whole field had it rained a good one or two inches that day before the game.

The result was a section of the field was over-watered and destined to become a bit slick, especially with cooler October temperatures. Periodically we used to have issues with drought and there would be hard spots on the turf. So, we had a mixture of hard spots and areas that became more wet than normal.

Washburn Rural won the football game 14-0. After the game several folks, mostly media folks, but also a Junction City Board of Education member, took issue with the field situation.

In an article written by Brent Milleson, Daily Union newspaper's sports editor, which was titled, 'Stupid human tricks' make fair play difficult.' His article started with this statement, "Junction City has found itself playing in muddy conditions several times in recent years when it's been dry virtually everywhere else in the state."

Now, I couldn't prove or disprove this conspiracy theory associated with other schools. I do think that it had occurred enough, in the perception of some Junction City folks, that it was no longer viewed as a product of natural causes. But I can assure the world that Washburn Rural did not purposely water a playing field.

Milleson goes on to write that the most recent example of this theory was the recent WR vs JC football district game. He mentioned it had occurred at Manhattan in 1987. His feeling was that the Junction City teams of 1981 and 1987 shared common traits with the 1981 Blue Jay squad - speed and quickness. According to Milleson he says more than just a little speed and quickness.

He claimed that one way to "neutralize" that speed is muddy field conditions. He also mentions that, as a coach or a fan, you realize you're not always going to get ideal field conditions. But he says, "if the conditions are less than perfect, let it be as a result of Mother Nature, not stupid human tricks."

There were differing perspectives by two journalists who covered the factors surrounding the game story and they were vastly different. One appears to be more opinion, not supported by facts.

Milleson points out that Kansas was in a drought. A serious one and cites the Topeka Capital Journal as a source for that information. John Feldt was the deputy meteorologist in charge at the National Weather Service Topeka's office at the time. Milleson acknowledges it did rain in Topeka on Thursday but says Feldt described the rain west of Topeka as getting only a couple of drops. Washburn Rural is southwest of Topeka and may have recorded slightly more than a couple of drops.

Milleson's description of the field appeared to be a slight exaggeration. He says the Junction City coach, Jerry Stuckert, and the fans were perplexed and puzzled by a field that was a muddy mess. In fact, he called it an oasis of mud. He claimed grass was no where to be seen in some areas in the middle of the field. Each sideline area was playable but the middle part of the field was a joke, he reported.

As a school administrator who attended that game, I can tell you that when the teams took the field the field was not a muddy mess.

A contrasting article by Capital-Journal sportswriter Kevin Haskin was titled, "Muddy field at Rural wasn't a factor."

Haskin provides a bit of background that Milleson apparently neglected to look into or include in his story. He reports that earlier in the 1991 season there were coaches wondering about the hard playing surface at Washburn Rural's stadium. One local coach jokingly wondered it someone had been practicing off-road stunts on the field with a three-wheeler.

The summer before the 1991 season there was an attempt to plant new grass as the field was plowed in the spring before and reseeded. He goes onto say the Auburn-Washburn district could not budget the maintenance, the water cost, etc. to properly develop a hardy stand of grass by fall football season.

What was left was a very barren, rock hard field which, in the fall of 1991 may have been a factor in three hand injuries to players playing games at Rural. Bowen noted that conditions involving a freshman game the week before the Junction City game was the reason for the decision to soften the rock-hard surface before the varsity game.

Unfortunately, a malfunction in the watering mechanisms caused one section of the field to receive too much water and that was according to Bob Gladfelter, Washburn Rural's athletic director.

"We were watering our field Thursday night with a special water wheel that covers areas that our sprinkler system does not," Gladfelter said. "Because of the drought, we've been concerned about the field being hard in spots where the sprinklers don't reach."

Because of a malfunction to the wheel due to a pressure drop, the wheel got stuck in one place. It was discovered between 9-10:00 PM on Thursday evening by a maintenance person checking the field. Additionally, according to a local meteorologist in Topeka he said that area received one-tenth of an inch of rain Thursday night and five-hundredths of rain fell Friday morning.

Before the game Washburn Rural administration spoke to Junction City's administration and to the game's officiating crew about playing on the field. Washburn Rural's Gladfelter said, "By no means did we intend to do more than just soften up (the field) for safety's sake."

After the game, the schools' athletic directors spoke on the phone on Tuesday and the Junction City AD said that Gladfelter had, "assured me this was not done on purpose to try to take away our (Junction City's) speed. He says it was an accident. I hope he's telling the truth. He probably is."

The Friday game night crew of officials deemed the field playable.

Following that Friday night game the Junction City principal sent a letter to the Kansas State High School Activities Association addressing it to two of their administrators, Nelson Hartman and Kaye Pearce. The principal called the letter a "summary of why we feel it necessary to vent our frustration."

With the letter they also sent a copy of Milleson's article from that Sunday's paper. The Junction City principal posed this question to the KSHSAA: "Was the field watered down on purpose? Nobody from Junction City knows for sure, but many hold the perception that it was done intentionally due to the following reasons:

1. Our (Junction City) coaches were told at least three different reasons why the field was wet – there should only be one explanation for the wet field.

2. A member of our (Junction's) Board of Education, while attending a Marching Band Contest on Saturday, overheard some parents from Washburn Rural telling some parents from Pittsburg: 'We took care of Junction City by watering down the field.'

3. We were not informed ahead of time about the conditions of the field.

The letter went on to say, "This was a crucial game for both schools. Consideration should have been given to relocating the game. But since we had no prior knowledge of conditions of the field, this left us thinking that we have been once again victimized by a mistake that could have been corrected so that neither team could benefit from the situation. We do believe by playing the game at Washburn Rural, without letting us know the conditions of the field, gave Washburn Rural an advantage."

But in the Capital-Journal article Washburn Rural Athletic Director Bob Gladfelter said the field was not that muddy. There were "no puddles on the field and no mud sticking to the shoes," Gladfelter told the sportswriter.

What did Coach Ron Bowen have to say? The Topeka sportswriter had to ask the hard question even though he said in the article it was ludicrous to believe that Bowen would tamper with field conditions to try and gain an advantage.

So, Coach Bowen, would you deliberately tamper with a field to gain and advantage over an opponent? Bowen's response was, "No way."

Bowen's perspective of the field conditions, "The field was not that bad. There was a little bit of standing water on the north side from the 10 to the 30-yard line. But back when it used to rain, if it rained an inch there'd be more water on the field than there was Friday.

"The screw-up points a finger at our program and that's not good," he said. "We had no intention of gaining any kind of advantage with a wet field. They'd have hollered at us worse if that field would have been in the same shape it was Wednesday," Bowen commented. Meaning if the field had been as hard as concrete.

Folks at Rural thought the rationale behind Junction City's complaint was shaky any way. Why would Rural want to slow anyone down with a muddy field when its leading rusher, Maurice Givens, was a state-class sprinter in track and field. Arguably, the fastest player on the field that Friday evening.

"There's not anybody on their team who makes as many cuts as Mo (Givens) makes," Bowen pointed out. "And if anybody is going to slide, it's Mo. From what I saw on film of the Junction City backs there is no juking. They just flat ran hard."

And it's neither here nor there, but in the 1991 district games Junction City lost to Manhattan, Washburn Rural and Topeka West. Which did not mean they did not have a good football team, but it further supports sportswriter Kevin Haskin's assertion, "Not to brag, but I picked Rural by 14 points without taking any kind of game conditions, or excuses, into account. Rural won by 14. Play the game again- under a dome, in a pigpen or on Junction City's immaculately manicured field- and I'd expect the same outcome."

One thing for certain Ron Bowen never has, nor never had to cheat to gain an advantage for a football game. He's a tremendous football coach, but his character is even more fantastic. A believer in let the best team on Friday night win. Or if we aren't the best team, let's hope we are more prepared and ready. His success has nothing to do with sprinkler systems.

1991 not only saw controversy, but it also marked Washburn Rural's ascent into 6A classification based on their enrollment. Kevin Haskin did the obligatory interview of Coach Bowen in the August 30, 1991 Capital-Journal article. Bowen took opportunity to provide a candid response about moving to 6A. "I hope these Class 6A powers take it easy on us since we're the new kid on the block," Bowen said.

Rural had always played 6A competition, but the major difference was with their new district assignment. They would have to make their way through Topeka West, Junction City and Manhattan to qualify for the playoffs.

The 1991 season saw three quarterbacks competing for the job. Senior Dallas Barth was back along with junior Mark Longhofer. Newcomer Michael Atha, a sophomore, was also in the position mix. But Coach Bowen had always dealt with this situation with the team's best interest in mind. Whoever was not number one at quarterback, would simply be moved to another key position.

The quarterback would have good protection upfront with four returners on the front line. Lucas Yarnell was the most talented blocker a year earlier and he returns along with Todd McKinnon, Wayne Wheeler and Travis Emmons.

There was a stable of running backs returning who got to carry the ball some for the Junior Blues, Stanley Quarles who had the most yards the previous season, Maurice Givens and Jeff Ruediger. Levi Baucom was moved from a line position to fullback.

Defensively they moved Yarnell to linebacker to take advantage of his skills and size. Along with Baucom they presented a solid second level. The secondary was extremely strong. But there were holes to fill on the line.

1992 – AS CLOSE AS YOU CAN GET

I'm certain that there were doubters. Washburn Rural had a good run in 5A football classification, but now that they were 6A, the largest 32 schools in the state, could they still be great? Well, they could indeed.

Topeka Capital-Journal sportswriter Kevin Haskin wrote in his annual "forecast" and predictions of the Washburn Rural season that, in their initial year of 6A, had actually proven they could play with the big boys, mentioning that the previous year Rural advanced to the semifinal game. He mentioned that the '91 team handed out some lopsided victories once again allowing many kids to gain valuable game experience. He predicted that this year's version of the Junior Blues would likely go 7-2. Preseason predictions are fun, but not always spot on. He was close though.

In Haskin's preseason preview of the Junior Blues, he mentioned that Ron Bowen was offered a chance to predict how his own team would do in 1992. Of course, Bowen declined.

He told Haskin, "The last time I made a prediction was in 1961. I was coaching at Udall High School, and I thought we were going to be pretty good that year. We had our entire backfield returning that year," Bowen reflected. "What I forgot to look at was our offensive line. As I remember, we kind of struggled that year."

Haskin went on to mention that 32 years later Bowen fields a program that doesn't struggle too often. They were coming off a 9-2 record, an undefeated league record, and a playoff, semifinal appearance before stumbling to Garden City and committing an uncharacteristic seven turnovers to help the Buffaloes.

Reflecting on last season ending loss, "I don't even know if they the kids still think about it or not."

But he did acknowledge the benefits of a post-season appearance. "It always helps give a program a boost. And it helps to have an extending season with extra practice time," Bowen said. Rural had five starters to replace on offense and seven on defense. About replacing those key positions Bowen said, "It seemed like in the past when we had question marks, new people stepped up. That's what we have to expect this year."

Haskin mentioned that Bowen might like the linemen returning this year better than the Udall experience in 1961, Both offensive tackles returned with senior Todd McKinnon and junior Joey Hodgson were coming back, along with guard Kato Luedka. Joining them on the line would likely be senior center Sean Kennedy and junior guards Michael Baker and Kalub Emmons.

The backfield would have no returning starters but junior fullback Justin Howe saw action in the district game gaining 101 yards against Manhattan. Senior Korey Hale looked to be the tailback. Senior Mark Longhofer appeared to be the leading quarterback candidate. Bowen looked to move backup quarterback and fastest player Michael Atha to slotback.

The year before the Rural defense, traditionally strong, led the city schools in defense allowing only 163 total yards per game. However, one of the key returners for that defense would likely miss several weeks due to dislocating a tendon in his finger. Two other linebackers return Michael Baker and Matt Meens.

And the secondary all returned with Longhofer, Atha and Hale covering passes.

Putting pressure on the running attacks of the opponents and applying the pass rush would be Howe and Luedka, along with junior Bill Bailey or sophomore Chase Simms.

One thing about Coach Bowen, when I was the athletic director, I found him very easy to work with on our football schedule. Our Centennial League was a six-team league so five league opponents we scheduled each year. What changed the dynamic of the schedule occasionally was that often a league school would be assigned to our district. So, occasionally there were years when we needed one or two non-conference games in our first six scheduled weeks.

Remember, in 1989 Washburn beat Salina Central, coached by Marvin Diener, in the 5A state championship game in a real head knocker. In 1991, just two years removed, Salina Central offered to schedule us for our opener. In 1991 we beat them a second time.

This time around, 1992, we went to Salina and lost to Central in the opener, 22-6. Not particularly the way you want to start your season – with a loss- but Central gave you a measuring stick to determine what kind of a team you might have.

And that season Rural ran off a string of nine straight wins after losing the opener and immediately bounced back in week two and defeated a very good Shawnee Heights team 29-20.

In week number three this team faced an always tough league opponent in Emporia High. And even though Rural had defeated Emporia the last three seasons they always played the Junior Blues very tough. This year was no exception. And it was always a concern to have to play them on their home turf, Emporia University's Welch Stadium.

Sportswriter Pam Clark covered the game for the Capital-Journal, and she said Ron Bowen didn't care much for his team's position in the first half. Her play on words was actually for, "field position." Emporia had a 6-0 lead at halftime, but Rural started all but one of their possessions over 80-yards from the Junior Blue's end zone. It's tough for a high school team to sustain drives of that length. Too much can go wrong. And on this evening it did. They couldn't move the ball and were three plays and out with a punt. Rural couldn't find a way to move the ball on the tough Emporia defense.

Clark reported that Bowen pulled quarterback Mark Longhofer aside before the second half kickoff. "I told him he's got to light a fire some way," Bowen related, "and he did."

With less than a minute left in the third quarter defensive back Longhofer stepped in front of a pass intended for the Emporia tight end and intercepted it at the Emporia 23, returned it nine-yards to the Emporia 14-yard line. Seriously good field position. Three plays later Junior Blue Terrel Meyers scored on a four-yard run. Bowen had recruited a soccer player to be the Washburn Rural place kicker, a sophomore by the name of Matt Tyler. The extra point would be the first time he was asked to kick in an actual football game. He split the uprights making it a 7-6 lead and that was all the scoring for the night.

"That's an awful lot of pressure to put on a kid who's never kicked under that kind of pressure before," Bowen said.

In week number four Washburn Rural used 271 yards rushing and 39 yards passing to defeat Hayden 34-16. Tailback Korey Hale had his best night thus far with 164 yards rushing on 10 carries. He also added three touchdowns scoring on an 86-yard run the first time he touched the football. He added a 65-yard touchdown run on the first play of the second half, then later added a 77- yard kickoff return for a touchdown. Michael Atha had a touchdown run and caught a pass for touchdown. Matt Tyler kicked and made four out of five extra point attempts and the night belonged to Hale and Atha and the Junior Blues. Hale was selected as the Topeka player of the week for his efforts. Bowen said, "He's kind of a deceptive runner. It seems like a lot of times he's still on his feet when you think he'd be down."

Week five was almost a repeat as Rural defeated Seaman 35-14 rolling up 342 total yards and did not have to punt the ball. Nine different Junior Blues carried the ball. This night was Junior Justin Howe's night, rushing for 138 yards and two touchdowns.

The Capital-Journal sportswriter Kevin Haskin credited the Washburn Rural offensive line mentioning Sean Kennedy, Todd McKinnon, Michael Baker, Kaleu Emmons, Joey Hodgson and Matt McPherson. Bowen credited assistant and offensive line coach Don Gifford with a little "do better" speech at halftime. Gifford was a little concerned that the line got a little complacent after taking a 21-7 halftime lead. Other than Howe's two rushing touchdowns three other Junior Blues found the end zone. Atha had a 10-yard rushing touchdown, Terrel Meyers had an 84-yard kickoff return for a score and Longhofer capped off the scoring with a seven-yard TD.

The last regular season game, game number six was with Highland Park and Rural, for the third straight week put up 30 points beating Park 37-14. Rural had captured their fourth straight Centennial League title and, after six games led the city statistically in both offense and defense. The Junior Blues averaged 307 total yards per game and scored at a 26.9 clip in those six games. Defensively they held teams to 199 yards per game and 13.2 points per game. You can win a lot of games with that lopsided statistical advantage.

But Rural was facing another tough district road – Topeka West, Junction City and Manhattan were in their district.

In their first district game they faced rival Topeka West who had a disappointing 3-3 record but would likely play with a lot of emotion when it came to trying to claim city bragging rights.

In Kevin Haskins Topeka Capital-Journal article he mentioned that Rural needed every inch of their field and, once again, relied on its defense to preserve the victory for them. In fact, it took a goal line stand with just more than a minute remaining to hold on for a 12-7 victory.

Rural had jumped out to a 12-0 halftime lead on two short Mark Longhofer touchdown runs, but a failed extra point kick and a missed two-point conversion left Rural at 12 points. So when West scored in the 3rd quarter and made their extra point suddenly it was anybody's game at 12-7.

Topeka West took over the ball on its own 31-yard line with 4:53 remaining on the game clock. Four plays later two big runs got West to the three-yard line, first and goal. West picked up one yard on first down, one yard on second down, but Cory Tarvin flew into the backfield and dropped their quarterback for a one-yard loss. It would be fourth and two from the two and the ballgame. The West running back went airborne near the goal line but was met in mid-air by linebacker Matt Meens and stopped about a foot an-a-half from the goal line.

"It's been a long time since we've come up with that kind of stand, and I'd say this was little too close tonight," Bowen commented after the game. That was not the only big stop that night. Earlier in the fourth quarter West had moved the ball to the Rural 16-yard line. But on a fourth-and-three play West was trying a bootleg by their quarterback, but linebacker Mike Blakely tackled him in the backfield before he could even turn to go the opposite direction.

Justin Howe had a big night rushing with 191 yards on 17 carries and Rural was 6-1 and an all-important 1-0 in district. Up next was Junction City.

Washburn Rural had to travel to Junction City after a home game with West. And this was just one year removed from the "water the field" game. You figured they'd be looking for revenge. Wrong year to get it.

According to the Capital-Journal article sportswriter Kevin Haskin quoted Coach Bowen as saying, "We were more worried about their passing game because that's how they hurt Manhattan – through the air." The Rural defense not only held Junction City to 52 yards passing, they stifled their run game to the tune of negative 10-yards rushing. The only score for Junction was a 17-yard touchdown run in the second quarter. Then Rural turned a 7-7 halftime into a 28-7 win with three second half scores. Tarvin scored in the first half on a one-yard run. In the second half Howe scored twice on runs of two and one yard respectfully. Atha added a twelve-yard touchdown run as well. Rural completed one pass but compiled 286 yards on the ground with Howe rushing for 139 of those yards. Rural was 7-1 and 2-0 in district play. The playoff game would depend on the outcome of the game with Manhattan.

In the game at McElroy Field Washburn Rural came out fast against Manhattan. Michael Atha broke the first play from scrimmage for a 52-yard touchdown to give the Junior Blues the early 6-0 lead. Terrel Meyers set-up the short field with a 32-yard kickoff return. Topeka Capital-Journal sportswriter Kevin Haskin asked Atha about his run after the game. "I figured they'd be keying on Howe and I just broke it wide open," Atha commented. "That got the momentum going. We've had good drives to start our last few games and that really helps," Atha said.

In between, Longhofer scored in the first quarter as well on a four-yard quarterback keeper.

Rural's vaunted defense held Manhattan to 61-yards on the ground and forced numerous punts that were not helping with their field position. The Junior Blues even blocked a punt when Matt Meens broke the line and got a piece of the ball and Tarvin recovered it at the two-yard line. Tarvin put the final points on the board with a one-yard score to make it a 19-point lead. Manhattan got a late 80-yard scoring pass play to put seven on the board.

Rural advanced to the 6A playoffs for the second year in a row and it was their eighth straight playoff appearance. The Junior Blues' first game in the playoffs would be Wichita North.

They say in any good season you can look back at some plays and even some games and recognize that a bit of luck can be involved for any good team to succeed and advance. In Wichita the Junior Blues got a taste of just that. The game was marred by turnovers, but luckily, every time Rural made a turnover, North would give it right back. In the second half senior Brennan Fagan recovered two punts that North fumbled and one led to a Junior Blue score. He was in the right place at the right time.

Rural was clinging to a 7-0 lead at halftime but their offense sputtered and made some mistakes. After the second fumble recovery by Fagan the Junior Blues only needed three plays to score their second touchdown and won 14-0 to advance to the semifinal game.

They were set to host their next opponent, but the Washburn Rural stadium did not have the seating capacity required for a 6A semifinal game. So, Rural arranged with Centennial League and Topeka neighboring school, Topeka-Seaman, to rent their facility to host the game with Dodge City who was undefeated. Rural would be playing an undefeated Dodge on a neutral field for a chance to make their fourth state championship appearance in 8 years.

For all intents and purposes it looked as if Dodge City might rain on the Washburn Rural parade. Dodge drew first blood with a short touchdown run. Then Rural scored on a Longhofer 15-yard scamper but Dodge answered in the second quarter with a 31-yard pass play that made it 7-14 at halftime.

According to the Capital-Journal article by Kevin Haskin who interviewed Rural captain and linebacker Matt Means, "Coach (Ron Bowen) told us at halftime to hold together as a team and just win the second half. It was pretty scary at the end because they'd been driving the whole game, but we came out like we wanted to take over."

Barely two minutes into the second half Mark Longhofer hit Matt McPherson with a perfect 63-yard scoring strike. Cory Tarvin ran in the extra point and the score was knotted at 14.

On the next Dodge possession Rural's defense stepped up and held Dodge City on downs and took over at the 38-yard line and proceeded to drive to their four-yard line. When that drive stalled, sophomore Matt Tyler came on and kicked the go-ahead field goal from 22 yards.

Haskin wrote that "in this case, take may be short for takeaway." The last two Dodge City turnovers were in the fourth quarter ending deep penetration and scoring opportunities for Dodge.

Korey Hale intercepted a pass in the end zone and returned it to the 31-yard line ending a Dodge City threat. Then with 1:45 remaining Mike Blakely made a tackle and forced a fumble that Justin Howe recovered at the Rural 20.

Dodge City had one more play with eight seconds left and the ball at the Rural 45-yard line but could not produce. The 17-14 hard fought win put Rural in the 6A championship game.

Waiting for the Junior Blues was Lawrence who looked invincible. They would be making their seventh straight appearance in the championship and were seeking their fourth straight championship. Odds makers probably would make Lawrence the favorite if Las Vegas got involved in Kansas high school football. But previous years of experience by teams and even their great traditions can be negated if the will is strong enough. And Washburn Rural's will was darn near strong enough.

This description of the Lawrence game perhaps gives the best picture. Longhofer said, "There was a huge "David and Goliath" storyline. And for good reason. Here we were, Washburn Rural, a school just two years in the 6A classification. A school with so much history and success at the 5A level. Our enrollment was about 850 students. Only four schools in 6A were smaller. Despite all that, we had advanced to the biggest game of our lives against, by far, the premier high school program at that time. Lawrence was the largest school in the state with an enrollment of over 1,800 students."

Longhofer went on to say that the Junior Blues may have benefited from being the underdogs in their previous playoff games against Manhattan, Wichita North and Dodge City. He also credits Coach Bowen's demeanor for helping them all and focus. "Coaching at an even keel was something he was good at," Longhofer reflected. "He made sure his team full of 16 to 18-year old knuckleheads were prepared mentally for the task at hand."

Another thing that Coach Bowen did to help put his team at ease was schedule a practice at Kansas State so the team could get in a large stadium and on the artificial turf. Longhofer recollected that Coach had a phrase "saucer eyes" when talking about a player's nervous response when put in an important situation. "Walking into that college stadium," Longhofer commented, "practicing on an unfamiliar surface and envisioning what it would be like to play in front of several thousand fans went a long way to minimizing us from getting 'saucer eyes' on championship day." Kind of resembles the famous movie "Hoosiers" doesn't it?

Longhofer remembers that the game did start out rough for the Junior Blues. Lawrence was driving the ball right down their throats for the first three plays after opening kickoff. Bowen called a timeout and trotted defensive coordinator Ray Glaze onto the field who calmly made some adjustments, and the result was a Washburn Rural interception in the end zone.

As quarterback Longhofer also recollects the first two offensive series for Rural going badly. Both possessions ended in Rural fumbles the first one Lawrence used to score and lead 7-0. Then Longhofer remembers Bowen calling "One Buffalo" an option running play similar to what the University of Colorado ran at that time. After a fake into the line and a pull and read by Longhofer, he pitched the ball to Korey Hale who outran some fast opponents to the end zone and the first quarter ended 6-7 Lawrence.

Longhofer remembers all the "bizarre" plays that marked the final three quarters. One such play occurred when Lawrence's all-state running back broke the line and what looked like it might go for a 49-yard TD. But Korey Hale caught him from behind, knocked the ball loose at the 10-yard line. Longhofer remembers being knocked on his butt, but the ball bouncing off his foot and rolling out of the end zone. Rural's ball via touchback. Lawrence put up the only score of the second quarter with a 33-yard field goal and it was 6-10 Lawrence Lions.

Longhofer remembers the ability of Coach Bowen and his staff to make halftime adjustments. And Rural came out to start the third quarter with a three-play drive. Longhofer for 38 yards on a counter-option play, Hale for a seven-yard gain and then Justin Howe rumbled 27 yards to pay dirt. Three plays, 72-yards against the top defense in the state and Rural took a 13-10 lead. Late in the 3rd quarter Lawrence answered with a scoring drive to take the lead 16-13.

Momentum shifted back to Rural when their defense forced Lawrence to punt early in the 4th quarter. On the snap Matt Meens shot a gap past the linemen and their second protective blockers to block the punt that rolled into the end zone. Meens bear-crawled the distance to cover the ball for a touchdown. Rural was on top 19-16 with eleven minutes remaining.

On the next Lawrence possession Rural's vaunted defense forced a three and out. After the last punt was blocked the Lawrence punter hurried his kick and it went off the side of his foot and gave Rural great field position near mid-field.

Rural went for the jugular on a bread-and butter play, the inside reverse to the slot back. Longhofer faked a pitch to the tailback and the slot back came back the other way for a reverse counter. Lawrence read the play perfectly and their linebacker was there to take the handoff instead and returned the turnover 50-yards for a TD making it 23-19 Lawrence.

With a little over five minutes left in the game Rural's last possession started on their 35-yard line. They would need to drive the ball 65-yards for a touchdown and time was a factor. The last drive had the game's BEST drama. There was a Lawrence interception that was nullified by a roughing the passer penalty to allow Rural to maintain possession of the ball and have a chance. A clutch screen pass was a big 24-yard gain and, on a 3rd and one, there was a bootleg call that the Lawrence defense sniffed out, but Longhofer was able to scramble, slide out of bounds at the 11 with 1:09 remaining on the clock.

The Junior Blues gained six more yards on an option and they had the ball on the five-yard line with 57 seconds remaining but had used two timeouts on the drive, leaving them with only one timeout left. Rural tried an option-dive play that Longhofer kept and lost a yard so, with the ball on the six, burnt their last time out. With no timeouts and just third and fourth down remaining, Rural was forced to try a couple of passes. The first glanced off the fingers of Mike Atha in the back of the end zone. A desperation last play to 6'4" Bill Bailey which was like a jump ball situation was knocked to the ground by the Lawrence secondary and ball changed possession with just 32 seconds left.

"While it was a devastating loss," Longhofer reflected," for me and for the team, I cherish the picture of Coach Bowen with his arm around my head and shoulders, consoling me on the field after the loss. He was like a father figure to me and so many players through the years. And in this time of heartbreak, he was there to lift me back up. A soul-crushing defeat was suddenly a little more bearable with his embrace and words of encouragement. I'll never forget it."

The championship game was a spectacular game with both teams giving their best efforts under tremendous pressure. There really was not a loser in this game. Rural just ran out of time and Lawrence made a great goal-line stand to preserve the 23-19 win. It looked like two prize fighters exchanging punches. And there was no knockout.

On the last opportunity by Rural the Junior Blues had to battle the Lions defense and the clock. They had no timeouts. Kevin Haskin, sportswriter for the Capital-Journal wrote that execution on the Junior Blues final possession was what helped them reach the five-yard line.

Perhaps the best quotes summing up the game came from the Lawrence side. Head Coach Dick Purdy told Haskin of the Capital-Journal, "We were getting a little concerned late. I don't think you'll see a finer football game. I think what happened is we had two teams with great athletes that overcame good execution."

And Lawrence linebacker, Max Cordova, told Haskin, "Washburn Rural deserves a lot of credit because they had us off balance. We were giving up a lot of yards, but when we had to, we got the job done. We stuck with our assignments and didn't let down. Both teams just played their hearts out."

Three of Washburn Rural's players were recognized as All-Class 6A selections.

Lineman, Todd McKinnon, Linebacker, Matt Means and Defensive Back, Mark Longhofer. Honorable mention honors went to Michael Atha, Justin Howe and Korey Hale.

McKinnon, Longhofer and Howe were all named to the first team All-Centennial League on both offense and defense. Other offensive players tabbed first-team All-League for Rural were Sean Kennedy, Kalub Emmons, Korey Hale and placekicker Matt Tyler. On defense Matt Means and Michael Atha were tabbed first-team All-League. Michael Baker was tabbed second-team All-League on offense as a lineman. Emmons, Chase Simms and Hale were second-team selections for defense.

Coach Bowen was selected as the League's Coach of the Year and was also tabbed as Topeka City Coach of the Year for the fifth time by the Topeka Capital-Journal.

All-City selections were Korey Hale, Justin Howe, Matt Meens, Mark Longhofer and Todd McKinnon.

In Kevin Haskin's article about Ron Bowen being selected City Coach of the Year a lot was revealed about Bowen and his demeanor towards teaching, coaching and life in general.

First the article was accompanied by a photograph of Bowen consoling quarterback Mark Longhofer immediately after the state championship game.

And he graciously answered the questions about did he second-guess his play calls in a game that came down to the wire like the Lawrence game. "Still am," Bowen responded. And when the reporter asked about some factors that may have contributed to the loss, Bowen said, "There's a lot of big if words in there. Early in the drive (the last one) we were lucky to get a late hit on the quarterback or we wouldn't have been down there at all."

Bowen was asked how long he'd stick around as a teacher and a coach. "You retire as a teacher you don't retire as a coach. But I wouldn't teach if I didn't coach," Bowen said. "When the state legislature makes it worth it, I probably will retire. If our pension was like the judges and the state legislators, I could probably afford to retire. But as long as I enjoy the kids, and I don't get on their nerves too much and they don't get on mine, I'll continue coaching."

One last comment about the game and life from Bowen was, "It's not life or death, even if you don't score from the 5-yard line." And it's that kind of perspective and candor that kept Bowen looking forward to other chances and other play calls. It's not life and death, it's a game. A great game.

As of the writing of this book 1992 still marks the most successful 6A football season in Washburn Rural history and this is nearly thirty years ago. It's always tough when your last game is a loss, but make no mistake, this game could have easily gone either way. I saw it with my own eyes.

1993- WOULD THERE BE REDEMPTION

H ow would Bowen and Washburn Rural rebound from the disappointing loss in the 1992 state championship game? After all, it was a totally new experience. Rural had won their previous three trips to the title game in 5A – 1985, '86 and '89. But this was the big classification and, as is always the case, graduation robbed some valuable players from the Junior Blues.

But, as Topeka Capital-Journal sportswriter Kevin Haskin points out there were some awfully good players returning for the new season. Seven offensive starters and eight defensive regulars return from the 10-2 season a year ago. And the march through the playoffs meant three extra weeks of practice for these returning players.

"We have a good bunch of kids coming back," Bowen said. "They worked hard, most of them over the offseason. They're trying to reach their goals. I don't even know what they are, but they better have them."

And, if history and tradition would have anything to do with continuing success, Rural would be taking a string of thirteen consecutive Centennial League wins into this season and would be bidding for their fifth straight Centennial League title as well. Ron Bowen would be coaching his 19th season at Washburn Rural and it was his 35th season coaching football.

Bowen lost a small, but talented senior class. There was a decision to make about who would play quarterback. Last year's slot back senior Michael Atha shared offensive snaps with senior Cory Tarvin and sophomore Mark McPherson was vying for playing time. There was some uncertainty but some talent at the quarterback position. Bowen wasn't even certain they would just utilize one player at quarterback or entertain playing two players equally.

And the previous year's fullback, who led the city in rushing from that position might just move to tailback. Justin Howe a 6'0" 210 lb. running back might play tailback. Seniors Kato Luedka and Nathan Rotler along with sophomore Damon Wright fit into the backfield plans as well.

On the line three-year starter Joey Hodgson anchored the line along with seniors Kalub Emmons and Bill Bailey who was the tight end in '92. Also vying for playing time were juniors Ryan Randall, Chris Hollar, Ryan Sigg and Senior Brent Senogles.

Matt McPherson could move from sharing tight end time to split end. Senior Thad Halstead and Chad Corcoran could also fill the wide receiver roles.

Although eight defensive players return there would be question marks because many would be asked to switch positions. Randall and Hodgson would likely be tackles while Emmons would move to nose guard. Bailey and Marc Deever likely would fill the defensive end spots.

The two defensive ends from a year ago, Howe and Ludka, would likely move to linebackers. Sophomore Geral Lewis would likely fill the other linebacker spot. Tarvin would be the key monster linebacker. Mike Blakely moved from linebacker to cornerback along with senior Aaron Dennison. Atha, who started at corner the year before, would be moved to safety.

In the season opener the Junior Blues had to travel to Salina Central, the same tough team that Rural opened with last season and lost their only game prior to the Lawrence championship game. Washburn Rural forced four fumbles and rode Justin Howe's 90-rushing yards and Cory Tarvin's 7-11 passing in his first game as the team's quarterback to a 14-7 road victory. Michael Atha scored both touchdowns on a one-yard run and catching a 10-yard pass.

In week two the Junior Blues used Howe's 197 yards of rushing and two touchdowns to defeat Shawnee Heights 21-8. Tarvin scored first after a fumble recovery by Bill Bailey. The line of Ryan Randall, Kalub Emmons, Ryan Sigg, Joey

Hodgson, and Bailey opened numerous holes for Howe and the other Rural backs to run through and protected Tarvin who was 5 for 10 for 77 yards.

In week three, the always tough Emporia Spartans were the Junior Blues home opener. And they would be playing on a brand new field just east of the existing one. In the summer an engineer condemned the wooden bleachers at McElroy that had been home to Washburn Rural football for nearly thirty years. There was some quick sidewalk work and metal bleachers installed on both sides of the new stadium. The track had been put in first.

Emporia was a gracious first guest as the Junior Blues defense pitched a shutout and Rural moved to 3-0 with a 19-0 victory. The offense was fueled by Aaron Dennison returning the opening kickoff 76 yards to the 14-yard line. That would be all the Junior Blues needed to help Tarvin score the first touchdown. Howe and Atha also added rushing touchdowns. Howe, Kato Luedka and Atha combined for 210-yards all on the ground.

The week four Hayden game was played in a solid drizzle and rain and Hayden fumbled the ball away on their first two possessions and botched a punt on their third. And Howe scored three first-half touchdowns on short runs. He added a fourth score in the second half and Washburn Rural downed Hayden 26-7.

The Topeka Capital-Journal reporters predicted a six-point win in week five with Seaman. Washburn Rural put up 368 rushing yards for a 42-12 win to move to a perfect 5-0. Four different Junior Blues scored touchdowns, Luedke (42-yard run), Atha (85-yard run and a five-yard run), Howe (a five and a one-yard touchdown run), and Dennison (10-yard run). Rural scored 35 second half points to never look back.

The final regular season game six would set the stage for district play in the final three games. Rural won the Homecoming game 21-7 over Highland Park assuring them their fifth straight Centennial League title. Howe had 165-yards rushing and two touchdowns. The Junior Blues got their first score on 46-yard pass Tarvin to Atha.

Waiting for Rural in the four-team qualifying district were Topeka West, Junction City and Manhattan.

Washburn Rural defeated a 2-4 Topeka West team 21-6. After West scored first the Junior Blues used a 40-yard Tarvin to Thad Halstead pass for a touchdown. At halftime it was just a 7-6 lead for Rural. Then Atha and Howe scored on short runs. Rural lead time of possession securing 13-first downs to West's eight.

Taking a 1-0 record to game two of district, Washburn Rural was looking to win and then a playoff deciding game with Manhattan. It almost didn't happen. The Junior Blues struggled the whole game and needed two overtimes to defeat Junction City 27-20. Junction City was usually a passing team, but they crossed up the Junior Blues defense by repeatedly and successfully running the football. The game ended in a 13-13 tie. Junction City got first possession and scored on a seven-yard pass play. The Junior Blues answered with a 10-yard possession capped by a one-yard plunge by Howe. Both teams made their extra point-kicks so it was 20-20 and a second overtime was necessary. This time Rural took another short drive into the end zone and made the kick for a 27-20 lead but Junction City also got a shot at the ball. Rural used two quarterback sacks to end the night for Junction City.

The only thing between Washburn Rural and their ninth playoff appearance was the Manhattan Indians. After an 8-0 start the Junior Blues would face a 7-1 Manhattan team. Manhattan won the game 27-0. In his Topeka Capital-Journal article sportswriter Kevin Haskin took a quote from Coach Bowen. "We got nothing consistent going," he commented. "We got outplayed, outhit and out-quicked on both sides of the ball." Rural was forced to punt the ball away nine different times and there would not be a playoff opportunity this season. After going 8-0 it was an abrupt ending to a great season. Manhattan would eventually lose in the semifinals to Derby by a 13-7 score. Manhattan, indeed, was a formidable team in 1993.

Nine Junior Blues along with Coach Bowen were selected as All-Centennial League. Bowen was Coach of the Year. Michael Atha was first team both sides of the ball. Joining Atha on offense were Joey Hodgson, Cory Tarvin, Justin Howe and kicker Matt Tyler. Joining Atha on the first-team defensive unit were Thad Halstead, Chase Simms, Mike Blakely and Kato Luedke.

Second-team offensive selections were Bill Bailey and Kalub Emmons. On defense selections were Emmons, Tarvin and punter Matt Tyler.

All-City first team selections were Atha, Hodgson and Howe. Bailey, Blakely and Tarvin were selected second team.

And Justin Howe was selected to the All-Class All-State team.

COACH BOWEN'S FINAL FOUR YEARS – 1994-1997 – TWO UP, TWO A BIT DOWN

1994 marked what would be the final freshman class to play four years for Ron Bowen. He would announce his retirement in 1997. Both he and Mary Lou would give up their Washburn Rural teaching coaching/ advising positions. Mary Lou was the longtime advisor for the Rural newspaper called the Blue Streak and was inducted into the Washburn Rural Hall of Fame in April of 2021.

And of course, Ron Bowen was at the helm of the football program since 1975. A total of 23 seasons rebuilding and leading the Junior Blue football program establishing a tradition of success.

And the last four years saw two good years of football and two not-so good football seasons record-wise.

In 1994, coming off an 8-1 season, the Junior Blues managed only one win that year. It was the worst year since 1975 and was only the third losing season since that time. And in one of those less than .500 seasons (1988) they still managed to qualify for the playoffs. Between 1988 and 1994 the Junior Blues only lost seven games total in a five-year span.

Once in a while, and every high school coach knows this, there will be some down years. Fortunately, there were two good years between each of these tough seasons. 1994 (1-8), 1995 (6-3), 1996 (8-1) and the final year of 1997 (2-7).

One can always wrack their brain to come up with reasons why the 1-8 and 2-7 occurred. And now, looking back, there would be lots of theories. Certainly, lots of variables. But rest assured two things DID occur. The Bowen-led coaching staff expected the same hard work and effort. The same self-discipline was instilled and nurtured and the young men likely enjoyed their experiences. Oh, don't get me wrong, losing is never any fun for anyone, but I'm certain that the same lessons were learned and maturity gained from each of the last four seasons, win or lose.

In 1994 Rural lost a one-score opener to Topeka West before losing by a wide-spread margin to Bishop Miege. Shawnee Heights ended a 14-year losing skid to Washburn Rural by beating the Junior Blues 33-6. Hayden and Seaman handed big losses to Rural as well. The lone win came at the hands of Highland Park as Rural beat the Scotts 21-6.

Washburn Rural dropped their three district games to Emporia, Junction City and Manhattan marking the worst season since 1975.

If the gas was out of Coach Bowen's tank, it didn't show as Washburn Rural bounced back in 1995 with a 6-3 record and only missing the playoffs due to the final game loss to Mahnattan.

In the preseason article in the Topeka Capital-Journal Coach Bowen told this year's edition of the Junior Blues who were following up a 1-8 season, the same thing he told the team following up the 1986 season a decade ago – "Forget about last season. We talked about it a little bit and I told them that's all history. It's in the past. In 1986 we just won the state and that was all history and so is last year."

The Junior Blues had lots of experience coming back and a powerful and speedy backfield with converted lineman at fullback and Damon Wright the leading rusher from the previous year back at the halfback. Other skill players returning were Steve Chooncharoen, Cody Snyder and Casey Hager.

Rural reeled off four consecutive wins beating Topeka West, Bishop Miege, Shawnee Heights and Hayden before losing their first two games of the season to Seaman 21-7 and dropping a 27-7 loss at the hands of Highland Park.

In their first two district games the Junior Blues beat Emporia 21-7 and Junction City in a 28-26 nail biter. All that stood in their way of a playoff berth was Manhattan.

The Indians laid a 27-0 shutout on Rural ending their season at a respectful 6-3.

In 1996 Washburn Rural returned a good nucleus and had a very good tailback set to make his mark this season, Cody Snyder. They opened with Independence and had a 40-7 win and continued their winning ways with a 35-3 thumping of Highland Park in which the Junior Blues ran the ball 47 times in the game for 214 yards. Snyder had his second 100-yard game with 119 on 21 carries. The Junior Blues defense forced six turnovers, five fumbles and an interception, and blocked a punt.

Their third victory was a close one in Emporia and they relied on Snyder's best game thus far a 31 carry, 203 yards rushing and a touchdown. Heath Farrar of Rural returned an Emporia fumble for a touchdown before the first half came to an end. Then Emporia got a Snyder fumble of a punt late in the fourth quarter and returned it 47 yards to draw within three points.

Rural won their fourth in a row against Hayden. Washburn Rural had two 100-yard rushers that evening with Snyder rushing for 22 times for 163 yards. Jason Beardslee carried 10 times for 124 yards. Quarterback Kaleb Hale added some balance with 6-8 passing for 112 yards with two touchdown throws and a rushing touchdown.

In the fifth week of the season Rural was to host Shawnee Heights for their Homecoming. Remember they had snuck up on the '94 Rural bunch and ended a 14-year losing streak. And it would have been an even longer streak, totaling 19 years in a row had it not been for the infamous "theft" that Coach Bowen used as his pre-game speech EVERY year. In fact, without the "theft" Bowen would have started his Shawnee Heights victory streak in 1975 and it would have ended in 1994.

Here's a summation of the 1979 infamous "theft" game told in Coach Bowen's own words:

"In 1979 we were leading Shawnee Heights by a 7 to 6 score. On the last play of the game Heights threw a pass into the end zone and we were called for a pass interference as the clock ran out. By rule, they were allowed one un-timed down.

"Here are the reasons I always referred to the game as a theft. First, the pass into the end zone was thrown from the right hash mark where the ball was spotted. The officials spotted the un-timed down in the middle of the field.

"Secondly, the field goal kicker was supposedly a sophomore who had played in a sophomore game and a junior varsity game earlier in the week. Players were only allowed (KSHSAA) to play in two games per week.

"The third and worst rule broken was they had 12 men on the field when the field goal was kicked and made which made the score Heights 9 and Rural 7. Washburn Rural player Tim Locke came running off the field yelling they had 12 on the field after the kick was made."

In 23 years they (Shawnee Heights) won two games counting the "theft."

In 1994 Heights earned their victory over Washburn Rural, they had a real good and a well-coached team. It just so happened that one of our former players, Matt Marple ('87) was coaching their offensive line. "They deserved to win that game," Bowen commented.

Before every Shawnee Heights game we all looked forward to the "theft" speech and the kids went out and took care of business every year but 1994.

In 1996 Rural routed Heights 30-9 and, yes, you can bet the pregame speech was about the "theft." And Snyder had 23 carries for 141 yards. It was his fifth game of 100 yards rushing and gave him 727 yards on the season with nine touchdowns.

Rural continued their offensive point explosions in the next two games beating Seaman 40-7 and Snyder had 24 carries with 180 yards and two touchdowns while helping the Junior Blues compile 350 total rushing yards. In the first district game Rural beat Topeka West 35-14 as Snyder put up 201 yards on 27 carries and two more touchdowns. The Rural defense was stingy allowing only 82 rushing yards. West managed to pass for 153 yards but Rural again had 305 total rushing yards.

The stumbling block came in week seven when Manhattan smacked Rural in the mouth 51-7. Cody Snyder, the 1,000-yard rusher sustained an ankle injury on the opening kickoff and was lost for the remainder of the game. This lopsided win put a real damper on the season and hopes for a playoff opportunity because Rural would need West to upset Manhattan and Rural to beat Junction City. The Junior Blues took care of what they could control and beat Junction 21-13, but their season ended with a solid record of 8-1.

In what would be Coach Ron Bowen's final season 1997 you would hope that there would be a story book ending with the seasoned coach having another shot at a state title, making the playoffs, having a glossy record and then ride off into the sunset towards the homestead and the farm. But this was no fairy tale. It was real-life. Real-life doesn't follow scripts. The Junior Blues ended the year 2-7. Even Shawnee Heights got a win over the Junior Blues and it was no theft. The two final wins came at the hands of Independence in the opener and against Seaman, a 31-14 final win for Coach Bowen. There was a six-point loss to Emporia in overtime, a one-point loss to Topeka West. But there would be no moral victories, just close calls which, with just a few breaks, could have been a four-game win season.

But in the long run it would be difficult to stain the distinguished football coaching career of one Ron Bowen. Rather than focusing on wins and chasing victories, Bowen always had a desire for his players to play well and compete. Chances are pretty good that if you stay in one high school in Kansas for 23 years and you have just four losing seasons and 19 winning seasons, with four state championship appearances, three state championships and make 10 playoff appearances, you can walk away and reflect on the successes associated with your leadership and feel pretty good about how things went.

It's a pretty nice feeling walking on the field each year knowing you had a chance to win a league title, make a playoff appearance and compete with some of the state's finest programs to culminate each season. Many high school coaches have had great careers without ever seeing a championship game. Not even had an opportunity to play in a championship game.

So maybe, just maybe, there are times now, on the tractor, as he discs his fields and gets ready to plant his seed, Coach probably replays a game or two or a dozen, or even a portion of a game and maybe he does things differently if he could. But for the most part the play calling was solid, the offense and defense were well-coached and the vast majority of athletes he had the opportunity to coach have grown into good men, solid contributors to their families and their communities. There lies the true measure of Coach Bowen's success. He always said he enjoyed his four years with each player, but he was much more interested in the next 40 years of their lives hoping they would develop into good men, respected men. And so many of them have.

STUDENT RECOLLECTIONS OF TEACHER/ COACH RON BOWEN

First let me say this is probably my favorite part of the book. Some of these stories and recollections from students, staff, former student-athletes and colleagues are their words. No prompting by me about what to write or share. In other words, there are some folks I contacted specifically asking if they would share stories about Coach. And there are those that came out of the blue, their own time, their own volition. These first three are unsolicited letters that were written to Coach.

Coach, no doubt, had a following of students who thought he was pretty special. They were not necessarily stars, nor were some even football players at all. These first three accounts are pretty special given those considerations. Special enough that Coach chose to share them with me and with you, as did the people who wrote them.

FROM FORMER STUDENT CARIE CROSBY MASSIE- "ML (COMMONLY KNOWN AS MARY LOU, RON'S WIFE,) AND COACH–

"As I sat at my school district's back-to school convocation (now a teacher) this year and listened to four senior students get up to talk about the difference their teachers, other educators, and school staff had made in their lives, I thought of you. As I sat yesterday at Chett's (a classmate who passed) funeral service and looked around at all my dear friends and felt pride for all that we all have become, I thought of you. I decided I couldn't let one more moment pass without telling you both the impact you have made in my life and others. Many conversations have been had and stories told about how you both helped to change opinions, behaviors, and the lives of the friends that I love, even in just the smallest of ways. I love that you have kept in touch with so many of your students and even those that were not your students from WRHS (Washburn Rural High School). Seeing you comment with such love and caring compassion on peoples' Facebook posts on a daily basis touches my heart. If only all teachers and students could see each other in this light and continued relationship after the short time frame of formal education. We see this from you and notice. We notice how much you care and pay attention to what happens in our lives and it matters. Thank you!

On an even more personal note, I want you, Coach, to know that you changed my life in high school. I'll never forget you and how you made me feel worthy of good things. You had a subtle, caring way of looking out for me that made me not want to disappoint you. I didn't have a father figure in my day-to day life, but when I would come to school and be around you, I knew that there was someone holding me accountable for who I really was and the person I wanted to become. And that day when I had to walk in front of all the student body and families as an elected Queen of Court candidate, and you brought your suit to work in case I needed an escort, I knew you were proud of me. This mattered! You mattered to me, and to all your students and players whether they realize it or not!

Thank you both for the teachers you were then and people you are now. You both are very special to so many!

Now, having said all this....... I hope you both are doing good as well as your family! My life is just as fun, crazy, stressful and wonderful as I could wish for it to be!"

Love ,

Carie

It's easy to see that it's the little, caring things and the consistent day-to day treatment of your students is what they remember. I especially like the Queen of Court assembly reference and Coach's willingness, without being asked, to wear a suit and escort her if needed. That's just one of many gestures of support from Coach Bowen. And he continues to be supportive of kids long after they have graduated. Weddings, honorary awards, funerals, etc. you may just find the Bowen's in attendance. It's a priority for them.

FROM ED BOZARTH WHO WAS TAUGHT BY MARY LOU BOWEN AND COACHED BY RON BOWEN IN 1960-61 AT CARBONDALE HIGH SCHOOL–

"Wonderful couple (the Bowens). They are what America stands for.

They are just a great team. They care about people. Always did, always have."

Bozarth and I discussed the small community and high school in Carbondale, Kansas. Bozarth said that the little school district didn't have a lot of money and resources, but he was very complimentary of three of the school board members at the time. According to Bozarth those three did their very best to get top-notch teachers in the tiny district. And he considers the Bowens as an example of those efforts.

Bozarth's brief experience with the Bowens as teacher and coach made a lasting impression on him. Many years later when Bozarth was a successful car dealership owner in Topeka he found a unique way to "thank the Bowens."

When first married Ron and Mary Lou owned a 1947 Ford Coupe. Ron referred to himself as a car man as he did what he could to customize the car. Many years later when Bowen was coaching in Topeka, he bought a 1948 Ford Coupe (same body style as the '47). Bozarth took their car and re-did it inside and out. And when asked about this gesture he wouldn't take much credit for it.

"That car was a gift on behalf of the thousands of students they helped in their careers," Bozarth stated. "That car was redone meticulously and put together with special order parts which represents the authentic nature of the Bowens. They are real people."

The parts were all made of steel, the fenders and floorboards, etc. Nothing on that car is fiberglass or aluminum.

As Bozarth and I talked, I mentioned how blessed Bowen and I and the rest of the coaching staff to have great kids to coach. Bozarth said, "There are differences in all high school coaches, but the majority have great kids to work with. And the differences between those coaches and Bowen was his focus and knowledge that he needed to play a significant role in developing those kids into, not only good athletes, but better people. And he was good at that. He not only won games he made sure kids he coached won in their lives later in life."- Ed Bozarth owner of the Topeka-Chevrolet dealership among others in the US.

One of the more interesting things I learned was when I interviewed former player Steve Russsell from Udall, 1960-1963. I knew what Coach Bowen had told me about his stint at Udall as their head coach. Basically it was during a transition for their football program. Because of the number of students in the school Udall was moving from six-man football to the traditional 11-man game when Russell became a high school freshman. The more I listened to Russell, the more I learned about him as a person and an athlete. Bowen took over at Udall when Russell was a junior. According to Russell he grew up on a farm. Russell said, "I would get up at 4:30 a.m. and milked cows and did my chores before school." Russell mentioned that he would finish football practice, "and return home to more chores."

I discovered that Russell was quite a talented athlete for a small town. He said, "I never left the field. I often times played several defensive positions and several offensive positions. Wherever Coach Bowen needed me. When I was a junior we were losing a game at halftime. We lost several games. But Coach Bowen told the team at halftime, 'I need someone at fullback who is tough and willing to carry the ball.'

Russell said he didn't offer, but out of the blue Bowen said, 'Russell, you'll play fullback this half.'

Russell said he told Coach Bowen, "Coach, I don't even know how to take a handoff. So, Coach told me which arm to have up if I go to the right and which one to have up if I go to the left." According to Russell he got 10 carries in the second half and gained about 150 yards.

"One big deal in Udall was our school band and FFA program going to the annual State Fair in Hutchinson, Kansas They would leave during the school day so Bowen told the team that he would hold football practice at 6 a.m. and told us all, you better be at practice, or you won't be playing in Friday's game. Well, five or six players missed practice, so we were short-handed. I played defensive end, but that night I played defensive line, some linebacker and some secondary too. He moved me where the need was."

When Russell graduated from high school he entertained several scholarship offers, even contemplated baseball scholarships. He eventually settled on Ark City, Kansas and the junior college located there then also ended up attending Northwestern Oklahoma. There he was an honorable mention All-American.

He still stays in touch with the Bowens and has attended many of Bowen's events over the years. He saw the second state championship in Manhattan, Kansas as Rural defeated Ark City. He was at Bowen's Shawnee County Hall of Fame induction in Topeka and he attended Ron and Mary Lou's 60th wedding anniversary celebration.

One of his fondest memories was when he was in college and Bowen rode to one of his college football games with his parents. "Him coming to my game impressed my parents and impressed me. He and Mary Lou are just good people. I enjoyed them a lot."- Steve Russell, Udall

FROM FRED CHANDLER 1973 AND 1974 VALLEY CENTER PLAYER–

"Coach, Congratulations on your selection into the Hall of Fame (at Valley). Your on the field record speaks for itself. But as important, I am so happy that for all the young lives you touched and helped mold, for all the awards and successes you have helped kids obtain, and for all of the great memories that people hold in their hearts, you are being recognized. I feel truly honored to have played for you. I honestly wish my boys could experience what I was lucky enough to experience. Congratulations again."

FROM LARRY "COWBOY" WIEZOREK (1976-1979) WASHBURN RURAL—

"I respected Ron Bowen and Ray Glaze. I wasn't much of a football player. Basically, I was a tackling dummy. It was just fun to be out there and play a little bit. I don't remember what Dick Patterson's role was at football, but it seemed like he was always out there. I respected all of them so much. Coach Bowen kept me out of so much trouble. He may have had a soft spot for me because I was just a farm boy. But Coach Bowen also would rough me up on occasions. One time he had me come at him to demonstrate how to avoid a blocker and he ended up throwing me aside pretty easily. He would take the "dip shits" like me and put us on special teams. I was like third string. I was little, but I was pretty fast. He found ways for me to see playing time."

"The man (Bowen) is really something to be admired. A great educator and a great leader. And someone to be admired. He kept me out of so much trouble. I was a leader in FFA and I got mad one time. They cancelled our FFA school assembly to have some Kansas City Royals come give an assembly. Me and another guy snuck off and I got one of my pigs and let it loose in the gym. Everyone, including the staff, knew I had done it so I was in trouble. Ron Bowen, Ray Glaze and maybe Don Schroeder (auto shop teacher) went to bat for me and went to Principal Dale Smeltzer and Dick Patterson, director of student affairs, and asked them to give me a break. Patterson came up with this plan. Rather than suspend me from school, he assigned me 10 hours of community/ school service. I was supposed to go to the student parking lot and pick up trash and clean-up the grounds around the building. I didn't much want to do it and I remember Ron Bowen saying, 'just do it; trust me on this.' So, I did it. Well, the thing they all knew and I didn't, was that I had already been named Kansas State Star Farmer of the year through FFA. If I had gotten suspended, I likely would not have been able to accept that award."

"Those guys, including Coach Bowen, cared enough and saw something in me that they felt like was worth saving. I will forever respect and admire those gentlemen."

"In fact I hadn't seen Coach Bowen for over 30 years and was back for Coach Glaze's memorial celebration. I went up to Coach Bowen and said, 'I'll bet you don't know who I am?' And Coach looked me directly in the eye and said, 'I know exactly who you are!' And I'll always remember that because I was certainly nothing special in football and he still remembered me." – Larry "Cowboy" Wiezorek

From former student David LaFond 1981-1984-Washburn Rural. Bowen referred to LaFond as the "motorcycle rider"-

"Boy, I don't know where to start.....

So, I was not the typical football player or three sport stud. I was a motocross racer and still am racing at age 55. I spent a lot of time with Coach Bowen in high school. I had him for three classes my senior year.

I loved busting my ass for that guy. He really motivated me to be a fierce competitor no matter what was in the way.

If it was a super shitty day he would say, 'Men, I have never seen a finer day.' That has stayed with me to this day. No matter what lies in front of you and no matter how hard it might be, get off your ass and go get after it.

I still love to do 'bear crawls' and 'up and downs.' Makes me smile and hurt at the same time.

Badminton battles against he and Glaze for our lunch cinnamon rolls were epic. Those two were pretty damn good.

Brisket ball in gym class and floor hockey with full body checks into the bleachers were awesome and he loved watching us battle.

I loved hanging out in that old nasty office of his and shooting the shit with him. I got hurt a lot racing motorcycles and always had a cast it seemed. I never missed gym class and he would let me participate no matter what. When I look back, he was a simple man that had an amazing work-ethic and it was not all about him it was about his KIDS. We need more Ron Bowens in this world.

Thank you, Coach Bowen, you are a legend." – former student David LaFond

FROM CHRIS TONER, FORMER WASHBURN RURAL FOOTBALL PLAYER (1980-1983), AND OFFICER IN THE MILITARY–

"Coach Bowen,

I wanted to thank you for taking the time to attend the Hall of Fame (for WR High School) induction ceremony. It meant the world to me that you were there to share this experience with me and to finally get an opportunity to thank you for being such a prominent role model.

Trust me when I say that your example played a huge part in my development as a leader in our Army and I owe much to you for that. The helmet (WR football helmet) is resting well in a high spot in our home – fond memories of teamwork, character, commitment, and friendship.

Very Respectfully,

Chris

I too had the privilege of knowing many of these former students. I met Chris Toner in eighth grade. He was a student who worked hard for what he got and was an undersized lineman and linebacker who worked equally hard to earn his playing time on the football field. He was tough. And when he said something, he carried it out and followed through, made good on what he'd say would occur. He had some innate leadership qualities, but educators and coaches like Ron Bowen and many others fostered and supported these qualities of leadership and Chris Toner became a very integral part of our armed forces. His leadership in Afghanistan was critical and heroic.

FROM FORMER WASHBURN RURAL STUDENT-ATHLETE TODD SCOTT - 1985-1988 AND HALL OF FAMER at FORT SCOTT JUNIOR COLLEGE AND ALSO PLAYED FOOTBALL AND GRADUATED FROM SOUTHWEST TEXAS STATE (NOW TEXAS STATE)–

"My first memories of Washburn Rural football were in the late 70's and early 80's. I remember watching Crow, Hughes, Yarnell, Filburn, Tantillo, Hamilton, Golden, Edson, Bleidissel and many others as an elementary and middle school student. I will never forget how excited I was to get #10 in flag football in 5th grade. Kevin Crow was my favorite player who also happened to date my sister. Unfortunately, I spent most of my time behind the bleachers at home games playing football with all my buddies. One memory on the football field that I will never forget is watching John Hughes throw a pass to Bob Steele to beat Emporia. Great game!!"

Going into the 1986 Season –

"We won the State Championship in 1986 because the 1985 team set the bar for us and we wanted to follow in the footsteps. We looked up to the 1985 seniors. They had tremendous talent and there is an obvious reason that most of the 1986 team watched the 1985 team from the sidelines. I think both teams had a great respect for the teammates that lined up next to them. We knew all our high school coaches before we were even enrolled in high school and always had tremendous respect for them. We did not want to let them down. Thankfully, we had a lot more wins than losses over the years."

My 1986 Season –

"We had a couple losses early in the season, but it was Bowen's Angels that set the foundation for the final championship run. We had to come together as a team and that moment will never be forgotten. Along the way to the championship, we had a torrential downpour in DeSoto. We had a "we don't like Rural" on TV the night before the district championship game against Shawnee Heights. The 20-degree game at KC Sumner in the Quarterfinals and then Semi Final at McElroy Field against Pittsburg was rocking. We were down at halftime and then we kicked it in during the 2nd half and we were on our way to the State Championship. I will never forget watching the video of all the students and parents rushing down to the field in the final seconds of the game. The State Championship was a beautiful day for late November. Much better than the ice storm against Kapaun the year before. Let's just say that we were well prepared and Coach Glaze had a big part of it. I am not sure they used the term swagger in November of 1986, but we had it. I remember seeing Ark City getting off the bus and they looked huge. When the game started, there was no doubt that speed was going to win that game."

"Coach Bowen was the ultimate father figure in all our lives. We never wanted to let him down in anything that we did, on or off the field. I remember a few talks with him when I was getting a bit off track. He would just have that look on his face and you knew that you messed up. He never had to say much. We knew. I hurt my shoulder the first game my senior year and he taped it up for me every practice and game for the reminder of the season. Looking back, I am not sure that I needed to be taped up by the middle of the season. I think it was a little bit of superstition and a lot more of me wanting to hang out with Coach Bowen before we went to the field each day."

"Many of the things we learned from our high school football coaches have defined who we are today. When we see each other, it is like we are 17 years old again. Loyalty and teamwork are traits that last a lifetime. We don't get to see our teammates as much as we would like to. One thing is for certain, if it is an event that our teammates are going to attend, two of the first people we see are Ron and Mary Lou Bowen."

"I coached youth football for 7 years and I am positive that our team was the only team in the league running the Slot-I all 7 years. We knew that if we ran the 255 Sweep play enough that the 120 Trap was going for a touchdown. We also knew our 5-2 Monster would shut down the run. Everything we did each week looked like a Washburn Rural practice schedule. I am sure that many of my teammates did the same thing in their youth programs. The apple does not fall far from the tree."

FROM FORMER WASHBURN RURAL STUDENT AND FOOTBALL PLAYER CHRIS WALKER (1985-1988) WHO PLAYED AT FORT SCOTT JUNIOR COLLEGE AND BAKER UNIVERSITY IN BALDWIN CITY, KANSAS–

"Coach Bowen is the ultimate father figure. He gives respect and trust and receives it back ten-fold. The leadership that Coach Bowen showed had a trickle-down effect. His assistant coaches followed his lead with ease and professionalism. His players understood with ease what being a leader was because they saw it every day. Coach Bowen expected discipline and teamwork and received it naturally from coaches and players. I truly believe that Coach Bowen developed leaders through these expectations, leaders who are more prepared for the trials and tribulations associated with the real world. I consider it a blessing to be able to play in this system under all of these powerfully influential individuals and cannot than them all enough. I love Coach Bowen for who he is and how he helped develop me."-Chris Walker 1985-1988 Washburn Rural alum played on two state champions

When you teach and coach young student-athletes you set out to attempt to impact their lives in positive ways. However, you don't set out to potentially be a factor in whether they live or they die. But that choice was faced by one of Ron Bowen's athletes in a remote part of Africa.

As a high school student Brad Elder was a 230-pound lineman for the Junior Blues (1983-1986) during their 1985 state championship season. Elder was a football player who also wrestled and enjoyed his sports. Probably what he enjoyed more was his love for biology and all things life science related. And this is the incredible story he told me.

Between his junior and senior year in college he decided to travel to Africa. After landing in Kenya, he decided to conserve his money and hitchhike south, eventually he was planning to join up with Jane Goodall, noted primatologist most known for her study of wild chimpanzees in Rwanda.

Tourists rarely cross paths with poachers. But Elder was not a normal tourist. He was backpacking and hitchhiking to save what money he had. Shortly before young Elder landed in Africa for his adventure, there was a crackdown on poachers in Africa poaching ivory. This put a strain on the poachers' income and a few turned their sights on robbing tourists. Shortly before Elder began his southward journey there was a young woman from Britain who was found dead in the vast savanna on an isolated two track path near her Range Rover. At the time there was speculation she may have had car problems and that lions killed her while she was stranded. It was discovered later that she was confronted by poachers, robbed and killed and left for the animals to disassemble. Elder and his group encountered the same group of poachers she did.

Poachers were out of jobs, but they didn't leave the African wild. So as Elder and three others began their trek in the four-wheel drive van, they unfortunately suffered mechanical problems. They had to illegally cross into some territories they were not supposed to be in to get a part. Unwisely they chose to sneak across the border from Tanzania back north into Kenya and inside the parks. Late in the afternoon, the group entered the strip of no man's land about 40 miles wide between the two countries. Their crossing was a remote, rarely used two track jeep-trail. As their trip resumed on the narrow road, there were steep ditches on both sides and a single poacher stepped out on the roadway, rifle in hand. The van stopped and was surrounded by other poachers. They opened the driver's door and attacked the driver with a machete. They opened the passenger's door and attacked him also. Elder was sitting in the back seat behind the passenger's seat with a female cousin of one of the two men in the front seats. The passenger was smacked with a machete as well. While the injuries were serious, both men survived.

The poachers were attempting to get in the van's sliding door but were not familiar with how this particular door opened and they became agitated. Trapped and scared Elder and the woman decided they better open the van door and try and talk their way out of the situation because they were unable to escape. The woman opened the door and was punched in the face. Then Elder was struck with a machete, thinking his arm may have been severed, but he was struck with the blunt end of the machete and had a deep contusion.

After getting three of the passengers from the van the poachers took money, shoes, and other items from them and then made them walk a couple miles into the brush. It was here the poachers went through the rest of the tourist's gear. From a high spot the poachers could see the van and see for miles the narrow roadway the vehicle was parked upon. It was also Elder's premise that they walked them this far from their vehicle so that, if they chose to leave them in the wild, it would be extremely difficult, if not impossible for them to make it back to their van too quickly if they made it at all. This would allow the poachers ample time to disappear back in the savanna and avoid the rangers.

The thorns and ground left the skin on their feet cut up resembling hamburger. Dense thornbush country is avoided even by lions as the trees and shrubs shed thorn laden branches. After two miles of walking barefoot through this everyone in Elder's party were leaving bloody footprints in the tall, dry grass. Away from the roadway and the van the poachers began to argue amongst each other. The leader, who spoke some English, was trying to talk the other members out of killing the tourists because he felt the authorities would pin the other murder (the British woman tourist) on them as well as this murder if they killed Elder and his partners. After a loud argument amongst the poachers which involved them shoving guns and pointing guns at each other, the poachers decided that they would not kill the travelers instead they let them go one at a time separated by about 10 minutes. It was pitch black darkness by this time so it was almost impossible to see anything as each were let go and made their own attempt to get to their van.

On the equator, the sun sets fast and before Elder made it down off the bluff, which was the stopping point, it was pitch black. It was intensified darkness because of the low cloud cover combined with NO lights withing one-hundred miles. Elder was the last one to be let go and, as he tried to navigate the steep ledges and shelves on the bluff Elder fell down a ledge and the poachers left him, presuming he was injured or possibly died.

Eventually after an excruciating long interval Elder was able to scramble up an incline barefoot, cut and bleeding. He manages to get up on top of the ridge and had enough energy to roll over onto his back. While he is exhausted, bleeding he lays on his back and starts to curse the powers to be asking "why me? What did I ever do to deserve this?" It had been over four hours since this ordeal started and he was bleeding badly from his feet. Every step was becoming a battle and his adrenalin had worn off and the pain was real and intense. He remembers thinking that the only control he had left was to just stop and stay put. He had given up by this point. Every move forward to this point was met with a real challenge that left him bloodier and defeated. He remembers thinking, in his exhaustive state, that just lying there and accepting his fate was okay. At least he knew how he was going to get past this point in his journey.

He was so exhausted and beaten he was not thinking logically about all the animals in the savanna that would eat him. So, he just laid there on his back defeated.

It was at this time he was looking into the darkness and the most real image of a man standing over him occurred. Elder says it was clearly Coach Bowen and he could hear his voice. He compared the experience to the one he had in football when an upperclassman knocked the air out of him and Bowen stood over him and said just as he thought he was saying now, "Pachyderm (which is what he called the big linemen) you gotta get up!" Elder was convinced Bowen was there with him. He also looked to his side, again into the darkness, and said he clearly saw the image of Coach Ray Glaze seated in his chair at the edge of the wrestling mat and he had his arms folded, wasn't saying a word, just shaking his head. Like he did with wrestlers when he wanted to convey this message to them- "you got yourself into this predicament, how are you going to get out of it?"

It was a pivotal point in the ordeal for Elder because he did get up, somehow managed to reunite with the other male from his group. They blindly walked their way back toward where they felt the roadway was, encountering thorn trees, swamp, and all the African wild can throw at you. They were nearly accosted and eaten by hyenas but a combination of singing and a sudden rainfall dissuaded the hyenas and after what Elder estimates was two additional hours finally found the rangers who almost shot them because they thought they might be setting them up for an ambush. They convinced them they were not poachers and were taken back safely, battered, bruised and cut to the safety of a lodge.

It was until the next day when Elder decided to write down the details of his ordeal that he recalled seeing Coach Bowen and Coach Glaze. It was a shock to him because the visions were so real at the time. But he also recollected the blue skies over Bowen's shoulder and the bleachers with wrestling fans in them when he "saw" Glaze. It was a stark revelation realizing the two men were not out in the savanna with him, but simply an aberration.

As of 2021 Brad Elder, Ph. D. Professor of Biology remains committed to causes in Africa and has returned to the wild. He has been an instructor at Doane University in Nebraska.

Elder adds, "I have been teaching for more than 30 years now and I see the impact of teachers and coaches all the time in my college students. The words, 'I have never seen a finer day' is a mindset that focuses me all the time." – Dr. Brad Elder 1986 Washburn Rural graduate and student-athlete.

Often, in sports, it more about the student-athlete that needed you more than your team needed them. And that's to go along with my saying, "It's not about what they will do for us, it's about what football will do for them." Here's a story about a young man who was at a crossroads his senior year and felt he had a big decision to make. Tony was a student aid for me and you'd be hard pressed to find a nicer young man. But Tony had the good fortune or the misfortune depending on your perspective to play behind some very talented athletes. That can cause an individual who hasn't fully developed yet to yearn for playing time.

FROM FORMER WASHBURN RURAL STUDENT AND FOOTBALL PLAYER TONY BURKS (1985-1988) WHO PLAYED FOOTBALL AT FORT SCOTT JUNIOR COLLEGE AND AT MORNINGSIDE COLLEGE–

"Coach,

I haven't seen you guys for a while. Which is good I guess, since we were meeting at so many funerals. For the longest time I have wanted to send you a short thank you. I'm sure you and Mary Lou already know how you have positively touched SO many lives. I want to thank you for touching mine. I doubt you remember a particular defining moment in my life. Wit so many students and players I am always impressed how you can even remember so many names. I don't even remember all of my teachers.

I certainly remember Coach Bowen and the day I tried to quit football. I've never been one for bluffing or doing things for attention so when I met with you in your office back in 1987 I had decided that I was quitting the team. You had taught me to be a man and I would only do it face to face. (I'm writing this letter because I would never be able to get this out without getting overly emotional.). It wasn't something I wanted to do but I felt it was the right decision. I don't remember all of the reasons, but I know I felt I wasn't contributing and perhaps I was wasting my time as well as yours, and taking up space that someone else should have.

You talked me out of it. Thank You. You somehow convinced college coaches to take a look at me. Thank You. When I went to junior college, I took the work ethic instilled at Washburn Rural and I out worked other more talented kids to secure my spot on the team. I earned a starting position and eventually a full scholarship at a four-year college (Morningside College). I fully believe it was the integrity and work ethic instilled in me (perhaps ran into me or bear crawled into me) at Washburn Rural.

I'll never forget that day in your office as it was a major for in the road of my life. I am glad you were there to keep me on the better path. I believe without a doubt, that path has led me to be a better man, husband, and father. I look at every day as the best day yet because, well, you know, "I've never seen a finer day."

I think of that day often and simply wanted you to know how much of my respect you have. Happy 2016. I hope it is filled with very fine days."

-Tony Burks WRHS 1985-1988

FROM FORMER WASHBURN RURAL STUDENT AND FOOTBALL PLAYER MARK LONGHOFER (1989-1993)–

Coach Bowen had the privilege of playing in four state championship games. And, although the Junior Blues won the first three, they lost a heartbreaker in 1992 ending up a few yards short at the hands of Lawrence. The quarterback for that group, Mark Longhofer had this to say about Coach Bowen.

"There are people throughout one's life that leave lasting impressions. Coach Bowen is one of those individuals. To me he was more than just a coach. He was a mentor. A mentor who taught me so many lessons about toughness, dedication, commitment, hard work and resilience. I never wanted to let him down. And while I felt like I let him down after falling short in the state title game, he helped me realize that couldn't be farther from the truth." – Mark Longhofer (1991-1993)

FROM AN OPPOSING CENTENNIAL LEAGUE COACH, DALE SAMPLE WHO WROTE THIS LETTER IN SUPPORT OF RON BOWEN'S NOMINATION FOR THE KSHSAA HALL OF FAME IN 2007–

Sample was a long-time coach at Topeka-Seaman High School and had great rivalry games against Ron Bowen and Washburn Rural. There was much respect between both men.

"I am writing this letter in support of Mr. Ron Bowen for induction to the Kansas State High School Hall of Fame. I coached football against Ron for eight years while at Seaman High from 1983-1990. Washburn Rural had some great teams during that period of time and we had a few great battles. HE was not only an excellent strategist and technician at coaching his players, he was a true gentleman. I remember several conversations outside the football season about offense, defense, special teams and player. Ron, along with his right-hand man, Ray Glaze, was more than willing to share ideas and strategy without hesitation. They knew that x's and o's were not what made an offense of defense work. The keys were execution and adjustments and there was no coach any better in that period of time than Ron Bowen.

Coach Bowen was a great model for young men. His personality and demeanor allowed for students, staff and other coaches to approach him without feeling invasive. Players knew when it was time to joke and when it was time to get serious. Ron made sure of that. He taught more than football. He taught life lessons and his players knew the most important lesson was 'do the right thing'. It is without hesitation or reservation that I recommend Ron Bowen for this honor. He would be a great representative for KSHSAA."- Dale Sample

FROM A COLLECTIVE GROUP OF WASHBURN RURAL ALUMNI PUT THESE WORDS TOGETHER–

"When we learned that Ron Bowen had been nominated for the Kansas State High School Activities Association Hall of Fame, we felt both privileged and honored to contribute to his nomination. Everyone has someone in their lives that leaves a lasting impression; someone that forever impacts their character. Ron Bowen is that person for us.

What may be surprising is the way in which he made an impact on our lives. His record on the football field stands for itself, but the tings that had the deepest impact had nothing to do with success on the gridiron. What we learned from him didn't come from an inspiring halftime speech, a dramatic second-half comeback, or even from winning multiple state championships. He taught us that it was the simple things – hard work, preparation, discipline, teamwork, sound fundamentals, positive attitudes, and strong ethics- that would make us champions in both football and life.

There was a saying Coach Bowen used almost daily – whether at the start of a class, practice or right before a game: 'Never seen a finer day.' We remember hearing this comment the most on days that always looked to bring the toughest challenge..... (two-a days at 6:00 AM or in 100-degree weather). And it never failed that we'd hear that comment just as we'd sit to stretch in the rain-soaked grass or the ice-cold snow. What we didn't realize at the time was that the comment that made us roll our eyes would become a driving force through the great times in our lives, and also motivates us through many challenging times long after out playing days were over. 'Never seen a finer day' has been used in several ways by former players; as a screen saver on a computer at work, taped to a bathroom mirror or a car visor, etc. One former player, who competed in bull riding, even had the quote etched into the belt buckle he wore when he rode.

While reliving our glory days one night, we all came to realize that the saying that became the theme to our 1985 championship season had a much deeper meaning, almost 'spiritual' as one of us described it. 'Never seen a finer day' represents the opportunity that each of us has to better ourselves every day, to appreciate that we're alive and that we have choice to take life's challenges head-on and choose what to make of them. It's truly amazing how a saying that simple can start the day on the right foot or change a perspective on a situation, especially during the trying times.

Needless to say, Coach Bowen was a person who always led by example. Some of us were fortunate enough to go on to play at the college rank and experienced many different coaches and coaching styles. We always knew that we had a great high school experience, but we didn't know how good we had it until we experienced other styles. Coach Bowen and his staff earned respect from the players, and also expected that the players respected one another. Although he could get excited from time to time, we never once heard him rant and rave or belittle a player in a manner that some witnessed in the college ranks, on other high school teams or on some of the TV shows highlighting high school programs today. He always handled the challenges, including challenging players, with a calm, cool demeanor. Situations were often settled with a direct glance, a simple comment or gesture – typically his cupped, open-hands out in front of his body which, in WRHS sign language meant that the player was to 'bear crawl' until he remembered what he was supposed to be doing. But it never took much, because of the respect he had from each of us. In short, he taught us through example that character isn't something that you talk about, it's something that you do. And respect isn't something that you demand, it's something that you earn.

We could go on and on about the stories of how Coach Bowen led by the examples of hard work and preparation. Everything from how we couldn't complain about early morning practices because we all knew that he had to drive an hour to get to school to how he delivered a load of grain in the morning prior to our team bus pulling off to play in the state championship game in Manhattan, Kansas. Whatever the task, Coach Bowen always asked us to give 100% effort, and then, just when we thought there was nothing left to give, asked us to give just a little bit more. Not only does that translate to success on the field, but to success in life where it often takes extra effort for success in a marriage or a career. While each student athlete's story might be different, the theme would be the same.

In closing, we'll share one last lesson. Coach Bowen always taught us that 'luck happens when preparation and opportunity meet.' Many of us have been very lucky and successful in life, no doubt due in part to the foundation that Coach helped to build. Ron Bowen has dedicated his life to preparing others for success. In our humble opinion, the KSHSAA is 'lucky' for the opportunity to have Ron Bowen nominated for its Hall of Fame." Sincerely, WRHS Football Alumni

It's also been said by many that Ron Bowen paid attention to ALL his students. He had expectations for all students and regardless of whether they were a football player or simply a student who was simply a young adult who was struggling to find their way, Bowen cared about their development. He cared about the person they were and were yet to become.

There was a set of twins at Washburn Rural and they earned the reputation of being a bit ornery and, on occasions a little resistant to authority. Jessie and Frank Robinson were much more interested in working with livestock or, as is the case now, working with concrete.

By Jessie's own admission, "My brother and I were a little on the ornery side. My brother always pushed things a little farther than I ever did and one day he talked back to Coach Bowen. We were freshman and....... well, you should talk to Frank about the particulars. I always respected Ron Bowen. Just respected him."

As Jessie recounts the story his brother swore at Coach Bowen during a PE class one day. Bowen knew that, if he took Frank to the office, he would surely be suspended. So, instead he gave Frank a rather large number of up-and downs to do. And after he completed them, he was welcome back to the class activities. I'm certain with the agreement that it would NEVER happen again. Frank respected Coach Bowen as well. It grew immeasurably after that incident.

FROM A FELLOW EDUCATOR WHO KNEW RON BOWEN VERY WELL. HE SERVED AS HIS ASSISTANT, HIS ATHLETIC DIRECTOR AND HIS PRINCIPAL WHILE BOWEN COACHED AND TAUGHT AT WASHBURN RURAL. BILL EDWARDS HAD THESE WORDS TO SHARE ABOUT COACH–

"I was fortunate to work with Ron Bowen for almost twenty years, in my roles as an assistant coach, AD, and school administrator. Ron was as consistent as a teacher and coach as you could ever wish. He believed in keeping things simple, teaching kids to both do things right and do the right things. He believed that all actions have consequences, most were good – but some not so good, and we all have to accept consequences. Ron constantly drilled into his charges that life is full of challenges. How each one responded to those challenges is the measure of who each one is as a person. True character shows up during times of adversity, and Ron believed our jobs as educators, teachers and coaches, was to prepare our kids for those difficult times. And kids – whether in the classroom, gym or field – LOVED Coach Bowen for who he is as a man"- Bill Edwards long-time Washburn Rural High School educator and in the school's Hall of Fame as a staff member.

Another athletic director that worked with Coach Bowen was Bob Gladfelter. Gladfelter also served as an assistant football coach prior to becoming the school's athletic director and he is a member of the state's tennis hall of fame as a coach.

BOB GLADFELTER HAD THIS TO SAY ABOUT COACH RON BOWEN–

"I had the privilege of knowing Mr. Bowen from being an assistant football coach and fellow teacher. He cared for all of his players and students and was always honest and direct with them. When asked how things were going, he would respond, "I've never seen a better day." I, for one, have never met a better man."

This from a parent, former school board member, Jeff Russell, who in 1989 was co-chair with is wife, Connie of the Washburn Rural High School Booster Club-

Russell remembers that before the 1989 state 5A championship game at Kansas University, he secretly had a few celebratory hats screen printed. Once the final gun sounded and the Junior Blues had defeated Salina Central in a very close, hard fought contest, Russell took it upon himself to find Coach Bowen and placed one of the hats on his head. The hats indicated 1989 5A State Champions on them.

Russell remembers more about the moment than just the hat. He recollected that Bowen looked at the hat, adjusted it and put it back on his head. When a reporter from the Capital-Journal found him for the post-game interview, Bowen apologized. He told the reporter, "I'm sorry, I didn't know anything about these; these were printed up by our Booster Club.

Russell told me that he viewed Bowen's actions to be ones of class and sportsmanship. In a celebratory moments after his team completed an undefeated, state championship season, he didn't want anyone to feel like he had anything to do with making them in advance and, more importantly, he chose to exercise humility for the Salina Central coaching staff, players and fans. He chose to think about good sportsmanship, and Russell said it would forever affirm what he already knew. Coach Ron Bowen was not one to brag, nor rub it in his opponent's noses. He had that much dignity. Always.

– Jeff Russell

THIS FROM LONGTIME FOOTBALL ASSISTANT (18 YEARS) AND RETIRED AUBURN-WASHBURN EDUCATOR SAM AUSTIN–

"I'll never forget receiving a letter From Ron Bowen in 1979 congratulating me on my undefeated freshman season at Jay Shideler Jr. High. I remember how it made me feel that the Washburn Rural High School head coach was taking the time to write a letter to me. That same year, Coach Bowen asked me if I would like to join his staff, little did I know it would be coaching with him for the next 18 years. I remember thanking Coach for the nice letter and told him it was easy to be successful with the talent that I had. He looked at me and in that gravely distinctive voice said, "yep but you gotta line 'em up in the right positions!"

I think that was one of the keys to Coach Bowen's success, he would put kids in the right position for their success and the team's success, if you had athletic ability, Coach was going to find a spot for you. Probably the best example of this was in 1985 with a kid named Tony Winslow, I used to call him Tony "Heisman" because he would always flash the Heisman pose to me. Tony was a good runningback but the problem was we had someone just a little better. Bowen approached Tony and said, "how would you like to touch the ball every play? Tony said, "anything for the team coach!" Bowen said, "Good, I'd like to try you at center". Though I joke about that, Ron didn't just tell a kid to go with a coach and try a new position, he sat the kid down and explained the importance of the move and how it was about "Team".

As an assistant coach you always felt important. Ron was a good listener and if he didn't like your suggestion, he would take the time to explain why. I never heard Ron Bowen ever get on a coach, he had a lot of respect for his assistants. Though there was the time I was standing on the sidelines and Coach Ray Glaze said something to the referee and then hid behind me. The official turned and threw the flag at my feet, the only thing Coach Bowen said was, "Sam we don't need that right now". I turned around and Coach Glaze had his hand over his mouth laughing. I was just glad the 15-yard penalty didn't cost us the game.

Ron Bowen was a class act. I remember telling him that I noticed he never cussed. He said, "tell me one good thing that would come from that?" Honestly, I couldn't think of one. Ron was always teaching, not only football but about life and making good decisions. I honestly believe that Coach Bowen would have given up all his victory's if it meant that every kid he touched would grow up to be a good husband, father, grandfather and outstanding member in the community.

When Coach Bowen asked me to introduce him for his induction into the Kansas Sports Hall of Fame, I was truly honored. It would be such a great opportunity for me to pay tribute to the man who taught me so much about the game and about life in general. After all, he had provided me with the best 18 years of my 35-year career in education."- Sam Austin assistant coach at Washburn Rural High School

BOWEN'S FAMILY HAD PLENTY OF STORIES–

Ron Bowen is a proud husband, father, grandfather and great-grandfather. If you have any doubts about his relationship with his family, mess with one of them. You'll find out that the mild mannered, good natured teacher/ coach and farmer can turn into a cantankerous cuss if pushed that direction.

He had a gleam in his eye whenever he talks about any of his kids. And they have blessed he and Mary Lou with grands and great grands. When they all get together, it's like a small regiment.

RECOLLECTIONS FROM OLDEST AND ONLY SON DAMON BOWEN–

The Bowen's oldest is also their only son, Damon. Damon was a wrestler and a football player at Effingham High School. One tough aspect of your father being a high school football coach, he's at work on his job while you are playing your Friday night games if you're not in the same school. During his junior football season, Damon suffered a very serious knee injury in the preseason scrimmage. He came back from it to eventually play some games as a junior and then played his senior season as well. Mary Lou made a special padding for his leg brace that allowed him to wrestle those two years.

Now, at the age of 57, Damon and his father are enjoying a different kind of relationship and plenty of time together. Damon helps his father with his farm chores. In fact, Damon said that he jokes with his dad about becoming his personal Uber driver and even came up with the fictitious name of "Two Dogs Uber Service" (there's a story behind that one that we'll just leave between the two Bowen men.) Damon calls it the uber service because, "In the winter we feed a lot of hay to the cattle. We are in and out of a lot of gates. Dad drives and I get the gates and cut the wrap off the bales."

Damon started his "farming career" at an early age in 1973 when the Bowen's first started working the current farm. Still residents and teachers at Valley Center for a couple more years, the two Bowen's, Damon just a young boy, would spend the summers farming on what now is the homestead. Since they weren't living on the farm, they stayed at Mary Lou's parents, Damon's grandparents, nearby and lived in their basement.

Damon recollects that his dad started calling his mother-in law "Granny" which Damon says, "she wasn't too crazy about that name at first." Later, when he and his sisters moved closer to Mary Lou's folks, he and his three sisters started calling her Granny. "I now have the honor of living in Granny's home and I miss her terribly still."

When you are the oldest you remember a lot of "firsts." You remember the first summers on the farm and the fun of living with your Granny. He also remembers the first bull that they raised from a calf. When the calf was born, "it was so big the heifer was having trouble having him so we got the neighbor to come help pull the calf.'

Damon recollects the size of the calf being huge. The neighbor who helped them pull it was Rich Gilkison, "so we named the calf 'Richie.' We raised him and used him as a herd bull and then dad called him 'Father Richard.'"

When you don't have livestock on your farm yet, you still have a valuable resource, so haying season became an essential part of the farm cycle. "When the folks first bought the farm," Damon recollects, "we didn't have any cattle so all the hay was put in square bales and sold in the winter. I wasn't big enough yet to be much help (with lifting bales) but I could steer the tractor while dad did all the loading and stacking on the trailer. At the barn dad would put the bales on the elevator and I was in the barn. When the bales piled up, I would bang on the elevator with a piece of pipe and dad would climb up in the hay loft and stack the bales. We put up somewhere near 3,000 bales a summer."

And as time went on, as boys do, Damon started to grow into a young adult. "When I eventually got older and bigger, we would pull wagons behind the baler and stack hay right out of the baler on the wagons. Dad and I took turns driving baler and being the loader and stacker."

As time went on and three girls were added to the mix, each one became capable of helping with this process. Damon remembers, "As the girls got older and helped with the driving and unloading onto the elevator."

Damon says his father, "finally came around to the concept of big round bales of hay." He goes on to add, "He was dead set against them at first, but then his help grew up." When you lose your "farmhands" you have got to make adjustments.

I asked about some early recollections pertaining to farm chores for the kids. And there was plenty to do and some of it labor intense. "The only livestock waterer was an antique hand pump with an electric pump jack added. But there was not any water near the barns where we needed it." Being a farmer requires you to be resourceful and Damon says, "Dad brought home eight pigs. We carried water from the bathtub to the barn in buckets, but not just ordinary five-gallon buckets. Dad brought home seven- gallon metal buckets from the Washburn Rural concession stand." These metal buckets were what the popcorn oil came in and they were heavy when full of water you had to carry for a distance.

Eventually Bowen came up with a closer watering source. Damon says, "Dad decided to put an electric well pump in to replace the old hand pump. So, we started digging by hand a well pit next to the well. The hole was probably 10 foot long and six foot wide. Probably about six foot deep." Here's where Damon's orneriness showed up. "At some point during the digging process I got the idea to throw water on dad while he was in the hole digging. He came up out of that hole and wrestled me down and rubbed my face in some nearby horse manure. I guess on a hot summer day getting soaked with cold water wasn't my best idea!"

One thing for certain is Damon has always been the one to liven up the chores, life in general. He has an affinity for humor and likes to have a good time even when the farm chores are hard. Some of his siblings, maybe even his folks, might refer to him affectionately, the instigator or the agitator. I think that quality we might just share. When I heard these stories and told Damon I was a little like him, not always using my "filters." His comment to me was, "Filters take all the fun out of life!"

ONE OF RON'S DAUGHTERS, M'LISSA SENT ME THE FOLLOWING IN 2021 WHEN I ASKED FOR SOME MEMORIES OF HER DAD AND FAMILY LIFE GROWING UP A BOWEN. M'LISSA BOWEN HALL–

"I think a lot of people only see that dad has a hard exterior, but he can be a softie. He's sentimental and he is caring, loving and loyal. He will stand up for, and defend you, even if you screw up.

I have many memories of spending time with dad, especially when he was young (before the other brats came along). Fishing, camping and hanging out at school with him – in the wood shop, riding in the drivers ed car and later at Washburn Rural in the gym when I had a day off from school. I always felt lucky if I got to ride home with him after a Friday night game. One of those nights a deer ran out into the road and dad yelled, 'duck!' Who knows if I ducked because I just remember thinking that it was a duck.

My favorite memory was recently brought to mind when my sister posted a particular picture online. When I was starting kindergarten, my baby sister had just been born. I'm not sure if they were home or still in the hospital, but dad was enlisted (or volunteered) to take me shopping for school clothes. I remember going to the store (I think it was Sears in Wichita) and picking out two dresses. I have pictures of them. I wore my favorite of the two for my school picture, but my favorite part was shopping with dad.

Hogs. Hog shit. We had hogs for a long time. Some were 4H projects. The farrowing creates had slatted floors so the waste would fall through below to be cleaned out. Not so bad unless you waited too long. I think there's a picture of me standing in liquefied crap. And don't forget the magots.

I even got to do some castrating. Moving hogs was quite a treat (not). Dad would be hollering to go that way, no, that way, no this way! I never could move fast enough in the right direction.

Summertime brought a variety of chores- gardening, haying, etc. One year, there was more velvetleaf than soybean plants. Dad made each of us girls (3 then) our own 'bean hook.' I don't remember how many mornings we went out to cut weeds before heading to swimming lessons, but I don't think we ever finished the field.

Football is life. I know this was true for dad, but I always felt that too. It was for the first 32-years of my life. As a little kid I always wanted to play football, but I had to settle for being a peewee cheerleader. I think I had more interest in dad's teams than in my own school and even considered transferring schools.

Mealtime was special, not only because we were together, but because of the stories. I always felt like I knew those people, most I never met. I know that dad played an important part in the lives of so many students. I suppose someone could be resentful of the time he spent with other kids, but I looked at it as sharing him with them. I was happy and proud to do it.

So, yes, football is life and when dad retired, as strange as it may sound, I felt like a significant part of my life had come to an end."

ANOTHER DAUGHTER, ANDREA BOWEN FINZEN HAD THESE RECOLLECTIONS OF HER FATHER–

"Dad was, for the most part, a quiet man. He usually didn't talk much that I remember growing up. When he did, you better darn well listen.

Although I knew about the oldest sibling, mom and dad's firstborn, Cindy Lou, who only lived six hours after she was born. I couldn't understand why important things couldn't happen on that certain date in September. I remember when my brother was going to get married and there was discussion about a certain date in September. Dad was adamant that it would not be that date. In fact nothing important could ever be held on that date. That date was taken- September 22, 1962. My mom has always said it rocked my dad tremendously. He had to make funeral arrangements and pick out a tiny little casket. I couldn't exactly understand it when I was young, but you better believe I do now.

My dad has always been a very private person. He obviously suffered each year, even after having four more kids. I don't think a person ever gets over such a loss, especially when it should never have happened. Mom said when Heather was born she looked a lot like Cindy. Probably why she's the youngest and spoiled. It's a family joke, but Heather admits it's true! I mean seriously, Heather is the only one he relented and bought a 'Hay burner' (horse) for. My dad would be holding his watch up in the air by now and saying, 'it's getting deep in here' and shaking his head and laughing.

One summer dad and I had a bass fishing contest at our pond. I beat him, although I'm fairly certain he let me. There wasn't always much time for fun in the summer because of the farm work. Heather and I did get to go to Wichita a few times when he had coaching conferences. It was a big deal because we got to stay in a hotel with a pool.

I remember standing by dad at a gate while he was looking at cattle. I don't remember what we were talking about, but he always called me 'Big Brown Cow Eyes' and I would tell him I don't have cow eyes. As I got older, he called me knot head. I say I come by my stubbornness somewhere, but truly, the knots were probably from him thumping me- 'you want me to put a knot on your head?'

My dad always had my mom's back. If we got into trouble or lipped off to mom, better watch out. As a kid I didn't think it was fair at all, but now I know it's something everyone wishes for in a marriage. Their marriage wasn't perfect, but it's one to be admired and I always wanted one like that. Mom was always dad's biggest fan. If she hadn't been cheering him on, hard telling how life would have been.

It wasn't always easy for us. As a teenager, you go through some trying times and I hated that they couldn't always be there for our events. I was up for football Homecoming queen (yeah, it's overrated, but at the time.....) and I knew dad wouldn't be able to be there, but secretly wished he'd show up (he was coaching in Topeka and Andrea was at Effingham HS). My brother, Damon, escorted me onto the field. He did have mom give me a silver necklace with a football on it, but the best part was his handwritten note, 'You'll always be my homecoming queen! Love dad.' That made it okay.

Life on the farm was busy. During the fall, we always got home well before the folks, so the chores were our responsibility. I remember having the meal fixed several nights before mom and dad got home. On their anniversary, September 8, I always tried to make a 'romantic' meal.

One night, while my little sis, Heather, and I were doing chores, it had rained and the cattle pen was knee high in slop! Well, Heather got over the fence to feed them but didn't bother taking the bucket with her. She asked me to get it and bring it in for her. Of course, I said, 'why didn't you get it yourself?' Not sure how, but a fight ensued in the knee-high crap. Damon just watched it go on. We ended up laughing, went into the house on the old back porch and stuck our clothes directly into the washing machine. We didn't even think about rinsing the clothes off first. Mom could have rung our necks. It was a 'helluba' mess (yes another of dad's sayings).

The first time I learned how to tell if dad was really mad and you better watch out was when the combine broke down and times were tights. So he took Heather and I in the grain truck up to the back patch to pick corn by hand. Suddenly we were hearing shots of gunfire. Dad got us in the truck and hightailed it out of the field. He chased those hunters down. I was sitting beside him thinking, 'we are going to die,' but not saying a word. Dad was so intense and when I looked at him, his ears were the reddest I've ever seen. He was literally hot on their trail. They finally stopped and he got out and you can imagine. (Ron later confirmed that they were a group hunting on his property without permission)

Mom let me go to Topeka one Saturday for a date. Well, apparently dad had different plans for me and wasn't happy that I had left. When I got home, he was pretty mad, so at 10 p.m. I was in the tractor with the disc in the field. About 11 p.m. the tractor tire went flat. We didn't have cell phones back then, so I started walking the two miles towards home in the dark. A neighbor was headed home, picked me up and gave me a ride the rest of the way. I was proud to say I was dad's field help. I helped both dad and Damon disc the fields. Missy did it once and took out a barbed wire fence, so I got to do it from then on. I take a little pride in that.

Putting up hay was a huge summer- time job. I would drive the tractor with the hay chute attached to the wagon. If you hit that bale just right it would turn and go straight in and up the chute onto the wagon. Dad and Damon were on the wagon stacking the bales. They liked to goof off and would get mouthy back there. So, anytime they directed stuff towards me, I just sped up, getting the bales going up the chute faster than they could keep up, me laughing and them learning a lesson.

A very favorite memory of football was when dad would get home from a game and set-up that old reel-to-reel projector in the living room to watch the black-and-white game films. The sound of that projector and watching him make those players run forward and backward while he studied every play. He would let me stay up and watch. I'd ask questions just to hear him talk.

Truth is, there are so many stories I could tell, but in a nutshell, I am honored to have grown-up on the farm, with the parents I had. Although I thought they were too hard on us at times, I suppose I wouldn't have wanted it any other way. We had morals, values, and a strong work ethic. There is not really much I can't do, or figure out how to do because of watching, learning and doing.

I know my folks had disappointments in some of our choices but those were all stepping-stones and taught us perseverance. We weren't a hugging, 'I love you' family. It was just a given. So, recently, when I was preparing to leave and my dad hugged me and whispered, 'I love you and I'm proud of you,' I bawled my eyes out heading back to South Dakota. He has done it every time since. It means the world to me."

THE FOLLOWING REFLECTION WAS PROVIDED TO ME IN 2021 BY DAUGHTER HEATHER BOWEN ADAMS–

"What do I want people to know about my Dad....just not sure where to start on that one, seems like most everyone you talk to who knows Dad, already knows he is stern, but he is a softy once you get past that exterior.

Don't be fooled by that strict, direct tone. The stern part is only because he values respect and honestly and does his best to instill that in people. His work ethic is beyond compare. He is soft, don't think he isn't, not on the pushover side but the kind heart. He expects you to do your best and knows that failure will come at times, that mistakes will be made, but what and how did you learn from it. I'm sure there were times when as a father he wanted to tell me what my decisions/choices in life should be, but what would I have learned, and how would I have grown if I didn't make those choices/mistakes on my own. Now that didn't mean you weren't expected to follow the rules but he was sure going to make sure you got lined out very quick. If you disappoint him, he will forgive you but you will learn a valuable lesson that is for sure.

Dad.......he won't say goodbye on the phone.....it's too final. He might say see ya later, be careful, alright, OK.... but never "goodbye". When I go to leave from a visit up home, I get a big hug and a kiss on the cheek with "I love you" whispered in my ear and a 'make sure you call when you get home"

He likes to go fishing, but he doesn't like to eat it. He can't stand chicken/turkey, he calls it "buzzard". When we were growing up he would eat popcorn on Sunday night. He has ice cream or some type of dessert everyday.

Favorite memories with my Dad, so many that's for sure but we will start with some favorites.

As a coach's daughter one would expect you to know everything and anything about the game, rules etc. Now it's not that I don't know the game, but I loved sitting in the living room behind Dad. He would set up the card table with the old film projector......I don't even know what that thing is actually called. But if memory serves me right, it folded up, anyway he would watch films on it. It made a clicking chattering noise as it played the films. I think it moved left to right on the unfolded screens. Gosh I'm going to have to ask if he still has that. But that was so fun for me to watch him watch that thing, back it up and take notes and back it up again. I believe that is why I would find myself at his games watching him up and down the sidelines coaching instead of watching more of the game.

Now, let's talk about horses.......oh wait he calls them donkeys or hay burners.

It's no secret that I have a love for horses but convincing my Dad to actually let me have my own and to show them was a tough one. I had some money in savings, but I needed another $400 to buy Faded Fox. So, Dad made me a deal. I had a first calf heifer that was going to calve, he said he would give me $400 dead or alive for whatever she dropped. Didn't matter, I could have the $400 no matter what. Well......I have learned a valuable lesson after that deal. Dad is a fair and honest man and his word is his word.......there was no bargaining on this deal. I tried, trust me I fought hard to get $800 when it was all said and done, but a deal is a deal......so just because she had TWINS does not me the money doubles. The agreement was "whatever she dropped dead or alive was $400".

Trips to WRHS, on days we didn't have school I looked forward to going to school with them. Being one of "Bowen's kids" was pretty awesome. I enjoyed watching him teach and hang out in the gym with him. I would bounce back and forth between Mom's classroom and the gym throughout the day. Sometimes I felt for those students of his because I recognized that tone in his voice. I remember this kid coming in the gym with earrings in his ears and to this day I still remember Dad telling him if he didn't get that out of his ear before he came out of the locker room he was gonna rip it out for him. He would also tell kids that he could put a bull ring in or a calf tag. Can't remember his choice of words but he made sure they knew he could take care of it for them.

Dentyne gum!! Dad always kept a stash in the car, but it was not for kids, well at least without permission. That's where Andi and I kinda got in trouble, because we would steal the gum on occasion, but one particular time we kinda, maybe.... OK we really got caught. Oh dang cat followed us in there and we kinda shut it in the door. Oh, the horror ....

Dad and I took a road trip to western Kansas, just so I could get another horse. It was just him and I going after another "hay burner", but he hooked up the trailer and away we went.

Storms – us kids would come downstairs in the living room if there was a tornado threat. Dad would stay up watching the windows or standing in the doorway. I can remember seeing his shadow through the night as he kept us safe.

Not sure if my siblings included this, but during our high school years all three of us girls, got selected as candidates for home coming. Naturally, Dad couldn't be there because he was coaching his own game, but he gave us all a necklace that had a football on it, letting us know he was there with us. Damon had the honor of being our escort since Dad wasn't able to be there, and the announcer always added a comment to our script with who Dad's team was playing that night.

LIFE ON THE FARM ACCORDING TO HEATHER–

"Did you eat today? Did you drink today? Don't you think your animals would like to?" words we heard often when we didn't take care of our chores. I admit I have used it on my children as well. You have the animals, its your responsibility to take care of them. Not only that but this is what we do, we farm and ranch, so they help "put food on the table, clothes on our back and a roof over our head." Yes, he has used those words and I live by them to this day.

I remember this one-time Mom was backing the car down to the gas barrel (we have those on the farm) I was standing down by the barrel and I started screaming bloody murder. Dad came running and Mom got the car stopped. Mom had run over a cat right in front of me, dang thing used up one of its nine lives though. You see it was down in one of the tractor tire ruts and so Mom somehow managed to go right over the rut without killing the cat.......but guess who was in trouble for screaming over a cat!!! Dad thought Mom had run over me, and oh boy was I in trouble. A cat's life was not as important as mine and I better not do that again.

"Find the friction point!!" one of his best sayings ever. Having been a drivers ed teacher, he made sure we all learned how to drive a stick shift. The hill two miles north of the house, was the lesson hill for sure. No matter how many times you rolled backwards, you were gonna keep trying, and find the friction point until you made it! We can all handle a stick shift to this day, give me the old dump truck and I can mash the gears.

Chores: we all had them to do, helping with the cows, and hogs (when we raised them). It was all part of living on the farm. We all learned how to drive a tractor and the safety that goes with it, from raking hay to disking a field. When I got Faded Fox, I was responsible for getting up before school and doing my chores before I left. I wanted the horse, which meant an extra animal to take care of so therefore it was my responsibility to make sure he was fed.

One time Damon was in charge of us while Mom and Dad were gone, it was a muddy mess in the lot, OK maybe more like soupy manure. Well Andi and I got into a fight, and before it was all said and done we were covered in soupy green slime. We hurried and got the mess all cleaned up, clothes and all. No sign of what had happened, but dear ol' Damon tattled on us. Fortunately, Dad just laughed Mom was a little concerned about the washing machine.

Pulling weeds out of the soybeans, Dad made these special hooks for us to use. I apparently didn't know how to operate them correctly because I got demoted to bathroom cleaning duty because I didn't do a very good job. Hee Hee Hee …….siblings still complain about that to this day. I mean seriously, I was in the air conditioning cleaning the toilet, like probably once the whole time. Hey, the baby is the favorite it's no secret, just ask them!!

I'll finish with this. When I got married and moved away, a long way away. I would call my Dad every Friday (game day) to wish him good luck. It became a Friday thing, that assistant coaches would ask, "did he get the call yet?" I can remember several times calling out to Coach Glaze's house because I hadn't been able to catch Dad at school.

I once wore a WRHS shirt into Emporia High and was asked by a coach in that building "kinda brave with that shirt on," I said "well Coach Bowen is my Dad so I guess I am." He responded, "that man is a legend!!" WHY YES HE IS!!!"

FROM MS. RON BOWEN- MARY LOU TO ALL THAT KNOW HER–

The one person that has been along for the entire ride, lived through all the same football seasons, spent countless hours in bleachers all over the state of Kansas and spent two hours a day in a car traveling to and from Washburn Rural with Coach Bowen, is his wife, Mary Lou. I think that makes her words awfully important.

"All you have to do is sit quietly in the bleachers in a somewhat isolated area, keep your children from being rowdy by supplying them snacks like all the other parents do. Right? Not by a long shot. Sure, your kids are supposed to be well behaved, and you are supposed to know all the other parents. After all, you are the football coach's wife! But hey, it really doesn't work that way.

I was number one fan, except for my mother and one of his aunts! Truth! Throughout their lives, those two ladies had his back. It was beautiful to watch. They made games as often as they could, or at least listened to the late-night sports reports.

But they weren't expected to keep the stat books each game as I was asked to do at one school. Folks were shocked, shocked, when I declined, telling them I could barely keep up with action on the field, much less who carried the ball, who clocked a defender and who tripped the quarterback! Besides, I couldn't find a sitter for that night, so I had little ones to control!

Through the years that followed, I learned a few more rules, plays, etc., and 'adopted' more sons every season. A few years I did end up as the team laundress, especially as not everyone washed white shirts and red pants separately! Coach really didn't want his team on the field in pink! One year it rained almost every Friday, resulting in ruining our home washer with sand and mud. That school district eventually equipped the locker room with laundry equipment. (Years down the road, pink socks or shirts were okayed in honor of cancer awareness.)

Those early years saw coaches wives, sometimes asking very personal questions, and it is really tough on first timers, as it takes years to become experts at fending those types of questions off. You will make friends, some really close ones, but even then, some information must be kept close. However, I would advise wives new to the role to take it slow, be stingy with personal info, but also be slow to turn down genuine friendship and honest offers to help. Most of it is honest and well intentioned.

For example, our first year at Udall, and Ron's first head coaching job, he was at the high school and I was teaching middle grades language arts. We were also expecting our first child. Long story short, things went wrong at delivery, and we lost our little girl, I spent long days hospitalized, and Ron had to handle more than teaching classes and a football season. We had no idea how quickly that small community would spring into action on our behalf. A community prayer service, food, housekeeping, offers of stored blood from the blook bank, if needed, flowers, visits,...... Some of those folks are dear friends to this day. The community is still one of our 'hometowns.' For many years after we left that area, one family, after asking our approval, made certain there were flowers on the baby's grave. Another blessing there was the birth of our only son, claimed by the community as one of theirs upon his birth.

Again, I advise, be wise, but be receptive to the fans' overtures. Most are sincere and caring.

We left Udall after five years to go to Leon, where one of Ron's duties would be to start a wrestling program and a daughter was born that fall. Of course there was little, if any, supply budget for wrestling, so once again the coach's wife stepped up. The uniforms that first year consisted of dyed long johns and sleeveless undershirts! Hey, they sufficed! And didn't look so bad, perhaps a little dingy by season's end. The wrestling program took off and is still respected, although known these days as Bluestem High School.

Valley Center beckoned next, and Ron again was challenged to start a wrestling program in addition to coaching football. The budget was not a problem there, and interest in the new sport was high, drawing a lot from football players. Both programs did well the seven years we were there. Again, we made a wealth of friends there, many remain as family to this day. Our last two girls were born while we were at Valley Center.

And then Washburn Rural beckoned next, and we found another home and family. You will have found that story in other pages of this book.

When I finished high school, I didn't plan to be a teacher, and I certainly had no inkling I'd end up a coach's wife! But that just goes to show how little we know at that early age. I wouldn't change anything about this life I have lived. I married a good man, who became a loving father, an excellent coach, a faithful friend, a helpful neighbor, and who has done well by me. I loved teaching, being a supportive coach's wife, knowing all the fellow staffers, and being a part of a bigger coaching family. I give thanks to the higher power who had plans for us." Mary

Lou Bowen who herself was inducted into the Washburn Rural Hall of Fame on Thursday, April 8, 2021 and as one of my colleagues put it, "she probably could have been inducted before Ron, because it isn't easy being a coach's wife. No, no it's not. But she accepted the challenge and embraced it.

#68 Mary Lou, Ron and Rocky the dog

YOU CAN TELL A LOT ABOUT A MAN FROM HIS WORDS–

At one point in his career Ron Bowen wrote a piece on his "Philosophy". His philosophy on football of course. A sport he's always loved, yet not always allowed to play it. In high school his folks would not allow him to play his freshman year. A bout with polio took away his sophomore year. After playing his final two years of high school he went on to college and attempted to play and did, but a back injury ended his playing days. But those experiences likely shaped Bowen's desire to coach the sport. As a result of his frustrations and struggles, thousands of young men benefitted from his love of the sport of football.

Here's bits and pieces of his philosophy.

"The sport of football mirrors life itself more closely than any other sport. It all starts with discipline, not only on the field, but in the classroom. Those young men who have good self-discipline, or are able to respond well to discipline, and have some athletic talent, can develop into respectable football players. That same type of discipline carries over into success in the work force or on to successful higher education and beyond.

Properly coached football is considered by many college and university clinicians to be the last bastion of true discipline in public schools.

Football has rules and regulations by which the game is played. The world we live in has rules and regulations that we must abide by or a penalty is assessed. Players get knocked down in football, and must regain their feet, must assess their situation, then go back and face a similar situation. Such situations occur in life. They may not get the job they applied for, the raise they were expecting, or they may even have an argument with their wife. Football prepares them to face situations that are not always pleasant.

In football players have to deal with a certain amount of pressure and stress – it prepares them for worse pressure and more stress later on.

Teamwork is a must in football. Players will be working with people from now on. The game of football itself puts parameters on area and time or you lose. Get the job done, you win. Losing is not a comfortable feeling, yet it must be faced from time to time. We all have lost loved ones and felt an emptiness from the loss. On the other hand, winning is fun and enjoyable and players learn how to handle success. They learn how to handle later successes.

Keeping respect for the game of football is a most important segment of life. There needs to be more involvement in football throughout this nation and less involvement in youth gangs, alcohol, drugs, owning a car and making car payments while in school.

Many potential players use the excuse they have to work or that they don't want to get hurt. The same young people will jump into their late model cars and zip out of the parking lot after school. The late Kaye Pearce, former director of the KSHSAA, at the 1990 Association of Football rules meeting said, 'Participating in football is 30,000 times safer than riding in a car.'

Owning a car and having a job just to support the car, including insurance payments, should not take precedence over participation in football. If the job were to help support the family or to keep them from being homeless, then it would be a different story.

The late General Douglas MacArthur in the book You Have to Pay the Price, by Earl H. "Red" Blaik said, 'Football has become a symbol of courage, stamina and coordinated efficiency. In war and peace, I have found football men to be my greatest reliance.' As a former superintendent of West Point, the General knew what he was talking about. We need to regain this symbol of courage by putting more emphasis on participation in the sport.

Theodore Roosevelt also recognized the need for competition when he stated, "The credit belongs to the man who is actually in the arena who knows the great enthusiasms, the great devotions, and spends himself in worthy cause; who at the best, knows the triumph of high achievement and who at worst, if he fails, at least fails while daring, daring greatly, so that his place will never be with those cold and timid sous who knew neither victory or defeat.'

Basically, my philosophy is that I want each of our squad members to find a place, knowing that if he is not a starter, or even if he plays very little, he is no less a person in my eyes. There are always those who are going to have more talent and will step to the front, but even those at the back of the line who stay with football will gain something from the program that will help them in life. I want them to find success as players and students. It would be great to see all players injury free, ours as well as our opponents. I want our team to be competitive (hopefully winning), physically and mentally tough, to play within the rules, have good fundamentals, be well-conditioned, hard hitters, and to have unquestioned sportsmanship.

I want them to take pride in being a member of the WRHS football squad. I want the younger squad members to keep improving, to carry on a tradition of quality football and quality representation of our school. In later year, I want them to look back on their high school football years as fun and worthwhile times. The game is for the young men who participate and the intrinsic values they acquire are carried with them throughout life." – Head Football Coach and educator, Ron Bowen

AND COACH BOWEN REFLECTS ABOUT THE MEMORIES–

"The writing of this book has brought back many memories of my younger years. Too many to mention all, however, I feel I need to cover some.

Marvin Mueller and Les Parker were in our wedding party and when we all were in high school together we were 'car nuts.' Mine a 1947 Ford Coupe that I had customized, Les and his 1940 Ford with flames painted on the hood an fenders, Marvin with his 1950 Chevrolet with a split manifold and dual straight pipes that I could hear him start when we lived a mile and a quarter away.

Then there is Jerry Miller, a fellow 1955 high school classmate, who convinced me to transfer from Kansas State University to Emporia. While there I became acquainted with the late Jim Wieuman, an Effingham High School graduate who arranged a blind date with a girl named Mary Lou Barnett who he pointed out while she was in the cafeteria lunch line with two of her friends. Most of us know how that turned out.

That '47 Ford Coupe that Mary Lou and I started our married life driving has long been gone. However, in the '70's we bought a 1948 Ford Coupe with the same body style as the '47. In 2006 the '48 was completely restored and painted a bright red in the body shop at Ed Bozarth Chevrolet in Topeka. As a former student of ours at Carbondale High School, Ed insisted on doing that for us. We will never be able to thank Ed and his wife Paula for that gift. It's a 'small world.' Paula's older sister Peggy was a classmate of mine at Hiawatha.

As I look back on my career as a teacher and a coach I wish to pay tribute to all who helped me along the way. Thanks to all the administrators, athletic directors, school board members, fellow teachers, secretaries, school nurses, custodians, cooks, district maintenance personnel, bus directors and bus drivers and athletic trainers. Thanks also to my many friends in radio, television, and print news media.

With the support of parents, cheerleaders, the backing of the student body and athletes who dedicated themselves to hard work, discipline, and positive attitudes, success happened.

A great amount of that success was due to the outstanding group of assistant coaches that I had the privilege of working with. I could not have been associated with a better group of men.

Lest I leave out the 'stripes' as there were many outstanding officials that I highly respected.

In my 34 years of coaching I developed lasting friendships with many opposing coaches.

On a very personal note, I thank my wife Mary Lou for all the years of sitting on bleachers in all kinds of weather. For supporting me, our coaching staff, and tolerating me on weekends when Friday nights didn't go too well. Thank goodness we had a lot of fun times.

Thanks to Damon, M'Lissa, Andrea and Heather for all their support through the years. Many times they kept the farm running when I was 50 or more miles away. Thanks for the 40th, 50th and 60th surprise anniversary parties, you 'sneaky' kids.

Lastly, I thank Chris Ridley for taking the time to research back through the years of newspaper articles, interviewing people and making the drive up to our farm to talk about the past. He spent countless hours assembling and writing this book. Thanks, 'Rid." Coach Ron Bowen

FROM THE AUTHOR

Author's commentary- If you can't tell by the substance of this book or by the philosophy Coach Bowen espouses, discipline. It was a key element of his team's successes. His success. And his methods of helping student-athletes develop self-discipline was consistently present and observable in any and all of Ron Bowen's teams. And in the classrooms and gymnasiums where he taught there was discipline. From Elkhart, Carbondale, Leon, Udalll, Valley Center and Washburn Rural he made an impact on so many folks. And it was more than just the traditional discipline that we think of when we think about stern expectations of conduct. His practice sessions were disciplined. They were well-timed out, not excessively long. There was a focus on repetitions so that good timing occurred. Players became confident in their assignments. He expected good conduct from players in their classrooms, on the football field and expected it to carry over to when they were in their communities.

Helping develop and stressing consistent discipline was Bowen's gift to his students and his players. It became such an integral part of his life and thus became a part of theirs- his students. Bowen appreciated the four years he was able to work with his football players and knew he had an element of control over them while they were students. But a young person's development of self-discipline would be something that would serve all his students and all his players for the rest of their lives. He always said that, while the four years he got to spend with his players and students was important to him, he still considered what they did with the other forty years after high school as a measurement of both his and their collective attempts to succeed. And that brought fulfillment and satisfaction. Not only theirs, but his.

I imagine that when Coach takes the time to reflect, he is proud of his team's successes. But imagine the joy he gets from hearing from his former players about their successes in life – their careers, their families, their communities. It was essential that every player felt like a part of something while at Rural. And, in keeping that same theme, no matter how successful they were at football they all had the capabilities and the tools necessary to be successful in life. So, yeah, the championships were wonderful; the wins that his players NOW get during the rest of their lives is equally as important.

My feeling is that school and sports create lasting memories. Lifelong relationships and a kinship like no other. That's why its important to let kids enjoy their school years to the fullest. That's why sports and activities are such integral parts of their experiences as youth. Life gets hard. Often times, it gets really hard. Being able to look back and call upon the discipline that you learned through studies, activities and sports is important. But the most important part is always being able to tap those relationships you worked so hard to develop with your teammates and with your coaches. They stand beside you literally and figuratively. Forever family.

Coach Bowen and Mary Lou continually show-up at significant life events of their former students. It's their way of saying they appreciated their student(s) and care about them as individuals. They care LONG after they graduate from high school. You may not find another pair of educators that cared more for their students and if you do find some they too are special teachers. And that caring attitude that comes naturally for the Bowens is a characteristic that helped make them the best mentors to so many of us who continue to see "Finer Days" in our own lives. Because of them.